MW00681062

China and Europe's Partnership for a More Sustainable World

Challenges and Opportunities

Transboundary environmental problems and European Union (EU)-China environmental trade, investment, and technical interactions are multi-dimensional, multinational, and multilevel. Delving into such themes to generate in-depth and policy relevant knowledge requires multi-country teams with broad disciplinary expertise using diverse analytical tools and methodologies. China and Europe's Partnership for a More Sustainable World is such a work. Rich and comprehensive, it sheds light on diverse topics like European investment in China's environmental sector, Chinese environmental FDI in Europe, environmental goods trade, EU and Chinese corporate social responsibility concepts, and biomass utilization and will be of immense interest to academics, businesspeople, and policymakers in China, the EU, and elsewhere.

– Jean-Marc F. Blanchard, Executive Director,
Mr. & Mrs. S.H. Wong Center for the Study of
Multinational Corporations, Los Gatos, CA, USA

This book offers new insights into an understudied and very important topic – EU-China relations in the environmental and energy field. The carefully researched chapters are rich in data and case studies and illuminating analysis. This book is of interest to academics, practitioners, and policymakers.

– Genia Kostka, Professor of
Governance of Infrastructure and Energy,
Hertie School of Governance, Berlin, Germany

A multifaceted, interdisciplinary enquiry into what actually drives bilateral investment policies and practices between the EU and China in their effort to pursue higher sustainability standards and the greening of their respective economies. This book has the rare merit of striking the right balance between theoretical and empirical research. While pragmatically recognizing the barriers to be faced, it offers direct insights into economic, legal and technological options, which can feed directly into policy formulation in both the EU and China, and adds a valuable building block to their joint aspiration for a mutually beneficial cooperation.

– Andrea Ricci, Vice President of ISINNOVA – Institute of
Studies for the Integration of Systems; Rapporteur of the EC
Integrated Roadmap of the SET Plan and Chairman of the
EU Transport Advisory Group for Horizon 2020, Roma

In this book you will find the interesting outcomes of a four-year EU-funded research project about the effects of EU-China cooperation in a very fast-moving field: renewable energies and environmental industries. As the research skilfully combines economic, legal and engineering approaches, the book is aimed at many readers – from academics and policy makers to general readers.

– Augusto Ninni, University of Parma, Parma (PR), Italy

China and Europe's Partnership for a More Sustainable World

Challenges and Opportunities

Edited by

Francesca Spigarelli
University of Macerata, Macerata, Italy

Louise Curran
Toulouse Business School, Toulouse, France

Alessia Arteconi
Università eCampus, Novedrate, Italy

United Kingdom – North America – Japan
India – Malaysia – China

Emerald Group Publishing Limited
Howard House, Wagon Lane, Bingley BD16 1WA, UK

First edition 2016

British Library Cataloguing in Publication Data
A catalogue record for this book is available from the British Library

ISBN: 978-1-78635-332-0
The research leading to this book was funded by the IRSES People Marie
Curie Action of the Seventh Framework Programme, European Union
FP7/2007-2013/ under REA Grant agreement no. 318908, POREEN.
This publication does not necessarily reflect the opinion of the EU.

Printed and bound by CPI Group (UK) Ltd, Croydon, CR0 4YY

ISOQAR certified
Management System,
awarded to Emerald
for adherence to
Environmental
standard
ISO 14001:2004.

Certificate Number 1985
ISO 14001

INVESTOR IN PEOPLE

Contents

Part II   Environment and Regulations

List of Contributors

Alessia Arteconi	Università Telematica e-Campus, Novedrate, Italy
Loretta Battaglia	University of Macerata, Macerata, Italy
Caterina Brandoni	University of Ulster, Newtownabbey, UK
Hongbo Cai	Beijing Normal University, Beijing, China
Elena Cedrola	University of Macerata, Macerata, Italy
Louise Curran	Toulouse Business School, Université de Toulouse, Toulouse, France
Eleonora Cutrini	University of Macerata, Macerata, Italy
Mi Dai	Beijing Normal University, Beijing, China
Jun Gao	Tongji University, Shanghai, China
Yulei Gao	Tongji University, Shanghai, China
Neil Hewitt	University of Ulster, Newtownabbey, UK
Mingjun Huang	University of Ulster, Newtownabbey, UK
Ye Huang	University of Ulster, Newtownabbey, UK
Christoph Lattemann	Jacobs University Bremen, Bremen, Germany
Yong Li	Shanghai Jiao Tong University, Shanghai, China
Fabio Lorusso	Istituto Universitario di Studi Europei (IUSE), Torino, Italy
Federica Monti	University of Macerata, Macerata, Italy
Lee Keng Ng	Curtin University, Sarawak, Malaysia
Giuseppe A. Policaro	University of Piemonte Orientale, Novara, Italy
Fabio Polonara	Università Politecnica delle Marche, Ancona, Italy

Ruxiao Qu	Beijing Normal University, Beijing, China
Paolo Rossi	University of Piemonte Orientale, Novara, Italy
Piercarlo Rossi	University of Piemonte Orientale, Novara, Italy
Federico Salvatelli	University of Macerata, Macerata, Italy
Francesca Spigarelli	University of Macerata, Macerata, Italy
Marco Spitoni	Università Politecnica delle Marche, Ancona, Italy
Ernesto Tavoletti	University of Macerata, Macerata, Italy
Katiuscia Vaccarini	University of Macerata, Macerata, Italy; Jacobs University Bremen, Bremen, Germany
Ruzhu Wang	Shanghai Jiao Tong University, Shanghai, China
Yanyan Wang	Tongji University, Shanghai, China
Lei Wen	Beijing Normal University, Beijing, China
Haitao Yin	Shanghai JiaoTong University, Shanghai, China
Yanping Zeng	Beijing Normal University, Beijing, China
Mingling Zhai	Tongji University, Shanghai, China
Changmian Zhang	East China University of Political Science and Law, Shanghai, China
Lihong Zhang	East China University of Political Science and Law, Shanghai, China
Qun Zhang	Beijing Normal University, Beijing, China
Xu Zhang	Tongji University, Shanghai, China
Xuemei Zhang	Shanghai JiaoTong University, Shanghai, China
Chunming Zhao	Beijing Normal University, Beijing, China
Haoliang Zhao	Tongji University, Shanghai, China
Hui Zhou	Shanghai JiaoTong University, Shanghai, China
Xiang Zhou	Tongji University, Shanghai, China

Foreword

In economic terms, the shift to Asia has been a fact since the beginning of this century. It is difficult to make generalizations for a continent of more than 4 billion people but Asian consumers are growing richer, with average earnings in many countries tripling over the past 10 years. China's economy represented around 5% of world GDP in 2000 and it may account for 25% by 2050.

In terms of economic development, history is accelerating: it took 155 years for Britain to double its GDP per capita, 50 years for the United States, and just 15 years for China. Over the last 10 years, Asia has accounted for half of the world's GDP growth. Forecasts indicate that Asian growth will continue to outpace Europe and the United States.

With economic growth coupled with resource consumption, one can expect more constraints on key resources. As people become wealthier, they use more energy (e.g., for mobility, air conditioning, heating, and computing), more water, eat and waste more food. Efficiency gains are often largely offset by the "rebound effect," whereby technological improvements ultimately lead to greater and not less consumption. This has been true for the electricity and in the transport sectors.

The recent progresses and new-found prosperity in China (and also in India, Brazil, and South Africa) may have knock-on effects on the demand for and availability of global resources. Global weather may become more volatile and severe (cf. hurricanes, disastrous flooding, extreme heat, and shortage of water) while rising sea levels could devastate low-lying cities like Shanghai and Hong Kong.

From a multilateral perspective, systemic governance of climate change has been agreed by 195 countries at the Conference of the Parties of the United Nations Framework Convention on Climate Change (COP-21) in Paris in December 2015. The conclusions of the COP-21 envisage a reduction of global greenhouse gas emissions to a level that limits the global average temperature increase to below 2°C or 1.5°C above preindustrial levels.

From a bilateral perspective, this book entitled "Going Green: China-Europe Partnership's for a More Sustainable Word" – published in the frame of the POREEN Marie Curie Action (*Partnering opportunities between Europe and China in the renewable energies and environmental industries*) brilliantly coordinated by Francesca Spigarelli – is emblematic of what two strong blocks can do together by combining their investments, cross-fertilizing their knowledge, and cocreating their futures.

The share of foreign direct investment, of megawatt of renewables installed, and the number of energy-efficient buildings are illustrative of the major changes taking place in Europe and China. The chapters of this book provide original analyses, recent key facts, and figures that pave the way toward more sustainability. This notion, sometimes called an oxymoron, covers the traditional economic, environmental, and social dimensions.

But in this trans-disciplinary book, sustainability also rightly addresses some sensitive legal issues like liability and corporate social responsibility. The chapters well integrate social sciences aspects (in the first two parts of the book) as well as science, technology, and engineering aspects (in the last part of the book). Addressing both theoretical and real-life practices, many lessons and opportunities can be drawn from this reading. From the European side, I will focus on five dimensions.

The European Union (EU) 2020 targets for greenhouse gas emissions reductions, for increasing the share of renewable energy, for improving energy efficiency, and for achieving 3% of GDP dedicated to research and innovation may be inspiring. The Energy Union is going in this direction.

Smart growth (fostering knowledge, innovation, education, and digital society), sustainable growth (making production more resource-efficient while boosting competitiveness), and inclusive growth (raising participation in the labor market, acquisition of skills and fight against poverty) are long-term leitmotifs that are good for people, the economy, and the planet.

The research efforts should stimulate technological but also social innovation and public sector innovation. Climate change, urbanization, and relative resource shortages may fuel a shift away from large coal power plants, petrol-engine cars, and energy-consuming buildings to decentralized renewable energy production, small electric and hybrid vehicles, as well as passive houses.

Global connectivity is changing how people live, how they work, and how they think. ICT, the Internet, and new mobile devices are and will continue to play a pervasive and transformational role. In 2000, there were around 700 million mobile devices, most of which did not connect to the Web. In 2015, there were 7.6 billion mobile devices worldwide, many of which are smart and connected to Internet. The European Digital Single Market follows common sense.

Europe needed over a century to develop the infrastructure to supply natural resources to the point of use: sewage farms, ports, electricity grids, pipelines, rail, and road networks. Making significant changes to this infrastructure will take decades. The new European "Circular Economy" paradigm means a shift toward reusing, repairing, refurbishing, and recycling existing materials and products. "Waste" can and should be turned into a resource.

These five dimensions are at the core of many EU–China collaborations like POREEN and URBACHINA (a collaborative research project on *Sustainable Urbanisation in China: Megatrends toward 2050*) that feed scientifically into the "EU–China Urbanisation Partnership." These initiatives should be seen in conjunction with more technologically driven projects, mostly in ICT, energy, and transport fields funded under the "Smart Cities and Communities," including with the large scale demonstrations, the so-called lighthouse projects.

In the near future, through Horizon 2020 – the European framework programme for research and innovation – further EU–China cooperation could take place on sustainable urbanization, on resource-efficient urban agriculture, and on innovating nature-based solutions in cities, especially to enhance the potential for international replication.

Green manufacturing and services, scaling-up of renewable energy, improvement of energy efficiency, sustainable agriculture, and low-carbon transport will certainly continue to shape the EU–China relationship. But resilience and trust should also underlie this relationship: Resilience for dealing with natural, technological, and human changes; trust among actors and institutions, shared conviction in the added value of the protection of collective goods like air, water, and public health.

Domenico Rossetti di Valdalbero
Principal Administrator at the European Commission,
Directorate-General for Research and Innovation

Introduction

For many years, the European Union (EU) and China have been developing a dialogue and effective cooperation initiatives on the need to address the environmental issues. They have found common ground on many key aspects and cooperation has been extensive in several fields. Diplomatic efforts have contributed to strengthen partnering opportunities between the countries.

The EU–China cooperation for environment protection has a quite long history. While the relation started as a mainly trade-oriented relationship, it has become a wide partnership, which has benefited from a sound institutional framework. The cooperation has embraced climate change issues, with strong linkages between energy security and environmental security.

There are several drivers for Europe's interest in strengthening environmental partnership with China. Europe has a comparative advantage in the field and has the opportunity to use this to gain bargaining power. China is a profitable market, both for the export of European environmental goods and for European firms seeking to invest locally. Moreover, helping China to diversify its energy mix and to improve its energy efficiency would have positive spillovers for the EU in terms of reduced global demand.

From the Chinese perspective, there are several reasons to engage with the EU, which include the latter's long experience in this sector and China's need to implement "more sustainable growth strategies." There are clear synergies between China's search for a more sustainable growth path and the EU's capacities in environmental protection and renewable energy technologies.

This book gathers some of the main findings of the EU-funded project POREEN on partnering opportunities between Europe and China in the renewable energies and environmental industries. As a Marie Curie action, POREEN's goal was to produce research results which inform policy, while improving knowledge and research skills. Research outputs were developed leveraging academic mobility in China and Europe, particularly of young researchers. Their common objective was to seek to highlight opportunities to expand and develop this important relationship in a way that moves both regions toward a more sustainable future.

In a four-year time frame, researchers analyzed the opportunities and potential to boost cooperation between China and Europe in this important area. They used a variety of research approaches and academic perspectives, combining economic, legal, and engineering perspectives.

The economic dimensions of the project included the identification of critical issues, gaps, and potential for bilateral foreign direct investments and trade in the broad area of green industries. Legal research had a similar objective, but focused on offshore oil and gas extraction, renewable energies, corporate responsibility, and environmental legislation. The team's engineering research relates to energy efficiency and carbon dioxide reduction, particularly concerning transportation and low-carbon buildings.

The book is structured into three interrelated and connected parts.

Part I has an economic and policy orientation. The seven chapters examine different aspects of trade and foreign direct investment relations between Europe and China, in the renewable energies and/or environmental industries. Bilateral trade and FDI flows are analyzed, also in the light of Chinese and European green policy and cooperation initiatives. Authors identify obstacles, barriers, and difficulties faced by European and Chinese firms in initiating, maintaining, and consolidating both trade and investment initiatives in China and Europe, respectively. Key factors and issues to be addressed to further stimulate EU–China trade and investment flows are also considered.

Part II addresses the legal framework of EU–China cooperation. The first two chapters describe the Chinese environmental protection system, analyzing both national laws and governance measures. Then, the focus is on three specific themes: the electric sector in China, Corporate Social Responsibility in a comparative perspective, and the legal framework for civil liability for environmental damages deriving from energy misuse.

Part III is focused on engineering-related research activity. Two main research areas are developed, both related to energy efficiency and carbon dioxide reduction: mobility and the transportation sector and low-carbon buildings. The four chapters in this part highlight the state of the art of the engineering research group in key areas (mobility and the transportation sector and low-carbon buildings) that might have a huge potential impact on bilateral cooperation between Europe and China. One topic is related to the use of methane and biomethane, both in its compressed and liquid form, as an alternative fuel to reduce the environmental impact and GHG emissions in the transport sector. In general, biomass as feedstock energy source in China and its potential has been evaluated in detail. Whereas on the topic of low-carbon buildings, the use of heat pumps and district cooling/heating networks have been considered in order to increase the energy efficiency for space heating and domestic hot water production. Moreover, smart devices in buildings, studied on experimental test rigs, for thermal comfort and consumption reduction have been presented.

Together these diverse inputs seek to contribute to a more integrated, coherent and effective approach to EU-China cooperation in the sector.

Francesca Spigarelli
Louise Curran
Alessia Arteconi
Editors

Part I
Europe and China Integration through Trade and Foreign Direct Investments

1

Policies That Promote Environmental Industry in China

Haitao Yin, Francesca Spigarelli,
Xuemei Zhang and Hui Zhou

ABSTRACT

Purpose — We aim to comb the current policies that have been developed to promote the environmental industries in China and analyze them in a comparative manner.

Methodology/approach — We mainly use the method of text study to study the existing policies that Chinese central government published to promote the development of environmental industry. We built a database of policies and regulations from 1979 to 2015 by searching the official website of the Ministry of Environmental Protection of China.

Findings — We find that the existing policies focus on command and control approaches. Policies are more oriented to the stage of production instead of stages of investment and consumption. They rely more on negative incentive when stimulating supply and positive incentive when encouraging demand. Based on existing academic wisdom, we suggest that Chinese government should pay more attention to environmental economic policy and to stimulating demand for environmental products.

Originality/value — Few studies provide a systematic overview of the policy systems that have been developed to promote environmental industry in China in a systematic manner.

Keywords: Environmental industry; policy; regulation; China; text study; research paper

Introduction

A cleaner and less energy-intensive development is a fundamental goal to be achieved for China. Public awareness, mostly in the urban population, has been rising on the need to have access to cleaner water, air, and soil, while the human costs of pollution are increasing rapidly (Lv & Spigarelli, 2016).

Sustainability of industrial growth as well as the health and safety of the population are priorities for the Government (China Greentech Initiative, 2013, p. 69). In the last years, all dimensions of energy security have been promoted, from availability of energy resources, applicability of technology, societal acceptability, to the affordability of energy resources (Yao & Chang, 2014).

The 12th five-year plan has set several measures to address environment issues in the country, which are considered as relevant as "economic restructuring" and "social equality." The Third Plenary Session of the 18th Communist Party of China confirmed and strengthened measures to support China's commitment and has placed environmental issues as the key reform priority.[1] Also, within the 13th five-year plan, the green growth is a priority. In the next five years, China is going to promote clean production, green and low-carbon industry systems, and green finance.

All measures set to promote energy saving, environmental cleanup, and the expansion of use of renewable energies are affecting demand and supply trends in China (China Greentech Initiative, 2013). Competitive national companies are growing in all relevant subsector of the green industry (Lv & Spigarelli, 2015). In this chapter, we focus on policies that have emerged in China to promote the development of environmental protection

---

[1]http://english.cntv.cn/special/18thcpcsession/homepage/index.shtml

industries. A better understanding of these policies and their potential impacts is essential for better policy coordination and future policy innovation, also in the light of international cooperation.

In the literature, researchers have made some efforts to combine this large and growing body of policies through categorizing them. Some understand these policies from the perspective of emphasized industrial aspects: energy saving, environmental protection, and resource recycling, while some classify them based on policy approaches; for instance, economic measures, technology measures, and regulatory measures (Ren, 2009) or macroeconomic policy, industrial policy, and pricing policy (Zhao & Hong, 2010). The classifications are developed mainly for a descriptive purpose, and often based on an ad hoc selection of policies. The existing literature does not provide much insight on policy effectiveness and does not attempt to reveal the linkage between policy approach and its effectiveness. Therefore, they cannot well serve the purpose of developing a better policy or a set of policies; that is, a prescriptive purpose.

Our study is a step to fill this gap. We collected all policies that China's central government has published to promote environmental protection industries from 1979 to 2015 and tried to look at these policies from different angles. Based on the academic observations that scholars have provided on the effectiveness of different types of policies, we offer suggestions for future policy development and implementation.

Chinese Environmental Policies: Looking at the EU and Moving Globally

In spite of its huge efforts in combating environmental pollution, China is still plagued with serious and increasingly challenging environmental issues. According to *the 2013 Report on the State of the Environment in China* (RSEC), China was the world's largest producer of COD and SO_2. China was also the biggest energy consumer, accounting for 22.4% of the global consumption (BP, 2014). Over-dependence on fossil fuels − 67.5% from burning coal and 17.8% from oil − made things worse. As reported by *the 2013 Global Carbon Project* (Carbon Dioxide Information Analysis Center, 2013), China has passed the EU for the first time in terms of per capita CO_2 emissions in 2013 and occupied a greater share (27.6%) of global emissions than both the United States (14.5%) and EU (9.6%). The severe environmental problems are a byproduct of China's tremendous economic growth in the past. It is now increasingly clear that environmental damages, for instance, huge resource consumption, ecological destruction, and frequent environmental accidents, are gradually becoming a constraint on future development and stability in China. Together with mounting domestic as well as international pressure for better environment and lower carbon emission, the efforts of Chinese government in environmental protection has intensified recently.

Controlling the growth of polluting industries, increasing pollution abatement investment, and developing environmental industry are the three main alternatives. The first two often imply increasing production cost or slowing down economic expansion, in conflict with corporate interests and the governmental goals of maintaining a reasonably high growth rate (Wang, Yin, & Li, 2010). Therefore, the third option of developing environmental industries is somewhat favored, and viewed as a way to better reconcile economic growth and environment protection simultaneously. As a result, recent years have witnessed a growing interest in the development of environmental industry.

Although promoting environmental industries as a strategy for sustainable development has caught attentions since early 1980s (Wang, 2012), it wasn't seriously explored by all levels of governments until 2010. On September 8, 2010, environmental protection industry was listed as one of seven strategic emerging industries that should be promoted in *the Decision of the State Council on Accelerating the Development of Strategic Emerging Industries* (DADSEI), and was unequivocally supported by the central government. Later, the 12th five-year plan, published in 2011, further states that environmental industry should be the top priority among all government-favored strategic emerging industries. The plan claimed that the total output of environmental industries should strive to reach 4.5 trillion yuan by the end of 2015, with a 15% average growth rate and accounting for 2% of GDP. This provided a new opportunity for the development of environmental industries in China.

After the DADSEI and the 12th five-year plan was introduced, a number of supporting policies and regulations were put into place. According to Zhang, Gao, Wang, Guo, and Wang (2014), about 550 policies regarding energy conservation and environmental protection were published during the period of

2010–2013, which occupy nearly half of the total (1,195 ones) since 1978 (Zhang et al., 2014). In this chapter, we study all environmental policies that are published by central government and are released on the website of Ministry of Environmental Protection (MEP) from 1979 to May 2015. We follow MEP's classification on its official website and summarize the number of different types of policies in Table 1. Policies from provinces or lower levels of governments are excluded, which explains why our number in Table 1 is smaller than that of Zhang et al.'s (2014).

While promoting internal change for environment protection, China is also looking at cooperation with international partner as an opportunity to learn and also to affirm its role on the global fight for a cleaner world.

A special role in the international landscape is played by cooperation with Europe. The EU and China have been co-operating on environmental issues for a long time. While the

Table 1:   Policies Issued by MEP.

Content	Number
Environmental laws	33
Regulations	180
Rules	489
Environmental economic policy	123
Environmental credit system policy	5
Environmental fiscal policy	58
Green taxation policy	7
Green credit policy	10
Polluting responsibility insurance policy	2
Green security policy	4
Green price policy	7
Environmental trade policy	4
Government green purchase policy	6
Eco-compensation policy	7
Emission trade policy	3
Others	9
Sum	825

Source: China's Ministry of Environmental Protection Official Website www.mep.gov.cn

relation started as a mainly trade-oriented relationship, it has become a wide partnership, which has benefited from a sound institutional framework (De Matteis, 2010, p. 457).

European interest in strengthening environment partnership with China can have several motivations (De Matteis, 2010, p. 464). China can be considered a profitable market, for selling European environmental goods. Moreover, helping China to diversify its energy demand and to improve its energy efficiency could help Europe in the competition for energy supply (Freeman & Holslag, 2009). On the other hand, China has several reasons to engage with the EU, which include the latter's experience in these areas and China's need to implement "more sustainable growth strategies" (Gill & Murphy, 2008).

At the moment, Europe and China cooperation is developed through three main channels and two specific programs (see Table 2).

Table 2:   Environment Cooperation Program between Europe and China: Main Initiatives.

Channels of Cooperation	Specific Programs
1. The Environment Policy Dialogue, at ministerial level. Since 2003 meetings have been taking place regularly, alternating between Brussels and China.	1. **EGP,** The EU-China Environmental Governance Program (2011–2015) In partnership with the Chinese Ministry of Environmental Protection, EGP aims to contribute to the strengthening of environmental governance in China through enhanced administration, public access to information, public participation, access to justice and corporate responsibility in the environmental field (http://www.ecegp.com/index_en.asp).
2. Bilateral cooperation mechanism on forests (BCM), between the Chinese State Forestry Administration and director level at the EC (since 2009).	2. **ESP,** The EU-China Environmental Sustainability Program Launched in September 2012, the project aims to support China's efforts to meet the environmental and climate change targets defined in the 12th five-year Development Plan. The specific objectives focus on the achievement of environmental sustainability through improved water quality and the prevention and control of heavy metal pollution and implementation of sustainable solid waste management.
3. The Climate Change Partnership, developed by Directorate General of the EC on climate action.	

Source: http://ec.europa.eu/environment/international_issues/relations_china_en.htm

EU-China cooperation is expected to be strengthened in the near future also considering outcomes of the recent COP21. All countries that are members of the United Nations Framework Convention on Climate Change (UNFCCC) – 195 nations, plus the EU – have agreed to adopt a new global climate agreement in Paris in December 2015, which will take effect in 2020.[2] Based on declaration of President Xi Jinping, China will "on the basis of technological and institutional innovation, adopt new policy measures to improve the industrial mix, build low-carbon system, develop green building and low-carbon transportation and establish a nationwide carbon-emission trading market."[3]

China has committed to strengthen cooperation with the EU to launch a nationwide carbon emission trading market in 2017.

Research Methods

Within the general international and national policy framework described in the previous paragraph, we mainly use the method of text study to analyze the existing policies that Chinese central government published to promote the development of environmental industry. The environmental industry in our chapter means the industries whose development clearly contribute to environmental protection, including the environmental protection services and the production of environmental protection products, resource recycling products, and environmentally friendly products (*2011 Report on the State of the Environmental Protection Relative Industries in China*).

We developed a database of policies and regulations that promote environmental industry through an effort of searching the official website of the MEP, which is responsible for environmental affairs and compiles almost all policies and regulations related to the environment protection in China from 1979 to May 2015. Totally, we find 825 policies published by the central government, which surely have something to do with environmental protection. Part of these policies may only remotely relate to the goal of promoting environmental industry. For instance, *"Regulations of the People's Republic of China on Nature*

---

[2]http://ec.europa.eu/clima/policies/international/negotiations/future/index_en.htm
[3]http://news.xinhuanet.com/english/2015-12/08/c_134896538.htm

Reserves" published by the State Council in 1994 aimed to protect the natural environment, but has little direct connections
with the promotion of environmental industry. We deleted such
policies and then analyzed the remaining 469 policies.

Analysis of Existing Policies for Promoting Environmental Industries

LAWS, REGULATIONS, RULES, AND ECONOMIC POLICIES: AN OFFICIAL TYPOLOGY

On its public website, the MEP classifies all its policies into four
types: laws (*Fa Lv*), regulations (*Fa Gui*), rules (*Gui Zhang*), and
economic policies. In contrast to economic policies, the first three
can be described as commonly known command and control
policies. Command and control policies rely on governmental
coercive power; on one hand, publishing policies that firms and
other organizations must comply with and on the other hand,
monitoring the regulated entities to make sure that the policies
are well enforced. The difference between laws, regulations, and
rules lies in their legal authority, with Laws the highest and rules
the lowest.

Figure 1 shows how the identified environmental industries
promotion policy fits into these four categories. It is clear that
related laws are quite few and rules dominate the existing policies. According to Figure 1, only three laws were passed: Cleaner

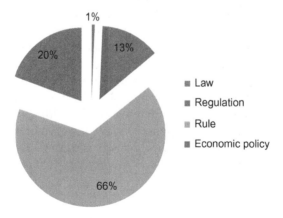

Figure 1: Laws, Regulations, Rules, and Economic Policies. *Source:* MEP
website www.mep.gov.cn

Production Promotion Law of the People's Republic of China (PRC) (2002), Law of the PRC on Conserving Energy (2007), and Circular Economy Promotion Law of the PRC (2008). Rules account for about 66% of the policies that promote environmental industries. The MEP has drawn up standards and technical requirements covering almost all aspects of environmental pollution, such as water, air, waste, noise, and soil pollution.

Although serving as the cornerstone of the regulatory systems for environmental protection, command and control policies have been criticized for its high costs (Tietenberg, 1985), enforcement difficulties (Yin, Pfaff, & Kunreuther, 2011) as well as the lack of incentives for innovations (Popp, 2003). In response to the weaknesses of command and control policies, two kinds of efforts have been tried. First, increase the penalty for regulatory violation to ensure compliance with command and control regulations. For instance, the "*Environmental Protection Law* (EPL)" was revised in 2014 to impose tougher penalties on violators. In order to deter violations like illegal discharge, Article 59 of the new EPL stipulates that violators who refused to correct their violations will receive daily fines with no limit. At the same time, detention punishment was first introduced for excessive discharge. According to Article 63, the responsible persons who allow building before approval will be heavily fined or detained. Moreover, for those violations that are so serious as to constitute crimes, Article 69 shows clearly that criminal responsibilities shall be affixed.

The second effort is to develop so called environmental economic policies, which attempt to utilize the market power and economic incentives to solve the enforcement, cost, and innovation issues. The most noted environmental economic policies include tax, subsidy, trade of emission rights, environmental insurance as well as information disclosure (Portney & Stavins, 2000).

Environmental economic policies emerged in China after 2006 and they now account for about 20% of all the policies. For instance, preferential taxation provides incentives to induce market capital to flow into environmental industries through reducing the tax burden of participants. It could take different forms including tax exemption, tax deduction, tax credit, tax offset, preferential tax rate, tax deferral, tax rebate, and the like. Article 27 of the "*Income Tax Law of PRC for Enterprises*" stipulates that the enterprises that engage in the eligible projects of environmental protection, energy conservation, and water

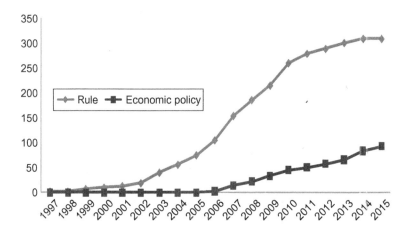

Figure 2: Number of Rules and Economic Policies over Time. *Source:* Authors' Coding of Policies at MEP website.

conservation can enjoy tax exemption or reduction. According to Article 33 and 34, the income that enterprises obtained through business activities that are in line with national industrial policies of comprehensive use of resources may be eligible for tax deduction, and enterprises that purchased and invested in equipment for environmental protection, energy, and water conservation, and safe production may be eligible for tax offset. Figure 2 shows the growth of environmental economic policies over the years and contrast it with the growth of rules. It is clear that although the number of economic policies grows very fast, but is still outpaced by rules. The existing policies for promoting environmental industry in China are still dominated by command and control policies.

INVESTMENT, PRODUCTION, TRADE, AND MARKET: A "VALUE CHAIN PERSPECTIVE"

Chinese government realized that the development of environmental industries needs efforts from all stages in the process of value creation, and therefore developed policies that incentivize each of these stages. In this subsection, we first give policy examples for each of the following stages: investment, production, trade, and market. Then we would step back, take a look at which parts have attracted more attentions and whether there is still space for improvement.

Investment

Obtaining investment stands as the first step to develop environmental industries. Chinese government brings forward various measures to encourage investment in environmental industries and discourage money from flowing into environmentally questionable industries. For instance, under the *Renewable Energy Law*, Chinese central government set up a special fund to back up the development of environmental industry. It can be used into two forms. First, it can be distributed as a grant to support the environmental technology R&D. Second, it can be used by environmentally friendly enterprises to pay part of their loan interest. This would help companies to lower their capital costs.

Another interesting policy is green credit and energy efficiency credit. In July 2007, State Environmental Protection Administration, People's Bank of China, and China Banking Regulatory Commission (CBRC) published the *"Opinion on Implementing Environmental Protection Policies and Regulations and Preventing Credit Risk,"* declaring the comprehensive entrance of green credit as a new weapon against environmental pollution. Green credit serves as a financial lever in the area of environmental protection. For environmentally friendly industries, financial institutions promise preferential low interest rates to encourage their development. But for polluting firms, banks punish them with lending restrictions and high interest rates. Through establishing the environmental threshold for loan access, banks cut off the original capital chain of high-pollution, energy-intensive firms, and channel money to environmental industries. However, in the early stage, the standard of green credit was vague because of the lack of a list of what is and isn't environmentally friendly. The *"Green Credit Guide"* issued by the CBRC in 2012 remedies the defect. The guide also sets a clear requirement for financial institutions that they must carry out the evaluation of green credit at least once every two years, as well as an effective supervision system. According to the data that CBRC released in 2014, the loan balance of 21 main banks on environmental protection projects are about 4.16 trillion yuan, accounting for 6.43% of the total loans (Yang, 2013). Studies have found that green credit policy has effectively encouraged companies to improve their environmental performance and help shifting industrial activities to environmentally friendly fields or/and environmentally friendly companies.

Following the footprints of green credit policy, to support energy-using units in improving energy efficiency and reducing energy consumption, *"Energy Efficiency Credit Guide"* was announced by the CBRC together with the National Development and Reform Commission (NDRC) in early 2015. The guide encourages financial institutions to support credit loan to energy-saving programs, and lists the standards and category of energy-saving programs that should receive favorable treatment.

Production

China used to be and still is a highly centralized country. It has a strong tradition in intervening in economic activities. In the efforts of developing market economy, this tradition has been weakened and the intervention takes more economic approach such as subsidy instead of direct administrative orders. Together with the label of "environmental industries have strong positive externalities," Chinese government widely used fiscal subsidies to promote the development of environmental industries, mostly on the stage of production.

According to the *"Implementation of the Central and Local Budgets for 2014"* submitted by China Ministry of Finance, a considerable amount of expenditure in the 2014 national account book has been used to subsidize environmental protection: 47.85 billion yuan for energy conservation and emission reduction, 11.55 billion yuan for air pollution control, and 17.62 billion yuan for natural forest protection. Taking the promotion of renewable energy development as an example, according to Article 20 of the *"Renewable Energy Law"* (REL) and the *"Renewable Electricity Pricing and Financing,"* renewable power plants are allowed to recover the cost above conventional power through feed-in tariff — a kind of cross-subsidization. Up to now, five large-scale subsidy programs have been implemented, and 1,770 renewable energy power plants have received subsidies. Except for renewable energy power generation, subsidy is also given to the construction of grid that connects renewable electricity and independent public renewable power systems.

Trade

As a huge open economy, Chinese governments also pay attention to the trade and develop policies to promote the export and import of environmentally friendly products, and to control and limit high polluting and energy-consuming ones. Basically, the policies use two approaches: one is using taxation to encourage or discourage the trade; the other is stopping or limiting the trade of certain products. As early as 1997, the State Council made a notice to adjust the taxation on imported equipment. The notice stipulates exemption from tariff and import-linked value-added tax for imported equipment belonging to government-flavored important programs, which include the development of environmentally friendly industry. In 2005, NDRC together with other core government departments (Ministry of Finance, Ministry of Commerce, Ministry of Land and Resources, General Administration of Customs, State Administration of Taxation (SAT), and MEP) announced "*Measures to control the export of some high energy-consuming, high pollution and resource products.*" The notice announced some measures to discourage the export and import of the environmentally unfriendly products, such as stopped approving processing trade contracts of some high-pollution products, canceled the export rebate of coal tar, hide, pelt and others, decreased the export rebate rate to only 5% for 25 kinds of pesticides, limited the exportation amount of resource products like rare earths and gasoline.

Most of the existing policies focus on controlling and discouraging the trade of environmentally unfriendly industry, which mainly refers to highly energy-consuming, highly polluting, and resource intensive products. There are several policies that clearly and directly promote the environmental industry in the trade or investment part in the process of value creation. The "*Catalog for the Guidance of Foreign Investment Industry (amended in 2007)*" issued by NDRC and Ministry of Commerce listed the recycling economy, clean production, and other industries into encouragement catalog, encouraging foreign investment into the environmental industry. Take the Sino-EU trade for example, the central finance budget arranged a special fund for the energy saving and emission reduction research corporation of Sino-EU small and medium enterprises, aiming to support the R&D corporation, technology innovation, and scientific achievement exchange in the field of energy saving and emission reduction. In 2011, Ministry of Finance (MF) and Ministry of Science and Technology (MST) issued a measure to manage the fund, and four million yuan was aided for 19 programs in 2013, among which 17 are R&D programs (MST). The government gives financial support to the corporation of environmental industry between China and Europe Union, but so far the support still stays in the stage of scientific research.

The trade in environmental industries continues developing. The export contract value of environmental protection industries in 2000 is 1.41 billion dollars and grows to 33.38 billion dollars in 2011, much faster higher than the growth of GDP (*Report on the State of the Environmental Protection Relative Industries in China in*, 2000, 2011).

Market

The last step in the process of value creation is marketing and sales. Chinese government has developed policies to help increase the market acceptance and popularity of environmentally friendly product. Increasing government purchase is probably one of the most commonly tools to encourage consumption of environmentally friendly products and services in the world. Since Chinese central and local budget departments first took "*green government purchase*" into practice in 2007, the government has been shifting its purchasing demands to energy saving and environmentally protection products, which successfully played a role model for the public. Moreover, the "*Notice about Building the System of Government Procurement of Energy Saving Products*" announced by the General Office of the State Council in July 2007 made it clear that, on the premise of satisfying the needs, energy-saving products must be the priority when governments use financial funds to conduct purchasing activities, which formally lifted government green purchase to be a mandatory requirement. At the same time, the notice also claimed to set up a priority product list for the convenience of all levels of governments to choose from.

In the latest "*Government Procurement Act*" (the State Council Order No. 658) passed by the 75th State Council Executive meeting on December 31, 2014, the Article 6 repeats the role of environmental factors in the government purchase process. Through establishing purchase demand standard, reserving procurement share and offering preferential price, government shall give priority to purchase products conducive to energy conservation and environmental protection, and thereby promoting the development of environmental industry.

Figure 3 describes how the existing policies distribute along the different stages of value chain. It reveals that 65% of the policies focus on production process, while only 13% of the mare oriented toward marketing and consumption part. Wang et al.

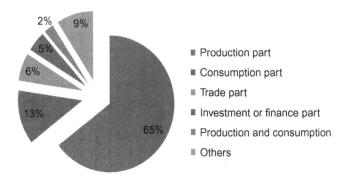

Figure 3: A Value Chain Perspective of Environmental Industry Policies. *Source:* Authors' Coding of Policies at MEP website.

(2010), in their study of China's policies on promoting renewable development, argued that the focus on production has resulted in excessive production capacity in renewable electricity, much larger than the lagged development of demand. As a result, it is observed that many renewable generators are not connected to the state grid and stand there idle for most of the time, or running at a very low operational efficiency. Yin (2014) further argued that many so called environmental industries, for instance the photovoltaic industry, are highly polluting and energy intensive in the production process. The PV products produce positive externality only when they are used. Therefore, government subsidies should be given the consumption or the use of PV products, instead of the production of PV products.

Therefore, we suggest that Chinese government should be careful when further promoting the production of environmental industries, especially through subsidy policies. Financial subsidies are legitimate only when they are used to reward realized positive externalities, which are often in the stage of consumption.

CARROT AND STICK: A PERSPECTIVE OF INCENTIVE APPROACH

From an entrepreneurial/firm perspective, switching to environmental industries often means giving up mature and often profitable traditional business and moving to a new field that is often full of uncertainty. Entrepreneurs may do not so, unless the government provide some incentives. In this paragraph we examine the identified existing policies from the perspective of incentive approaches that these policies have employed. "Carrot" points to positive incentive, that is, companies would be rewarded for their efforts of developing environmental industries. "Stick" points to negative incentive, that is, companies would be penalized for hinging upon environmentally questionable industries. We further differentiate whether the policies focus on supply or demand side. For example, the *Notice of Charging the Use of Plastic Bag* belongs to the category of negative demand because it discourages the demand for traditional but environmentally bad products.

Negative Incentive

For companies whose operations have harmful implications for the environment, negative incentives could create spaces or motivations for developing environmental industries. For instance, charging fossil fuel power plants a pollution fee for discharging SO_2 could benefit two environmental industries: first is giving renewable power generators a competitive advantage and second is by stimulating demand for desulfurization equipment and service.

To control environmental pollution, Chinese government began to charge pollution fee as early as 1980s. On February 28, 2003, the first legally binding and uniform standard for pollution fee, the "*Regulations for Levy Standard on Pollution Discharge,*" was issued. According to Article 3 of the regulation, governments at the level of county or above shall charge polluters for discharging waste water, waste gas, waste solid material and hazardous waste, or excessive noise, based on the pollution types and amounts. In 2014, the government undertook a major overhaul of the pollution charge schedule. The "*Notice on Issues concerning the Adjustment of Pollution Charge Schedule*" published by the NDRC, the Ministry of Finance and the MEP announced: for exhaust emissions, the rates of discharging sulfur dioxide and nitrogen oxide must be increased to no less than 1.2 yuan per equivalent before June 2015; for waste water, the discharge fees of COD, ammonia nitrogen, and five heavy metals (lead, mercury, chromium, cadmium, and arsenic) must be increased to no less than 1.4 yuan per equivalent. Both doubled the previous level, which reflects a less tolerant attitude of government to environmental contamination.

Positive Incentive

Many examples that we give in this section are positive incentives; for instance, subsidies given to environmental industries, government purchasing requirements, and so on. Some other examples include the use of eco-labels. The purpose of eco-label is to remove the information asymmetry between companies and consumers. With an eco-label attached, consumers can easily tell which product is produced in an environmentally friendly manner or which products are more energy saving during its lifetime of usage. On May 17, 1994, China Environment Labeling Product Certification Committee was established to formally implement the "China Environmental Labeling Plan," which is linked to the international "eco-label system." In terms of authentication method, the procedure has been conducted in strict accordance of the international standards of "ISO 14020," "ISO 14021," and "ISO 14024." Up to the end of 2012, more than 2,500 enterprises and over 45,000 products had passed "attestation of Chinese environment labeling," and the annual output value had exceeded over 200 billion yuan. Other examples include "Organic Food Mark" and "Energy Efficiency Label." If more and more consumers follow Eco-labels and choose to buy products that are good for environment, incentive will be created by millions of buyers to impel firms to consciously strive for cleaner production or developing more environmentally friendly products.

Figure 4 shows how the existing policies selected their incentive approaches. It reveals that the existing policies rely

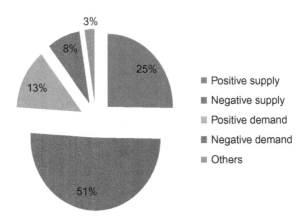

Figure 4: Incentive Types of Environmental Industry Policies. *Source*: Authors' Coding of Policies at MEP website.

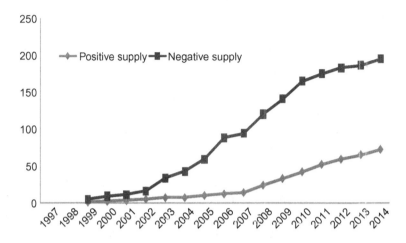

Figure 5: Growth of Negative and Positive Supply Policies. *Source*: Authors' Coding of Policies at MEP website.

more on positive incentives when targeting boosting demand for environmental industries and more on negative incentives when oriented to creating supply for environmental industries. Figure 5 demonstrates how the policies that use positive and negative incentives to promote supply change over time. It is clear that the approach of negative incentive is increasing at a faster pace.

Concluding Remarks

It is a daunting task to comb the policies that have been developed to promote environmental industries. The first challenge is the large number of policies that have been put in place. The second challenge is the complexity of these policies. A policy could target multiple stages along the value chain, and could use both positive and negative incentives. The third challenge is that few studies have been done to look at the impacts of these policies, especially from a comparative perspective.

We made a first step to fulfill this task. We collect these policies in an organized manner, and then examine these policies from different perspectives. As for the linkage between policy design and its effectiveness, we rely on the existing academic wisdom. The first observation is that China still relies on command

and control approaches to promote environmental industries. These approaches have been plagued with cost, implementation as well as incentive issues. Economic policies, when feasible, may be able to achieve a better result with a lower cost. The number of environmental economic policies is increasing in China. Efforts should be made to expand the use of these policies.

The second observation is that the existing policies focus primarily on the stage of production. This may lead to two undesired outcomes. First, the development of production goes much faster than demand, and therefore results in excessive supply. Second, the production process of environmental industries is not necessarily clean and energy saving. For instance, the PV industry is often viewed as environmental industry. But the environmental benefits from this industry will not realize until the products are used to replace traditional energy. The production process is polluting and energy-intensive. Therefore, we suggest that future policies should focus on the demand side; that is, boosting the use of products from environmental industries.

The third observation is negative incentive is used more often than positive incentive in the existing policies. We have no basis to suggest which one is better. Therefore, the observation from this perspective is no more than fact description.

Acknowledgment

We thank the financial support from National Natural Science Foundation of China (No. 71202071, 71322305, 71421002) and Ministry of Education of China (PSCIRT No. 13030).

References

BP. (2014). *Statistical review of world energy*. Retrieved from http://www.bp.com/statisticalreview

Carbon Dioxide Information Analysis Center. (2013). *2013 global carbon project*. Retrieved from http://cdiac.ornl.gov/GCP/carbonbudget/2013/

China Greentech Initiative. (2013). *China at a crossroad*. The China greentech report 2013. Retrieved from http://cgtr.chinagreentech.com/CGTIChinaGreentechReport2013.pdf

De Matteis, P. (2010). EU-China cooperation in the field of energy, environment and climate change. *Journal of Contemporary European Research*, 6(4), 449–477. Retrieved from http://www.jcer.net/ojs/index.php/jcer/article/view/242/233. Accessed on January 9, 2015.

Freeman, D., & Holslag, J. (2009). Climate for cooperation: The EU, China and climate change. Brussels Institute of Contemporary Chinese Studies. Retrieved from http://www.vub.ac.be/biccs/site/assets/files/apapers/Policy%20papers/Freeman_Holslag_EU_China_Climate.pdf

Gill, B., & Murphy, M. (2008). *China-Europe relations: Implications and policy responses for the United States.* A report of the CSIS freeman chair in China studies. CSIS. Retrieved from http://csis.org/files/media/csis/pubs/080507-gill-chinaeuroperelations-web.pdf

Lv, P., & Spigarelli, F. (2015). The integration of Chinese and European renewable energy markets: The role of Chinese foreign direct investments. *Energy Policy, 81,* 14–26.

Lv, P., & Spigarelli, F. (2016). The determinants of location choice: Chinese foreign direct investments in the European renewable energy sector. *International Journal of Emerging Markets, 4,* forthcoming.

MEP. (2000). *2000 report on the state of the environmental protection relative industries in China* (in Chinese).

MEP. (2011). *2011 report on the state of the environmental protection relative industries in China.* Retrieved from http://www.mep.gov.cn/gkml/hbb/bgg/201404/W020140428585697464457.pdf. (in Chinese).

MEP. (2013). *Report on the state of the environment in China (RSEC)* (in Chinese). Retrieved from http://www.mep.gov.cn/gkml/hbb/qt/201407/W020140707500480541425.pdf.

Popp, D. (2003). Pollution control innovations and the clean air act of 1990. *Journal of Policy Analysis and Management, 22*(4), 641.

Portney, P. R., & Stavins, R. N. (2000). Public policies for environmental protection. Resources for the Future.

Ren, Y. (2009). *The study of the environmental industry development in China.* Doctoral dissertation, Jilin University (in Chinese).

State Council. (1994). *Regulations of the People's Republic of China on nature reserves.* Retrieved from http://www.gov.cn/gongbao/content/2011/content_1860776.htm

State Council. (2010). *The decision of the state council on accelerating the development of strategic emerging industries (DADSEI).* Retrieved from http://www.gov.cn/zwgk/2010-10/18/content_1724848.htm. (in Chinese).

Tietenberg, T. H. (1985). *Emissions trading: An exercise in reforming pollution policy.* Washington, DC: Resources for the Future.

Wang, F., Yin, H., & Li, S. (2010). China's renewable energy policy: Commitments and challenges. *Energy Policy, 38*(4), 1872–1878.

Wang, J. (2012). Opportunities and strategies of energy-saving and environmental protection industries in the twelfth five-year plan. *Macroeconomic Management, 332*(8), 51–52 (in Chinese).

Yang, G. (2013). Energy saving and environmental protection industry meet major development opportunities. *Modern Industrial Economy and Information Technology, 51*(13), 6–7.

Yao, L., & Chang, Y. (2014). Energy security in China: A quantitative analysis and policy implications. *Energy Policy, 67,* 595–604.

Yin, H. (2014). The future of energy. *South Reviews, 511*(7), 95 (in Chinese).

Yin, H., Pfaff, A., & Kunreuther, H. (2011). Can environmental insurance succeed where other strategies fail? The case of underground storage tanks. *Risk Analysis, 31*(1), 12–24.

Zhang, G., Gao, X., Wang, Y., Guo, J., & Wang, S. H. (2014). Measurement, coordination and evolution of energy conservation and emission reduction policies in China: Based on the research of the policy data from 1978 to 2013. *China Population Resources and Environment, 24*(12), 62–73 (in Chinese).

Zhao, X., & Hong, D. (2010). Historical evolution and future prospect of China's energy saving policy. *Soft Science, 24*(4), 29–33 (in Chinese).

2

The Environmental Goods Trade between China and the EU: Development and Influencing Factors

Ruxiao Qu and Yanping Zeng

ABSTRACT

Purpose — This chapter seeks to analyze trade in environmental goods between China and the EU and highlight prominent problems and future opportunities.

Methodology/approach — We explore trade empirically, based on the definition of environmental goods proposed by OECD and database from UN COMTRADE (HS96).

Findings — We find that value of trade in environmental goods between China and the EU has increased from $2.759 billion in 1996 to $42.446 billion in 2012, with an average annual growth rate of 21%. Trade is concentrated in Germany, the Netherlands, Italy, France, and Belgium (together accounting for 82%). China has a trade deficit in most categories of environmental goods. Overall, although trade in environmental goods between China and the EU has increased rapidly, the trade structure is unbalanced and the competitiveness of China's environmental goods trade is still low.

Practical implications – This chapter provides a robust basis for analysis of trade in environmental goods between China and the EU.

Originality/value – Discussions on environmental goods trade are complicated by a lack of clear definition and lack of consistent data. This chapter provides a clear and consistent data set in order to have a robust basis for analysis of this important phenomenon.

Keywords: China; Europe; environmental goods trade

Introduction

In recent years, with rapid development of the global economy, enormous problems of environmental impacts have emerged. Countries around the world have begun to pay close attention to these problems. Meanwhile, China's environmental protection industry also has been developing rapidly. Since China joined the WTO in 2001, its total trade volume of environmental goods has increased markedly and its international competitiveness has improved continuously. At the same time, trade in environmental goods has increased strongly between China and the European Union (EU), which is the global leader in the environmental protection industry and renewable energy development (Sinclair-Desgagné, 2008).

Developing trade in environmental goods between China and the EU has a lot of benefits. On one hand, it is not only conducive to the development of the environmental industry and the enhancement of environmental technologies in China but also promotes its domestic economic development and improves the quality of life. Therefore, it is very important to better understand the main developments in trade in environmental goods between China and the EU, its structure, problems, and future opportunities. However, discussions on the issue suffer from the lack of a clear definition on what constitutes environmental goods trade. The objective of this chapter is to provide a clear and consistent data set in order to have a robust basis for analysis.

Literature Review

Generally, environmental goods can be divided into two categories: first, goods for primary and industrial processes in areas of merchandise sewage treatment, air pollution control, and other fields and second goods which can reduce negative impact or have a potentially positive impact on the environment during the production and processing of other goods or in energy production. However, due to the comprehensiveness of environmental activities, there is still no definition of environmental goods that is internationally agreed. According to OECD[1] (1999), environmental goods refers to primary industrial products and processed industrial products that are used to provide environmental services, such as sewage disposal, solid waste treatment, air pollution control, etc. Meanwhile, the OECD and the EU Statistics Bureau also jointly proposed a general framework for the classification of environmental products. In addition, APEC also proposed a list of environmental goods in 2012[2] (Steenblik, 2005).

Studies on environmental goods trade have mainly focused on the liberalization of the trade in environmental goods and trade policy of China (Chen, 2008; Wan, 2011; Zhong, 2010). Specifically, Chen (2008) focused on the significance of international trade in environmental goods for the development of environment industry in China; Zhong (2010) analyzed the impact of liberalization of environmental goods trade on developing countries from tariff revenue, domestic industry, and international interests and other aspects. Wan (2011) focused on environmental goods trade by studying preliminarily the negotiations on offensive and defensive interests of China of environmental goods in Doha Round Ring. However, no research specifically analyses the development and future opportunities of trade in environmental goods between China and the EU.

---

[1] OECD (1999, pp. 9–13).
[2] http://www.apec.org/Meeting-Papers/Leaders-Declarations/2012/2012_aelm/2012_aelm_annexC.aspx

Methodology

To unify the definition and classification of environmental goods, this chapter exploits the definition proposed by the OECD (see Table A1). In addition, to avoid errors caused by different statistical standards, the trade data comes from United Nations commodity trade database (United Nations COMTRADE database) with unified HS code (96) from 1996 to 2012. This time period was chosen as it covers the years both before and after China joined the WTO, and thus the period when trade in all products grew most rapidly. Trade is reported in unadjusted dollar values.

Bilateral Trade in Environmental Goods between China and the EU Countries

With the development of environmental industry in China, its international competitiveness has increased gradually, in line with total trade value. As leaders in the industry of renewable energy and environmental goods, EU countries are important trade partners of China in the sector. Therefore, it is valuable and significant to investigate the development and main situation of trade in environmental goods between China and the EU.

OVERALL TRENDS

According to data from the United Nations Commodity Trade Database (UN COMTRADE), total trade value in environmental goods between China and 28 countries of EU has increased from $2.759 billion in 1996 to a maximum of $55.878 billion in 2011, which represents a 20-fold increase (Figure 1). The trade deficit has exhibited a similar trend in recent years. The share of environmental goods in all commodities trade was fairly stable at around 6% until the late 2000s, when it rose, peaking at 10% in 2010 before falling again more recently. The average annual growth rate of trade value in environmental goods between China and the EU was 21% during the period, although very variable annually (Figure 2).

This growth is linked to the establishment of policies to encourage the environmental goods industry in EU countries, as well as the development of the environmental goods industry and

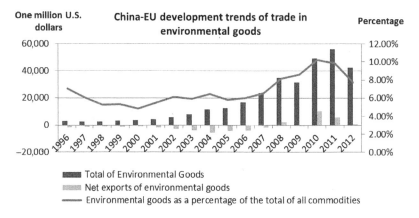

Figure 1: Trends in Trade in Environmental Goods between China and the EU. *Source*: Authors' calculations from UN COMTRADE database.

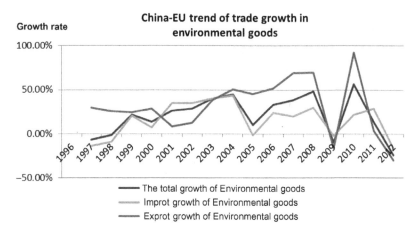

Figure 2: Growth in Trade in Environmental Goods between China and the EU. *Source*: Authors' calculations from UN COMTRADE database.

improvement of international competitiveness in environmental goods of China. However, following the global financial crisis in 2009 and debt crisis in Eurozone, trade value fell by 10%, in 2009 from $34.876 billion to $31.458 billion. We see a subsequent gradual revival in trade, as the global economy recovered and the EU implemented rescue measures to address the debt crisis. Trade reached $55.878 billion in 2011 although it fell again in 2012. Overall the figures show that trade in environmental

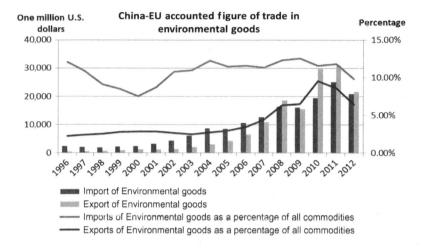

Figure 3: Trends in Export and Import Trade in Environmental Goods between China and the EU. *Source*: Authors' calculations from UN COMTRADE database.

goods between China and the EU is generally on a positive trajectory and should have great potential in the future.

Looking at the figures in more detail, we see that import and export trade in environmental goods has exhibited different trends. Before 2008, China's imports always exceeded its exports to the EU, with the highest deficit ($5.492 billion) seen in 2004 (Figure 3). However, in 2008 exports exceeded imports for the first time and over the following years in 2010 and 2011 trade surpluses were significant, although in 2012 flows were once more rather balanced. Meanwhile, the share of environmental goods in China's total imports has historically been greater than its share of total exports indicating that trade in environmental goods between China and the EU has tended to be more concentrated on import trade, although that is changing, as we see in the later figures. The proportion of environmental goods in China's total exports has increased in recent years and the growth rate has been greater than that of import trade (Figure 2).

TRADE STRUCTURE BY PARTNER

Figure 4 presents the main partners among EU countries and the share of environmental goods trade with China.

As shown in Figure 4, the main EU trade partners of China in total trade in environmental goods are Germany (39%), the

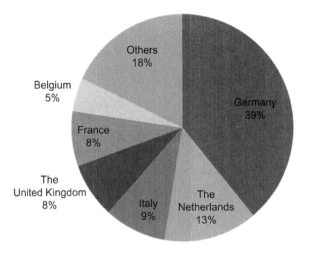

Figure 4: Key EU Partners of China's Trade in Environmental Goods. *Source:* Authors' calculations from UN COMTRADE database.

Netherlands (13%), Italy (9%), the United Kingdom (8%), France (8%), and Belgium (5%). Trade with these key partners represents about 82% of EU trade in environmental goods with China, indicating that the concentration of China's trade in environmental goods in EU countries is quite high.

Prominent Problems in Trade of Environmental Goods between China and the EU

Based on the above analysis, environmental goods trade between China and the EU has shown a strong development as a whole. However, there are still some problems worth noting, such as an unbalanced trade structure, differences in competitiveness of import and export, and trade frictions and barriers.

IMBALANCES IN TRADE IN ENVIRONMENTAL GOODS BETWEEN CHINA AND THE EU

As we know, trade between China and the EU occupies a very important position in China's foreign trade, which has a pivotal role in the economic growth of China. The total trade volume between China and the EU reached $547.7 billion dollars in 2012, although the trade volume of environmental goods accounts for only 7%. There is certainly potential for expansion in this share.

Moreover, the structure of environmental goods trade between China and the EU has often been quite imbalanced. Although, environmental goods export from China to the EU has grown rapidly in recent years, it still accounts for a lower proportion of the total exports than trade in the other direction. Furthermore, China had a deficit in environmental goods trade from 1997 to 2007, although that situation has tended to reverse since the financial crisis. Currently, the situation is fairly balanced, but it is unclear what direction trends will now take.

LOW COMPETITIVENESS OF CHINA'S ENVIRONMENTAL GOODS

From the point of the overall development of China's environmental industry, although it has grown rapidly and there are a large number of enterprises trading in environmental goods and providing environmental services, the economic benefit is still low due to the small size of the enterprises. Besides, the environmental industry is still in the process of developing, thus, its technology and competitiveness in global market is relatively low (You & Wen, 2014). Moreover, from the point of view of the system, the enterprises providing environmental services are often closely linked to the government and thus often lack modern management systems. This makes it difficult to compete with the advanced countries of EU (Gong, 2014), and hampers further expansion of environmental goods trade.

Lastly, from the perspective of international and national policies, the lists of environmental goods which are most widely used are from OECD or APEC. Both of these emphasize capital and technology intensive goods, which tends to result in developed countries having an absolute advantage in environmental goods trade. The average applied tariff rate of the environmental goods in the two lists in developed countries is generally lower than developing countries, which will inevitably hamper the trade of developing countries.

TRADE FRICTIONS AND BARRIERS IN ENVIRONMENTAL GOODS TRADE BETWEEN CHINA AND THE EU

Finally, although on one hand, EU countries have underlined the importance of environmental protection, developing environmental industry since the beginning of the 1980s, on the other, these policies often become an important reason for the trade frictions or trade disputes with other countries. In particular, some of the policies are considered to amount to "green trade barriers" for the export of China's environmental goods (Luo, 2012), which hinders the further development of environmental goods trade with the EU.

Furthermore, trade barriers to trade in environmental goods between China and the EU still exist. In the list of environmental goods from OECD, the applied tariff rate in developed countries is much lower than that in developing countries. The biggest gap of the applied tariff rate was registered in 2001, when the applied tariff rate for environmental goods trade was less than 1% in developed countries, while it was 10% in developing countries (Balineau & de Melo, 2013). However, with the rapid development of environmental industry, the tariff rate of environmental goods is tending to fall in both developed and developing countries. This provides a supportive international context for the further development of environmental goods trade between China and the EU.

FUTURE DEVELOPMENT OF TRADE IN ENVIRONMENTAL GOODS BETWEEN CHINA AND THE EU

Against the background of economic globalization and the rapid development of the environmental industry and trade, the development of environmental goods trade between China and the EU has many benefits. On one hand, it is not only conducive to the development of the environmental industry and the enhancement of environmental technologies but it can also promote China's domestic economic development and improve quality of life. Our analysis indicates that trade has expanded extensively in recent years on both directions and, although China has historically had a trade deficit with the EU, in recent years it has managed to develop exports such that in the most recent year of analysis (2012) it had a small trade surplus.

In terms of the future, there are several reasons to believe that the expansion of China-EU trade in this sector would be beneficial. Firstly, developing environmental goods trade between China and the EU can further promote the development of the formers' environmental industry. Much of China's environmental industry focuses on pollution control. The export of environmental goods provides the opportunity to increase revenues and wealth creation in the environmental industry. Therefore, the development of trade in environmental goods, especially export trade, is extremely important to developing the environmental industry and improving the quality of China's economic and social development.

Secondly, developing environmental goods trade between China and the EU can improve the technical level of environmental protection in China. China has a very large potential market demand, which appeals to developed countries of EU, but direct sales of environmental goods or technology from developed countries face some barriers. Encouraging the introduction of advanced environmental technology through commercial transfer can promote secondary development or adaptation of environmental technology.

Thirdly, developing environmental goods trade between China and the EU can promote China's domestic economic development and improve the environment. Concerning the trade in environmental goods trade between China and the EU, although exports have expanded, China remains dependent on imports. The latter can not only increase the quantity of environmental goods and enhance the quality of environmental services, but also improve the living environment, reduce costs and government spending. At the same time, it may stimulate the progress of the environmental technology of domestic enterprises and encourage inventions and creations of environmental technology, thereby further increasing the size of the environmental industry and enterprises and improving efficiency.

It is obvious that the liberalization of the trade in environmental goods has the potential to benefit both sides, but the liberalization requires mutual efforts. Therefore, China should use its own advantages, push forward the development of the trade in environmental goods between China and Europe and maximize the mutual benefits in accordance with the features of European market.

In conclusion, as the position of China's environmental industry is improving in the international trade market, however, there is a need to grasp further opportunities, enhance the competitiveness of environmental goods, and develop environmental goods trade, especially with the EU. Eventually, environmental industry will become a new growth point of China's international trade.

Acknowledgments

This chapter was funded by People Program (Marie Curie Actions) of the European Union's Seventh Framework Program FP7/2007-2013/ under REA grant agreement n° 318908.

References

Balineau, G., & de Melo, J. (2013). Removing barriers to trade on environmental goods: An appraisal. *World Trade Review*, *12*(04), 693–718.

Chen, Y. (2008). Opportunities and challenges of opening the environmental goods and services market. *Statistics and Decision*, *6*, 103–105.

Gong, Q. H. (2014). Estimation of global advantage and competitiveness of China's environmental goods. *Practice in Foreign Economic Relations and Trade*, *3*, 76–79.

Luo, W. (2012). Impact of environmental regulations on trade competiveness of China's environmental goods. *Modern Business*, *11*, 30–36.

OECD. (1999). *The environmental goods & services industry: Manual for data collection and analysis*. Paris: OECD Publications.

Sinclair-Desgagné, B. (2008). The environmental goods and services industry. *International Review of Environmental and Resource Economics*, *2*(1), 69–99.

Steenblik, R. (2005). *Environmental goods: A comparison of the APEC and OECD lists (No. 2005/4)*. Paris: OECD Publishing.

Wan, Y. T. (2011). The research of interests of attack and defense of our country in the Doha round environmental negotiations. *International Trade*, *2*, 112–117.

You, H. B., & Wen, J. (2014). Analysis on export competitiveness of China's environmental goods. *China Opening Journal*, *4*, 14–17.

Zhong, J. (2010). Analysis on the factors of environmental goods and services trade liberalization: Perspective from developing countries. *Henan Social Sciences*, *6*, 140–142.

Appendix

Table A1: Statistical Framework of Environmental Goods and Service.

	Second Class	Third Class
A. Pollution management group	Production of equipment and specific materials	Air pollution control
		Wastewater management
		Solid waste management
		Remediation and clean-up of soil, surface water, and groundwater
		Noise and vibration abatement
		Environmental monitoring, analysis and assessment
		Other
	Provision of services	Air pollution control
		Wastewater management
		Solid waste management
		Remediation and clean-up of soil, surface water, and groundwater
		Noise and vibration abatement
		Environmental R&D
		Environmental contracting and engineering
		Analytical services, data collection, analysis, and assessment
		Education, training, information
		Other
	Construction and installation	Air pollution control
		Wastewater management
		Solid waste management
		Remediation and clean-up of soil, surface water, and groundwater
		Noise and vibration abatement
		Environmental monitoring, analysis and assessment
		Other

Table A1:   (*Continued*)

	Second Class	Third Class
B. Clean technologies and products group	Production of equipment, technology, specific materials, or services	Clean/resource-efficient technologies and processes Clean/resource-efficient products
C. Resource Management group	Production of equipment, technology and specific materials, provision of services, and construction, and installation	Indoor air pollution control Water supply Recycled materials Renewable energy plant Heat/energy saving and management Sustainable agriculture and fisheries Natural risk management Eco-tourism Other

Source: OECD (1999, pp. 9–13).

3

International Integration and Uneven Development: An Enquiry into the Spatial Distribution of Foreign Firms in China

Hongbo Cai and Eleonora Cutrini

ABSTRACT

Purpose – The objective of this chapter is to provide a first assessment on the evolution of spatial distribution of foreign firms in China.

Methodology/approach – We examine the overall changes in the location of foreign firms in China over the period 1999–2009. Then, we distinguish two time periods, 1998–2001 and 2002–2009 so as to analyze whether foreign firms' agglomeration across regions has changed significantly after the China's entry into the WTO (2001) and the first launch of the Chinese government policies to develop western internal areas.

Findings — Our analysis suggests that foreign-invested enterprises (FIEs) with higher foreign capital shares are more geographically clustered in coastal regions than other enterprises with lower foreign capital shares. This group with the highest intensity of foreign involvement in firm capital also experienced the most relevant changes over the decade of our analysis becoming more localized between the core-periphery divide (coastal provinces and the rest of mainland China).

Research limitations — The main limitation refers to poor data availability, data matching problems, and measurement errors in the database used, as highlighted by Nie, Jiang, and Yang (2012).

Practical implications — A general analysis of location patterns and the role of public policies may inform foreign companies in their entry strategy in the Chinese market.

Originality/value — Very few studies have explored location patterns with detailed geographical data and, at the same time, with data disaggregated by foreign ownership shares.

Keywords: Industrial agglomeration; foreign firms; entropy measures; regional inequalities

Introduction

The development process from low to high income is far from ubiquitous within countries as producers tend to prefer some places (cities, coastal areas) to locate their firms. An excessive spatial agglomeration of production and wealth then entails introducing policies that make living standards of people more uniform across space.

With the economic reform, in 1978, China abandoned its traditional import-substitution model in favor of the export-orientated one. Thereinafter, the country experienced a miraculous economic growth which was accompanied by increasing disparity between coastal and internal region.

The reason why it is important to understand the location of foreign firms and FDI is that it is supposed that inward FDI (and openness to trade) are among the possible main explanations of such increasing regional disparities. In fact, FDI location tend to mimic the spatial distribution of economic activities resulting in their clustering in largest metropolitan areas and regions with better infrastructure and access to foreign markets. Empirical evidence for China tend to confirm this view (Chen & Fleisher, 1996; Fujita & Hu, 2001; Gao, 2004; Ge, 2009; Lin, Lee, & Yang, 2011; Ma, 2006; Wei, Yao, & Liu, 2009; Wen, 2007; Zhang & Zhang, 2003 among others).

In this context, preferential development policies – notably the Western China Development Program (GO-West), first launched more than 10 years ago – was designed to foster a catching-up process of western peripheral less-developed areas, thereby promoting a more balance internal economic geography.

This chapter aims to provide a comprehensive analysis on the evolution of spatial distribution of foreign firms to gain some insights on whether these policies may have been effective in reducing the core-periphery divide or whether, instead, the location advantage of coastal regions has not changed much over the last decade, possibly because of cumulative agglomeration economies. We distinguish foreign firms by the share of foreign capital in total capital to assess whether higher foreign control may be associated to higher agglomeration in capital regions and coastal regions (to have better access to the foreign markets) or in peripheral regions to gain the benefits and incentives provided by the "Go-West Development Policies."

The remainder of the chapter is organized as follows. The section "Literature Review" surveys the background literature, the section "Policy Development in FDI Policy and Regional Development" provides an overview of FDI policies and policies to address uneven development and growing disparities within China. The section "Objectives, Data, and Methodology of the Chapter" offers details on data and the method we adopted. The section "Findings" presents our empirical results and the Section "Conclusions, Shortcomings, and Proposals for Future Research" provides some concluding remarks.

Literature Review

In the China reform program, FDI was regarded as a modernization drive and a major source to promote country's economic growth. Although, the country's experience over the past three decades highlighted the adverse facets of globalization, particularly in relation to the difficulties encountered in spreading the benefits of globalization within the entire territory. In fact, after the economic reform the Chinese manufacturing industry became more geographically concentrated, particularly in the coastal areas since they are endowed with a better access to external markets. Ge (2009) suggests that, beyond the presence of natural advantages and skill endowment foreign trade and FDI significantly affected the increasing industrial agglomeration in China during the period 1985–2005.

Early studies for China suggest that the globalization through trade and FDI contribute to widening regional income disparities within the country (Fujita & Hu, 2001; Wei et al., 2009; Wen, 2007; Zhang & Zhang, 2003). Moreover, further support on the positive relation between agglomeration of FDI and widening income disparities between coastal and non-coastal regions in China is provided by Lin et al. (2011) who found that FDI tends to exhibit a higher impact on productivity in coastal regions than their non-coastal counterparts. Besides, FDI gave rise to increasing wage inequalities between coastal provinces and internal provinces (Ma, 2006).

While it is generally acknowledged that foreign trade and foreign investment are, *ceteris paribus*, positively associated to regional growth (Chen & Fleisher, 1996; Gao, 2004), this does not imply that FDI has determined such high spatial disparity, since causation may also run from regional disparities to FDI. FDI may intensify the existing spatial agglomeration of industrial activities since foreign firms tend to locate where localization or agglomeration economies could be reaped (Bobonis & Shatz, 2007; Bode, Nunnenkamp, & Waldkirch, 2012) and/or where other foreign investors have previously established their production plants (peer effect in the host country) (Mukim & Nunnenkamp, 2012; Nunnenkamp & Mukim, 2012).

Our work also draws some insights from a recent line of research within the new economic geography (NEG, henceforth) framework dealing with the relationship between international integration and the location of economic activities within countries. While some models reach the conclusion that international openness ultimately fosters the dispersion of economic activities within the countries (Fujita, Krugman, & Venables, 1999; Krugman & Livas, 1996), others authors, turning back to NEG's seminal framework (Krugman, 1991), tend to support the idea that internal agglomeration would arise as international economic integration proceeds (Crozet & Koenig-Soubeyran, 2004a,

2004b; Monfort & Nicolini, 2000; Paluzie, 2001). Basically, the outcome on the spatial distribution of economic activities and wealth depends — in theory — on how the process of integration into the world economy constitutes a rupture of the existing tension between centrifugal and centripetal forces. Further models differentiate between industrial location consequences and demographic distribution patterns that economic integration brings about. Basically, they suggest that openness leads to dispersion of urban population and concentration of particular industries characterized by strong linkages (Fujita et al., 1999; Venables, 2000).

It is not surprising that China was one of the most studied cases on the issue, since it experienced both increasing trade integration and FDI and growing spatial agglomeration within the country during its miraculous economic growth in the past decades. Consistent with the importance of port city location highlighted by Overman and Winters (2003) and in the theoretical literature (Fujita & Mori, 1996), coastal Chinese provinces hosting major export markets have become home to many manufacturing industries, and foreign investment have been attracted mainly by this area because of market access considerations (Bao, Chen & Wu, 2013; Wen, 2004).

Policy Development in FDI Policy and Regional Development

THE EVOLUTION OF FDI POLICY IN CHINA

In the initial stage, the FDI policies focused on coastal economic open zone and special economic zone. Pilot export zone was opened up in Guangdong and Fujian in 1979, in 14 coastal cities in 1984, in Hainan Island in 1988. In 1991, the Shanghai Pudong Development was established.

According to some scholars, the early-reform policies to attract FDI may have facilitated the skewed distribution of FDI across regions. "One important reason for the skewed distribution of FDI across regions is the early reforms that focused on opening up four special economic zones in Guangdong and Fujian in 1980, 14 coastal cities in 1984, Hainan Island in 1988 and Shanghai Pudong Development Zone in 1991. Of course, there are fundamental reasons why the coastal cities were selected as open zones. Compared with the inland areas, the coastal regions had a more productive agricultural and industrial base, a more efficient transportation system, better environmental and human resources, and above all, an easier access to China's largest investors, especially Hong Kong" (Yao, 2006).

Since the 1978 reform and opening up, China ended the long-term self-isolation foreign policy, started re-integration into the world economy. Of course the Chinese government has gradually accelerated the pace of attracting FDI. In the initial stage (1979–1984), the government recognized the benefits of FDI for the economic development, then actively attracted foreign capital inflow by various ways. During this period, the Chinese government improved laws, regulations and policy system of the FDI utilization in China, and set up a special department (Foreign Investment Commission, the Ministry of Foreign Trade) for FDI utilization and management. The introducing of foreign capital was gradually become standardized and more sustainable.

Through years of exploration and practice, China entered the initial development phase (1985–1991) of attracting FDI. During this period, the government's restrictions on FDI gradually relaxed. While broadening the channel of using foreign capital, China also consciously focus on industrial structure of FDI and guided foreign capital flow to specific industries. The Chinese government promulgated the "twenty-two" regulation ("Regulations of Encouraging Inward FDI") in 1986, and further increased concessions for foreign capital in land, labor, taxes, etc.

With more standardized FDI utilization and management and implement of preferential policies, China entered the phase of rapid development (1992–2000) of attracting FDI. In early 1992, Xiaoping Deng's Southern Talk clarified a clearer target of market-oriented reform and declared the determination of open expansion. In the same year, the government expanded the scope of opening port cities along the river, inland border cities and the provincial capital cities, and made policy support in many industries. Total use of FDI reached $ 323.3 billion during that period, when in addition to continue to intensify efforts in attracting FDI, it also formulated corresponding measures for the problems in last phase. The Chinese government gradually implement national treatment on foreign-owned companies, and further regulate tax and businesses voucher system on foreign-owned companies.

Since China joined the WTO in the end of 2001, FDI utilization showed steady development state (2001–2006). Emphasis changes from amount to quality, efficiency and structure of the foreign capital. In this stage, the government adjusted the categories of industries encouraged or restricted for FDI. By expanding the allowed areas, tax incentives and other means it encouraged foreign capital heading in central and western regions and encouraged foreign-owned enterprises to cooperate with state-owned enterprises.

Since 2007, the quantity of FDI that China attracted continues to increase, and the quality also improved steadily. China revised and launched many laws and regulations that involving foreign capital in China. Chinese government also transferred from "blind draw" to "reasonable use" in the hope that FDI can play a more important role in promoting industrial upgrading, structural optimization, technological innovation, regional balance, and other aspects of development. China also started to pay attention to introduction of advanced technology, management and high-quality talent, and guided foreign capital to invest in more high-level manufacturing, and rising industries like environmental friendly, new energy.

Recently, the "Catalogue of Priority Industries for Foreign Investment in Central and Western China" released by the China's National Development and Reform Commission and the Ministry of Commerce, is inserted in the Go-West Policy development strategy. The program was launched in March 1999 and gave rise, in the first phase, to an inadequate growth, essentially concentrated to two urban agglomerations (Chengdu e Chongqing). In the second phase, development plans for three special economic zones were set out in the western areas (Chongqing-Chengdu, Guanxi-Golfo di Beibu, Chuangzhong-Tianshui). Then, in the third phase, policy of development was specifically designed for central regions and focused on specific sectors: wheat production, transport, high-technology equipment, energy, and raw materials.

The new Catalogue encourages foreign-invested projects in selected industry and service sectors, and it is organized by province, covering 22 out of the 31 administrative partitions in Mainland China. The aim is to rebalance the economic structure of Chinese provinces, through economic incentives (e.g., fiscal incentives, lower labor cost, tax exemption for imports of machinery and equipment, lower tax rates for profits) in selected sectors for each provincial-level regions (e.g., Anhui: medical devices and key components; Henan: motor vehicles parts and components; Gansu: tourism, transport infrastructure; Shanxi: pension and medical care, raw materials; Chongqing: agriculture and forestry, transports; Inner Mongolia: solar power generation equipment).

POLICY FOR REGIONAL DEVELOPMENT AND REGIONAL DISPARITIES: A JOURNEY THROUGH THE CHINA'S FIVE-YEAR PLANS OVER THE LAST THREE DECADES

The policies to help reducing regional disparities and promote dispersion of economic activities within the country can be seen as a part of the China's leadership effort to reduce various sources of imbalances of the Chinese economy (Bowles, 2012). Once the financial crisis highlighted the vulnerabilities of export-led model of economic development, a consistent set of domestically driven policies aimed at reducing income inequality and external vulnerability were designed to move China onto an endogenously-driven development path. The short-term stimulus package introduced in response to the 2008 worldwide economic crisis, add economic support to the medium-term policies ("Go-West" strategy) to assure a greater role to domestic consumption as a growth driver and reduce external vulnerability and income inequality (Bowles, 2012).

As for territorial development, our journey through the Five-Year Plans allows to highlight the various attempts to shift from an exogenous model of development to an endogenous one.

The Seventh Five-Year Plans (1986–1990) and the successive Five-Year Plan (1991–1995) first adopted a growth pole strategy aims at favoring spatial agglomeration in the coast, with the expectation that the promotion of the coastal region would have activated linkages and multiplier effects that eventually have trickled down in other peripheral regions (central and western provinces) (Perroux theory of "growth poles" behind, Perroux, 1950, 1966). Many foreign-invested firms were concentrated in the export processing and manufacturing areas in the special economic zones, the open cities and Hainan Island.

A first recognition of the need to "pay greater attention to supporting the development of inland areas" is found in the Ninth Five-Year Plan (1996–2000). The theory of endogenous development and strengthening of existing comparative advantages appear as the first theoretical foundation of the designation of seven economic zones across the country, although from the China's 10th Five-Year Plan (2001–2005) a top-down approach resurfaces in the western development strategy, an attempt to reduce economic development disparities in 12 western provinces and two adjoining Prefectures in Hubei and Hunan provinces. This was to be achieved through a combination of central government investment, directed credits from state bond issues, the introduction of preferential policies to induce non-state and foreign investment, and fiscal policies. Moreover the 10th Five-Year Plan marked the beginning of a consistent policy thrust over the past 10 years, to move to a more balanced growth path in which consumption plays a greater role and investment and exports a lesser role, also stressing the importance of the service sector. In this context, the provision of social security are viewed as mechanisms to reduce savings rates and boost consumption. Starting from the 10th (2001–2006) to the 12th Five-Year Plan (2011–2015) several measures have been introduced to improve wealth and support internal demand (e.g., pension scheme in urban areas, increase of employment in urban areas, improve medical and health-care services, increase of minimum wage rate, and net per capita income for urban and rural population). These measures may have, from a territorial point of view, the potentiality to increase the urban-rural divide instead of reducing it. The strategic role of specific territories has recently been explicitly acknowledged by the China's central government in the 11th Five-Year Plan (2006–2010). The plan specifically mentions three industrial areas requiring focused attention to protract national economic development: the Yangtze River and Pearl River Delta regions and the Binhai new coastal city area in Tianjin. This is the first time that any Five-Year Plan has recognized regions smaller than large aggregates of provinces, and portends policy development at a far more appropriate regional scale (Kamal-Chaoui, Leman, & Rufei, 2009).

Objectives, Data, and Methodology of the Chapter

We analyze the location patterns of foreign firms by considering the province-level disaggregation. We group foreign firms according to the proportion of foreign capital (0–25%, 25%–50%, 50%–75%, and more than 75%).

The data in the chapter comes from Chinese Industrial Enterprises Database (CIED), which was established by the China National Bureau of Statistics. The sample ranges from state-owned industrial enterprises and non-state-owned industrial enterprises above designated size. The database is the most comprehensive firm-class database, including overview data as well as financial data of enterprises, more than a total of 130 indicators. "Industrial" in CIED means three categories: "extractive industries," "Manufacturing," and "Electricity, gas and water production and supply," from "China National Economic Industrial Classification." Here the manufacturing account for 90% and above. The database covers all state-owned industrial enterprises and above-scale non-state-owned industrial enterprises. It has been largely used for studies of industrial organization in China (Nie, Jiang, & Yang, 2012 for a critical review).

Table 1 summarizes the enterprises number and the share of state-owned, collectively owned, private, foreign-invested (including Hong Kong, Macao, and Taiwan) enterprises during 1999–2007. Over the period 1999–2007, the number of firms covered by the database per year increases from approximately 160,000 in 1999 to about 330,000 in 2007. Table 1 describes, for each year, the total number of enterprises and the proportion for the same year, according to the ownership's type, such as state-owned, collective, private, foreign owned.

The table shows the remarkable modification of the Chinese industrial structure. The share of state-owned and collectively owned enterprises has declined significantly, dropping from 66% in 1999 to less than 10% in 2007. But the share of private enterprises has increased substantially from less than 20% to more 70%.

Table 1:   Evolution of Firms by Capital Ownership (Number and Share), 1999–2007.

Year	State-Owned		Collective-Owned		Private		Foreign-Owned		Total
	Number	Share	Number	Share	Number	Share	Number	Share	
1999	52,817	32.86	53,507	33.29	27,757	17.27	26,652	16.58	160,733
2000	44,665	27.66	49,383	30.58	39,192	24.27	28,240	17.49	161,480
2001	36,781	21.67	42,528	25.06	59,208	34.89	31,178	18.37	169,695
2002	31,570	17.55	38,237	21.25	75,884	42.18	34,208	19.02	179,899
2003	25,157	12.93	32,334	16.62	98,698	50.74	38,318	19.7	194,507
2004	27,403	9.89	26,896	9.7	165,864	59.85	56,976	20.56	277,139
2005	18,520	6.86	23,875	8.84	171,603	63.53	56,112	20.77	270,110
2006	16,209	5.4	20,983	6.99	202,417	67.43	60,585	20.18	300,194
2007	11,724	3.5	19,355	5.78	236,823	70.68	67,174	20.05	335,076

Source: Adapted from Nie et al. (2012).

For a more detailed description of changes in FDI in China, we divided firms according to regions as well as the proportion of foreign capital, which would be first, according to the administrative division code, the enterprise will go into one prefecture-level city, then according to proportion of foreign capital, it is divided into four intervals: 0−25%, 25%−50%, 50%−75%, and more than 75%, and we calculate the number of the enterprise in each interval. Thus, we could know the number of foreign-capital enterprises in each region and each interval.

Findings

The increasing disparity between coastal and internal regions is one the key feature of Chinese economic development in China. Table 2 displays the evolution of firms by share of foreign ownership.

For the entire sample period, most of the enterprises are in the interval 0−25%. The average proportion of these enterprises is 48.9%, almost half of the total. There are the fewest enterprises in interval 50−75%, the average proportion is 15.6%.

In our sample period (1999−2009), the development of foreign capital into China can be split into two periods.

Table 2:   Number of Firms by Year and Share of Foreign Capital (% of Total Capital).

Year	<25%	25–50%	50–75%	>75%	Total
1999	26,072	17,202	10,196	5,616	59,086
2000	37,843	416	235	155	38,649
2001	6,124	9,393	12,119	8,588	36,224
2002	4,123	7,837	4,022	18,938	34,940
2003	51,942	19,862	14,868	10,876	97,548
2004	25,919	9,911	7,427	5,430	48,687
2005	25,952	9,922	7,430	5,434	48,738
2006	25,972	9,931	7,434	5,438	48,775
2007	26,013	9,939	7,429	5,433	48,814
2008	24,541	9,514	7,141	5,242	46,438
2009	25,825	9,864	7,382	5,405	48,476

In the first period (1999–2003), the FDI fluctuated roughly. The number of foreign-capital enterprises decreased from 59,086 in 1999 to 34,940 in 2002 and grew to 97,548 in 2003 within a short time. The share of the group with the proportion of foreign capital below 25% changed most dramatically. In 2000, the number of enterprises in this group account for 97.9% of all the foreign-capital enterprises, then the proportion fell to below 17% and grew back to 53.2% in 2003.

In the second period (2004–2009), the foreign capital share became rather stable. From 2004 onwards, there are total around 48,000 foreign-capital enterprises. The distribution of firms across categories defined according to the foreign capital share remains almost unchanged. The largest group was still that with less than 25% (52% of all the foreign-capital enterprises). The other groups also kept stable, 20% for interval 25–50%, 15% for interval 50–75%, and 11% for interval above 75%.

One may wonder what the reasons are behind the higher variability in the period 1999–2003, and why the sample across categories becomes more stable since 2004 onwards. One reason is that the dataset suffers from data matching problems and measurement errors. Particularly, as it was recognized by Nie et al., 2012, there are some differences between the data before and after 2003 in the CIED.

We also advocate the following possible reasons behind this result:

1. Since 2000, the world economy showed weak growth momentum, the world's major stock markets continued to fall. With the end of the fifth wave of global mergers and acquisitions, as well as Enron, WorldCom and other large US and European enterprises' scandal, the investors' confidence suffered a heavy strike, making many multinationals to take a "small but efficient" investment strategy. Therefore, international direct investment in 2002 and 2003, following declining trend of the global cross-border mergers and acquisitions, continued to show decreasing trend.

2. China's entered the WTO in 2001, so there may be some fluctuations and unpredictability on China's foreign policy. In order to avoid losses caused by them, foreign investors, to a certain extent, choose the way of diversification.

3. In March 2002, the Chinese government announced a new "Guidance for Inward FDI Industries," and abolished the 1997 version. In the new catalog, some of the traditional

popular FDI areas, such as mining and quarrying, manufacturing, electricity, gas, transportation and other are classified as restricted or prohibited, which interrupted the growth trend of FDI in these traditional area.

The spatial distribution of foreign firms across Chinese provinces in 2009 appears as not dramatically different than in 1999. Still in 2009, almost half of foreign-invested companies are concentrated in the most industrialized provinces along the eastern coast (Guangdong, Shandong, Jiangsu, Zhejiang, Liaoning, Hebei, and Fujian) (Table 3).

In line with previous studies, we suggest that further agglomeration toward coastal provinces still continue to be the case during the study period. Particularly, we found that eastern region

Table 3: Geographical Location of Foreign Firms in China, by Provinces.

	1999		2003		2009	
	n	%	*n*	%	*n*	%
Beijing	512	0.9	844	0.9	417	0.9
Tianjin	504	0.9	860	0.9	427	0.9
Hebei	2,854	4.8	4,768	4.9	2,371	4.9
Shanxi	1,383	2.3	2,302	2.4	1,140	2.4
Inner Mongolia	1,020	1.7	1,478	1.5	732	1.5
Liaoning	3,179	5.4	4,976	5.1	2,466	5.1
Jilin	1,461	2.5	2,324	2.4	1,154	2.4
Heilongjiang	1,621	2.7	2,478	2.5	1,227	2.5
Shanghai	528	0.9	924	0.9	459	0.9
Jiangsu	4,629	7.8	8,054	8.3	4,001	8.3
Zhejiang	3,572	6.0	6,350	6.5	3,157	6.5
Anhui	2,556	4.3	4,208	4.3	2,098	4.3
Fujian	2,193	3.7	3,784	3.9	1,885	3.9
Jiangxi	1,815	3.1	3,058	3.1	1,516	3.1
Shandong	4,522	7.7	8,014	8.2	4,021	8.3
Henan	3,689	6.2	6,244	6.4	3,102	6.4
Hubei	2,850	4.8	4,448	4.6	2,215	4.6
Hunan	2,861	4.8	4,706	4.8	2,331	4.8
Guangdong	5,436	9.2	9,100	9.3	4,529	9.3

Table 3:   (*Continued*)

	1999		2003		2009	
	n	%	*n*	%	*n*	%
Guangxi	1,638	2.8	2,410	2.5	1,186	2.4
Hainan	187	0.3	328	0.3	164	0.3
Chongqing	423	0.7	714	0.7	355	0.7
Sichuan	2,695	4.6	4,418	4.5	2,191	4.5
Guizhou	1,086	1.8	1,782	1.8	883	1.8
Yunnan	1,171	2.0	1,650	1.7	816	1.7
Tibet	218	0.4	334	0.3	166	0.3
Shaanxi	1,283	2.2	2,142	2.2	1,060	2.2
Gansu	1,431	2.4	2,248	2.3	1,117	2.3
Qinghai	405	0.7	572	0.6	283	0.6
Ningxia	350	0.6	510	0.5	255	0.5
Xinjiang	1,014	1.7	1,520	1.6	752	1.6
	59,086	100.0	97,548	100.0	48,476	100.0
Coastal provinces	28,116	47.6	48,002	49.2	23,897	49.3
Central provinces	18,236	30.9	29,768	30.5	14,783	30.5
Western provinces	12,734	21.6	19,778	20.3	9,796	20.2

accounted for over 49.3% of total foreign-invested enterprises in 2009 (it was 47.6 in 1999). Instead, the share of total firms decreased in western provinces (from 21.6 in 1999 to 20.2% in 2009) and central provinces (from 31% to 30.5%).

Table 4 depicts regional shares by groups of firms in three points in time: 1999, 2004, and 2009 (Table 4). It shows that foreign-owned firms with the uppermost share of foreign capital (>75%) displayed a stronger preference for coastal regions (relative to the reference group that is the overall sample of firms). Foreign firms – with the highest capital share held by non-residents (above 75%) – located in coastal regions represented 62% of the total firms belonging to the same group in 1999 and further rise to 67.2% in 2009 (Table 4). As we have seen, for the entire sample of firms, we found that the analogous share is lower and increase less markedly during the observation period (from 47.6% to 49.3%) (Table 2). Similar considerations are valid for the other group with majority control (50–75%).

Table 4: Changing Spatial Distribution across Regions by
Groups of Firms.

	1999	%	2004	%	2009	%
>75%						
Coastal	3,510	62.5	3,646	67.1	3,632	67.2
Central	1,290	23.0	1,109	20.4	1,102	20.4
Western	816	14.5	675	12.4	671	12.4
Total	5,616	100	5,430	100	5,405	100
50−75%						
Coastal	5,623	55.1	4,246	57.2	4,222	57.2
Central	2,853	28.0	1,918	25.8	1,911	25.9
Western	1,720	16.9	1,263	17	1,249	16.9
Total	10,196	100	7,427	100	7,382	100
25−50%						
Coastal	9,076	52.8	5,169	52.2	5,149	52.2
Central	5,012	29.1	2,861	28.9	2,844	28.8
Western	3,114	18.1	1,881	19	1,871	19.0
Total	17,202	100	9,911	100	9,864	100
<25%						
Coastal	9,907	38	10,916	42.1	10,894	42.2
Central	9,081	34.8	8,963	34.6	8,926	34.6
Western	7,084	27.2	6,040	23.3	6,005	23.3
Total	26,072	100	25,919	100	25,825	100

On the opposite side of the distribution, we found the group
with lowest foreign stake, which is composed by the larger number of firms compared to the other groups. This group of firms
displays the most ubiquitous distribution across the three regions
(Table 2). The eastern provinces account for the highest share
(from 38% to 42%) but the divergence with the rest of the country is less pronounced than in the other groups of firms. Central
regions host 34.6% of total firms in the group, while western
provinces accounts for a decreasing number and share of firms in
the same group (from 27% to 23%).

The spatial distribution of the second group (from 25% to
50% of foreign share) across the three regions is the most similar
to the geographical distribution of the entire sample and it is
characterized by the higher stability. While the share of the two

eastern and central region remained almost unchanged (52% and 29%, respectively), it is worth noting that only for this group, the importance of western provinces (18.1% in 1999) has slightly increased in relative terms (by one percentage point) during the period 1999–2009, even though not in absolute terms.

Conclusions, Shortcomings, and Proposals for Future Research

Economic growth in China has been accompanied by an unbalanced internal geography as in the experience of many rapidly industrializing countries. The concentration of economic activities and FDI has increased, especially in the more dynamic regions (metropolitan and urban areas) and in the Economic and Technological Development Zone (ETDZ).

With the deepening of reform and opening up as well as with the entry of large scale of FDI, it shows obvious bias, and the gap between developed and developing regions is difficult to narrow. FDI regional agglomeration is closely related with strategies of economic development since the reform and opening up in China. It took coastal eastern regions as a pilot, slowly moved forward to inland. Despite the government effort, the persistence of the west-east gradient in foreign capital remained high. As it is confirmed by our analysis, the westward trend of foreign capital is inconspicuous. We advocate that the main reasons of such immobility are related to regional differences in institutional factors.

1. In mid-west, the human capital and the industrial supporting is not as well as that in the east. Furthermore, the fundament facilities are not complete and human resources are insufficient. These factors make the foreign capital unwilling to transfer from the east to the mid-west. Besides, because of the information asymmetry, the foreign investors are not familiar with local governments in the mid-west. They do not want to take the risk of being tricked. This also restrains the FDI transfer.

2. When China began to introduce FDI, many FDI industries were directed to the east, which accelerates the development of manufacturing in coastal areas in the east to high stage of the industrial chain and also makes the coastal areas in

the east the manufacturing center in China, and even the "world factory." In the meantime, in the mid-west, and especially in the west, the manufacturing industry suffered a continued downswing. For the low-end raw material manufacturing industry, the aggregation shows more obvious dependence on ecology and natural resources and it is becoming more fragile by the strengthening of legislation on environment protection.

3. Although there may be FDI spillover and technology transfer, the western is far from being a center of attraction for manufacturing FDI. Also, because of the central "buffer zone," China's strong spatial gradient feature determines that for the majority of the mid-west – especially western regions – it is difficult to reap the benefit of FDI spillover and technology transfer.

4. Foreign investors, especially manufacturing enterprises tend to invest in locations that have convenient transportation and import and export havens. High communication density is especially of the basic condition to attract foreign capital. The eastern significantly performs better than the mid-west in these respects. The difference of human capital between the different areas is also an important factor affecting foreign investors.

References

Bao, C., Chen, Z., & Wu, J. (2013). Chinese manufacturing on the move: Factor supply or market access? *China Economic Review, 26*, 170–181.

Bobonis, G. J., & Shatz, H. J. (2007). Agglomeration, adjustment, and state policies in the location of foreign direct investment in the United States. *Review of Economics and Statistics, 89*(1), 30–43.

Bode, E., Nunnenkamp, P., & Waldkirch, A. (2012). Spatial effects of foreign direct investment in US States. *Canadian Journal of Economics, 45*(1), 16–40.

Bowles, P. (2012). Rebalancing China's growth: Some unsettled questions. *Canadian Journal of Development Studies/Revue canadienne d'études du développement, 33*(1), 1–13.

Chen, J., & Fleisher, B. (1996). Regional income inequality and economic growth in China. *Journal of Comparative Economics, 22*, 141–164.

Crozet, M., & Koenig-Soubeyran, P. (2004a). Eu enlargement and the internal geography of countries. *Journal of Comparative Economics*, forthcoming.

Crozet, M., & Koenig-Soubeyran, P. (2004b). *Trade liberalisation and the internal geography of countries, vol. multinational firms' location and economic geography* (pp. 91–109). Cheltenham: Edward Elgar.

Fujita, M., & Hu, D. (2001). Regional disparity in China 1985–1994: The effects of globalization and economic liberalization. *Annals of Regional Science*, 35, 3–37.

Fujita, M., Krugman, P., & Venables, A. J. (1999). *The spatial economy: Cities, regions and international trade*. Cambridge: MIT Press.

Fujita, M., & Mori, T. (1996). The role of ports in the making of major cities: Self-agglomeration and hub effect. *Journal of Development Economics*, 49, 93–120.

Gao, T. (2004). Regional industrial growth: Evidence from Chinese industries. Regional industrial growth: Evidence from Chinese industries. *Regional Science and Urban Economics*, 34, 101–124.

Ge, Y. (2009). Globalization and industry agglomeration in China. *World Development*, 37(3), 550–559.

Kamal-Chaoui, L., Leman, E., & Rufei, Z. (2009). *Urban trends and policy in China*. OECD Regional Development Working Papers, 2009/1, OECD publishing.

Krugman, P. (1991). *Geography and trade*. Cambridge: MIT Press.

Krugman, P. R., & Livas, R. E. (1996). Trade policy and the Third World metropolis. *Journal of Development Economics*, 49(1), 137–150.

Lin, C.-H., Lee, C.-M., & Yang, C.-H. (2011). Does foreign direct investment really enhance China's regional productivity? *The Journal of International Trade & Economic Development: An International and Comparative Review*, 20(6), 741–768.

Ma, A. C. (2006). Geographical location of foreign direct investment and wage inequality in China. *World Economy*, 29(8), 1031–1055.

Monfort, P., & Nicolini, R. (2000). Regional convergence and international integration. *Journal of Urban Economics*, 48, 286–306.

Mukim, M., & Nunnenkamp, P. (2012). The location choices of foreign investors: A district-level analysis in India. *World Economy*, 35(7), 886–918.

Nie, H., Jiang, T., & Yang, R. (2012). *A review and reflection on the use and abuse of Chinese industrial enterprises database*. MPRA Paper No. 50945. Retrieved from https://mpra.ub.uni-muenchen.de/50945/

Nunnenkamp, P., & Mukim, M. (2012). The clustering of FDI in India: The importance of peer effects. *Applied Economics Letters*, 19(8), 749–753.

Overman, H. G., & Winters, L. A. (2003). *Trade shocks and industrial location: The impact of EEC accession on the UK*. Mimeo, University of Sussex.

Paluzie, E. (2001). Trade policy and regional inequalities. *Papers in Regional Science*, 80, 67–85.

Perroux, F. (1950). Economic space: Theory and applications. *The Quarterly Journal of Economics*, 64(1), 89–104.

Perroux, F. (1966). L'economia del XX secolo, Comunità, Milano.

Venables, A. (2000). Cities and trade: External trade and internal geography in developing economies. In S. Yusuf, W. Wu, & S. J. Evenett (Eds.), *Local dynamics in an era of globalisation: 21st century catalysts for development*.

Wei, K., Yao, S., & Liu, A. (2009). Foreign direct investment and regional inequality in China. *Review of Development Economics*, 13(4), 778–791.

Wen, M. (2004). Relocation and agglomeration of Chinese industry. *Journal of Development Economics, 73,* 329–347.

Wen, M. (2007). Foreign direct investment, regional market conditions and regional development. *Economics of Transition, 15,* 125–151.

Zhang, X., & Zhang, K. H. (2003). How does globalisation affect regional inequality within a developing country? Evidence from China. *Journal of Development Studies, 39,* 47–67.

4

The Liability of Foreignness of EU Environmental Protection Companies in China: Manifestations and Mitigating Strategies

Lee Keng Ng and Louise Curran

ABSTRACT

Purpose – The objective of this chapter is to explore the experience of EU companies in the environmental protection sector in China focusing on their difficulties and the mitigating strategies mobilized.

Methodology/approach – We adopt a qualitative, case study approach, using interview data to explore the liability of foreignness (LOF) experienced by the companies studied and the strategies adopted to overcome LOF.

Findings – We found examples of all categories of LOF identified by Eden and Miller (2004), among our case study companies, but the most problematic and persistent were discrimination hazards. Companies adopted various strategies to cope with LOF, including maximizing the use of local employees, developing relationships with local and national government actors, and establishing partnerships with local companies. None had chosen a combative legalistic approach to the unfair treatment they had suffered.

Research limitations – The relatively small number of cases (six) limits the generalizability of our findings. However, we are convinced that the size of our case companies and their long experience in China mean our findings are well grounded, although more research is needed.

Practical implications – The experience of our case study companies can help to inform the strategy of companies interested in entering and developing the Chinese market.

Originality/value – Very few studies have explored LOF through a case study-based qualitative approach. This research therefore helps to supplement findings from more large-scale quantitative analyses. In addition, there is little research on the LOF of foreign companies in China. Given the growing importance of the market, we believe the question merits further analysis.

Keywords: EU-China FDI; environmental industry; liability of foreignness; company strategy

Introduction

The objective of this chapter is to explore the experience of EU companies in the environmental protection (EP) sector in China, focusing on the difficulties experienced, which we link to the concept of liabilities of foreignness (LOF). The Chinese market context should have a great potential for EP companies, given the rapidly evolving domestic awareness of the need to address environmental problems (CCICED, 2013) and increasingly stringent government action to encourage change. However, the institutional distance between the EU and China remains high. International Business (IB) theory would thus suggest that companies will experience difficulties dealing with the challenges which tend to emerge due to that distance (Eden & Miller, 2004; Zaheer, 1995). This chapter explores the question of how institutional distance impacts on international business operations in this context and how companies deal with subsequent difficulties.

Our analysis is informed by case study evidence from six EU companies in the EP sector in China.

The chapter is structured as follows. We will firstly outline the existing literature on LOF of relevance to our chapter and highlight the gap in the literature which we seek to address. This is identified more precisely in the following section on the objective of the chapter, which also outlines our methodology. We summarize our key findings in the following section, before concluding and providing some indications of the limits of our research, as well as some propositions for further work.

Literature Review

Hymer (1976) posited that foreign firms incur costs when operating outside their home country – the costs of doing business abroad (CDBA). These are the cost of gathering information to better understand the country's economy, language, law and politics, and the cost of discrimination that firms face from local government, customers, and suppliers. In her study of these costs, Zaheer (1995), developed the concept of the LOF. Her study found that foreign firms often perform more poorly than local competitors and have a lower chance of survival.

This LOF is associated with four costs: "*... costs directly associated with spatial distance; firm-specific costs based on a particular company's unfamiliarity with and lack of roots in a local environment; costs resulting from the host country environment; costs from the home country environment*" (Zaheer, *op. cit.*, p. 343). Zaheer's study suggests that overcoming LOF involves both exploiting organizational capabilities and adopting local isomorphism (following the organizational practices of the market).

Zaheer's work has fostered extensive scholarship, well summarized in a recent literature review (Denk, Kaufmann, & Roesch, 2012). For example, Daamen, Hennart, and Park (2007) undertook case study research of four Korean MNEs subsidiaries in the Netherlands to explore the causes of LOF and whether it could be circumvented through certain strategies. Costs associated with foreignness included staff relocation costs; high local staff turnover; loss of several business opportunities; and litigation fees because of managerial errors.

LOF has often been linked to distance – both spatial and institutional. For example, Boeh and Beamish (2012) studied the liability of distance between 1,171 Japanese-US, parent-subsidiary dyads and found that firms with high dyad travel time tended to favor market entry through joint-venture, so as to reduce monitoring cost, while firms with more international experience tend to choose a location that is easier to access. Institutional distance (ID) has also been widely used in studies of LOF. Eden and Miller (2004) consider ID to be a key cause of LOF and postulate that it affects the entry modes that MNEs will choose. This proposition is supported by Xu and Shenkar (2002), who find that LOF can be reduced or overcome by adopting an appropriate entry mode and carefully selecting the host country.

Several scholars have sought to disaggregate the sources of LOF and the means to address these. Eden and Miller differentiated between the unfamiliarity, discriminatory, and relational hazards of doing business abroad. "Unfamiliarity hazards" are linked to lack of knowledge and experience and the related difficulties and misunderstandings created. "Discriminatory hazards" emanate from the host country's government, consumers, and the general public, due to distrust and antipathy toward foreign firms. "Relational hazards" represent the extra efforts needed as a result of internal and external organizational transactions. Certain types of LOF – especially unfamiliarity, mainly relate to the incidental costs of doing business, which are non-discriminatory in nature and can be minimized as MNEs learn to cope with the idiosyncrasies in the host country (Pedersen & Petersen, 2002; Sethi & Judge, 2009). Others, linked to discriminatory regulatory and political contexts are more difficult to address.

In terms of the evolution of LOF, several scholars have found that LOF can be reduced over time (Pedersen & Petersen, 2002; Zaheer & Mosakowski, 1997). Zaheer and Mosakowski (1997) assessed the extent of LOF of firms in trading rooms over a 20-year period and found that the exit rate of foreign trading firms tend to reach the exit rate of local trading firms after 16 years. Pedersen and Petersen (2002) also studied LOF over a long time period and found firms that have a high learning engagement tend to perceive high market familiarity and thus LOF is seen to decrease over time.

Finally, some scholars have pointed out that foreignness is not always a liability. Sethi and Judge (2009) hold that IB literature has focused too much on the LOF, without considering the benefits derived from that status. They develop a concept – the Assets of Foreignness (AOF) – which includes host country pro-foreign investor policy such as preferential subsidies, tax holidays, etc. as well as branding and quality of foreign firms, which are often perceived to be better than local firms.

In summary, in the IB context, foreignness can be considered both a liability (LOF) and an asset (AOF). Firms in international ventures are likely to be challenged by restrictions based on their foreignness, imposed by both host institutions and the host marketplace. Certain LOF, such as host country laws, are regulatory in nature and can be relatively easily understood, because the rules are codified. On the other hand, interpreting the response from the host marketplace is more difficult and complex because it is experiential.

Much of the existing research that has been done on LOF takes a predominantly quantitative approach, seeking to explore the effects of LOF on key performance indicators related to profitability and efficiency (Elango, 2009; Li, Poppo, & Zhou, 2008; Miller & Eden, 2006). There has been limited qualitative research seeking to explain how such hazards impact on emerging market multinational enterprises (EMNEs) as they expand or to explore how they react. In addition, much of the key work on LOF has been undertaken in developed country markets (Elango, 2009; Pedersen & Petersen, 2002; Zaheer, 1995). Very few researchers have focused on emerging markets. Although some work has been done on LOF for Chinese companies investing in Europe (Curran & Thorpe, 2015; Klossek, Linke, & Nippa, 2012; Li-Ying, Stucchi, Visholm, & Jansen, 2013), we find no substantial work on the issue of investment in the other direction.

Luo and Mezias (2002) pointed out some years ago that a better understanding of LOF requires further investigation of specific situations. However, few scholars have responded to this observation. This chapter seeks to contribute to the literature on LOF by undertaking such an investigation, looking in detail at experience of companies in a specific emerging market institutional context.

Objectives and Methodology of the Chapter

As highlighted in the review of the literature above, there is limited work that has used the case study approach to explore the LOF experience and still fewer studies that explore experience in emerging markets. Specifically, we know very little about the LOF faced by EU firms in China where the institutional distance is perceived to be high. Given China's growing importance as a market, this is a curious omission.

This chapter seeks to address this research gap by exploring the experience of a number of companies in a specific sector evolving on the Chinese market. We focus on the EP sector because, firstly, each sector has a very specific regulatory framework and institutional context and by holding the sector constant, we avoid variations due to regulatory distance between sectors. Secondly, the EP sector is one where there is clearly emergent demand in China (CEC, 2013), so there should be pull factors, in terms of market demand, which create a dynamic for EU companies, which are relatively well placed and competitive in the sector.

The specific research questions we explore are:

1. To what extent has LOF affected EU companies in the EP sector operating in China?
2. What are the key strategies used by EU firms to deal with LOF in China?

As indicated above, we adopt a qualitative methodology which addresses the micro level of companies. Although qualitative research methods have been relatively little used in the international business literature (Peterson, 2004), the case study approach is well adapted to elucidate the "how" and "why" questions in research (Yin, 2002). Case studies have been used in all types of business research including exploratory, descriptive, and explanatory (Bonoma, 1985; Ghauri & Gronhaug, 2002; Yin, 2002).

The six case studies reported in this chapter were undertaken on European companies which had entered and were operating in China. These were two French waste management companies, three United Kingdom (UK) sustainability companies, and one Finnish environmental technology company. We interviewed top managers, operational executives, and project managers from each company in 2014–2015. Each interview lasted between 90 and 180 minutes. Interviews were transcribed and key observations from managers coded, in terms of the key aspects of LOF observed and their mitigating strategies. Table 1 provides brief

Table 1: Key Details of Companies Involved in the Study.

Description/ Companies	A	B	C	D	E	F
Home country	France	France	UK	UK	UK	Finland
Year of establishment of parent	1880	1853	1946	1971	1938	1961
Age of establishment of parent	135	162	69	44	77	54
Year of entry into Hong Kong	1989	2000	1976	–	1993	1990
Year of entry into China	2003	1994	1984	1994	2000	1990
Chinese market entry strategy	M&A	M&A	Greenfield	M&A	Greenfield	Greenfield
Geographical distance (km) between parent and China	9,131	9,131	8,150	9,207	9,207	7,232

details of the six companies studied, all of which took part in the study on the basis of anonymity.

Institutional Distance (ID) between the EU and China

In order to put our research into context, it is important to highlight the high institutional distance which companies from the EU face in China. Kostova (1996) defines institutional distance (ID) as the extent of dissimilarity between the three institutional pillars – regulatory, normative, and cognitive – of two countries. In the case of the EU and China, dissimilarities arise from the vast distance in geography, absence of a common language of communication, varying stages of economic and political development and very diverse cultures. These factors will tend to influence the world view of business people and the way they interact with each other. Table 2 provides some indicative figures, which underline institutional differences.

Table 2: Indicative Governance and Institutional Indicators
2014.

Worldwide Governance Indicators	EU Average Score	China Score
Political stability and absence of violence/ terrorism	82	27
Government effectiveness	95	47
Regulatory quality	94	43
Rule of law	95	40
Control of corruption	94	47
Favoritism in decisions of government officials	15	22
Efficiency of legal framework in settling disputes	18	49
Efficiency of legal framework in challenging regulations	17	47
Transparency of government policymaking	25	33
Ethical behavior of firms	13	55

Source: The World Bank (2014). World Economic Forum. Global
Competitiveness Report 2014–2015.

The figures highlight the high variance in the governance and
institutional environment between the EU and China. The lower
scores of China in all governance indicators (except political
stability) reflect a weaker institutional environment than the EU.
While relatively close in terms of favoritism and transparency in
policymaking, the two are rather far apart in several other indicators, most notably ethics. Although distance remains constant
between the two actors, it is clear that the direction of movement
is likely to affect the LOF experienced.

To better understand the cultural distance (normative and
the cognitive pillars), Hofstede's Cultural Dimensions provide
some insights (The Hofstede Center, 2015). The EU does not
exist as an entity in the scoring system, but if we use France and
the UK as indicative, we find that China exhibits scores on
certain dimensions which are diametrical opposed. China is
much lower on individualism (20 vs. 71 for France and 89 for
the UK) and higher in long-term orientation (87 compared to 63
and 51, respectively) than the other two.

Finally, in terms of the legal framework, the business environment for foreign companies is regulated by the FDI Law. In
the case of the EP sector in China, extensive relevant regulation is

in place. Companies have to comply with the overarching Environmental Protection Law (EPL), which has recently been revised and the various environmental laws applicable to the EP industry. Moreover, regulations can vary locally. This regulatory context increases the interaction between government institutions and the companies to ensure compliance.

In conclusion, the EU and China are not only geographically distant, they also differ in culture, language, political regime, and level of institutional development. These differences impact on the institutional distance between them and may affect the growth and survival of firms. The following section will explore the extent of these difficulties and their impacts on strategy of our case study companies.

Findings and Discussion

The findings in relation to our two research questions are summarized in Table 3, which provides an overview of the key LOF experienced and the mitigating strategies adopted by the six companies studied. In terms of our first question "To what extent has the LOF affected EU companies in the EP sector operating in China?" all of the companies we interviewed had experienced difficulties directly related to their "foreignness." These conform well to the categories of LOF defined by Eden and Miller (2004). Unfamiliarity hazards were mainly related to cultural differences and the communication difficulties these created, both within the company and between the company and its customers. When it decided to produce in China in 2014, Co.F was disadvantaged by its unfamiliarity with the heat pump market in China. The application process for the license to manufacture took longer than expected because of requests for additional documentation that was not explicitly indicated.

Relational hazards were mainly linked to the distance between the companies and the local authorities, as well as their customers and partners. This was particularly problematic in the EP sector, as it is a highly regulated sector where permits and licenses are commonly required and where links to local institutions help to anticipate and manage the changing context. Co.E experienced several relational hazards. When the ex-pat management decided to start the sustainability business in China to service the local business community, a local manager was hired. This was because the British managers had limited relational

Table 3: Summary of Findings.

Company	Key Manifestations of LOF	Mitigating Strategies
A	Distance from key regulatory authorities	Instigate training for Ministerial personnel on waste treatment
	Unfair treatment in bidding for contracts	Educate local government. Focus on quality of their services
	Cultural misunderstandings	Train local employees with European skills
B	Unfair treatment in bidding for contracts	Use local employees when building relationships with local government
	Unfair treatment in enforcement of regulations	Use government to government contacts to seek to address corruption
	Cultural misunderstandings	Train local employees and build on their local knowledge
C	Distance from authorities	Exploit high-level ties between the home country and China to help build relationships
	Unfair treatment in licensing	Work with local partners which have the relevant certifications
	Cultural misunderstandings	Exploit digital exchanges and cross subsidiary training to build an internal company culture and exchange experience
D	Distance from authorities	Maintain a "courtesy distance, not far and not near" to protect its Class A environmental impact assessment (EIA) license, the only foreigner that owns this license
	Unfair treatment in performing EIA and due diligence	Focus on servicing multinational clients to realize the full benefits of a Class A EIA license. (There are 191 local companies which own the same license)
	Unfair treatment in accessing FDI and soil remediation	Focus on the most challenging EIA projects, which generate higher revenue and less local competition because of lack of technical skills and expertise
	Cultural misunderstandings	Minimize cultural misunderstandings by appointing local employees at all levels
E	Distance from authorities	Leverage the Parent company's high-level connections with the central government to reach out to government funding agencies that promote the adaptation of green production methods

Table 3: (*Continued*)

Company	Key Manifestations of LOF	Mitigating Strategies
	Cultural misunderstandings	Use locals to build relationships and interact with other local developers, architects, contractors to develop the sustainability business
F	Distance from authorities	Leverage good relationship with an SOE customer to create relationship with the Ministry. Meet officials frequently to discuss environmental protection and technology trends
	Unfair treatment in licensing	Accede to unreasonable compliance demands by making changes to the process during testing (*"nothing to be done about it, other than complying and waiting for approval"*)
	Cultural misunderstandings	Use local Chinese-English interpreters who are full time employees to communicate with distributors, end users and government officials

experience because of the language barrier. They did not have "guanxi" – as local networks are known in China. They have also had difficulties managing local staff due to differences in attitudes. As a result, they not only had higher staff turnover, a problem several other companies underlined, but they also have had legal problems with their staff. They recently lost a costly legal case against three local employees accused of agent opportunism.

The most difficult and persistent hazard identified by all companies was discrimination. For example, Co.C, in spite of long years' experience in China, still hadn't received the building license required for their engineers to "sign-off" drawings. Company A has over 40 years of experience in operations in China and yet still opted to use local partnerships in waste projects, to leverage partners' networks in winning and managing new projects. They acknowledge that calls for tender were often structured in such a way that foreign companies were effectively excluded. Co.F considered that they often had to accede to unreasonable compliance demands in order to ensure that their projects went ahead. When they applied for a license to manufacture environmentally superior heat-pumps, in spite of a long history in the market and local legitimacy, the process of issuing the license to manufacture was very slow. Co.F was forced to wait another winter to test the heat pump. Discriminatory inspection procedures caused difficulties for Co.B. They reported that local officials checked every item in detail when inspecting them, but were more lenient with local companies.

The issue of unfair treatment through discriminatory support for local competitors was also highlighted. Aside from favoring local actors in tenders, which was widespread, but also not necessarily specific to China, there were other, more subtle means of disadvantaging foreign actors. Co.A was effectively excluded from certain markets because it could not compete with the prices that were offered by the SOEs, which have strong financial and support from the government. Co.B's operation has suffered because corrupt officials deliberately caused bottlenecks and delays by not performing the necessary engine inspection, reflecting lower control of corruption in the Chinese institutional context, as outlined above.

In terms of our second research question: What are the key strategies used by EU firms to deal with LOF in China? The companies we studied often adopted quite similar methods to overcome their LOF. Several dealt with unfamiliarity by leveraging their existing networks before entering China. Cos.A and B benefited from the infrastructure of their parent and sister companies and were thus confronted with less unfamiliarity and relational hazards (Eden & Miller, 2004). In Co.C, the same group of people who developed the Hong Kong office were responsible for the first project in China in 1984. The LOF experienced was reduced by prior exposure of a similar culture, such that cultural distance was lower. This is consistent with previous research which indicates that unfamiliarity hazards can be overcome through learning (Pedersen & Petersen, 2002).

In addition, most companies internalized local knowledge by recruiting and integrating a large proportion of local staff and training them in western management and technical practice. For example, in Co.B, the foreign MD used local employees to deal with customers, as they are well positioned to "challenge and argue" with them because they are able to understand each other's nuances. This also helps to avoid "losing face" if the foreign MD turns down any request for monetary rewards in exchange for getting work done, reflecting higher ethical concerns in EU companies.

In terms of relational hazards, most companies made conscious efforts to develop their "guanxi." On a project level, Co.A exploits its group-level network to find trustworthy local partners, who have good connections with local government. Furthermore, conducting official training programs to educate and empower the Environment Ministry officials with technical knowledge has helped to foster inclusiveness and reduce the unfamiliarity of Co.A's operations (Pedersen & Petersen, 2002). However Co.B's relationship with government departments declined over time, indicative of an increase in LOF. This could be attributable to the diminishing effect of the firm's competitive advantage on the market, after 17 years. Local actors had been able to acquire or copy similar process-based proprietary knowledge.

In terms of the discrimination hazards experienced, in theory, several companies could have requested the EU to pursue a case against China in the World Trade Organization (WTO), as there were clear examples of institutionalized discrimination against foreign operators, in defiance of China's WTO commitments. However none had chosen this route. All considered that a less combative approach, based on local networking and proof of competence through experience, would lead to greater openness over time. In terms of the evolving institutional context, several informants felt that their patience was being rewarded and that the context was becoming more open. The new EPL aims to level the playing field and hence it is expected to reduce the LOF faced by foreigners in the EP sector. The recent anti-corruption campaign targeting governmental officials, also indicated that the Chinese government was serious about increasing governmental transparency. From an institutional perspective, the fact that transparency was increasing and corruption falling, meant that the ID between the home and host context was reduced (see Table 2), which would be expected to reduce LOF.

Several companies leveraged their local contacts to reduce discrimination. Co.A's partner is an SOE which owns the Industrial Park where their plant is located. The officials who undertake routine plant inspection are embedded in the same state-led organizational culture as the partner. Thus, they tend to treat Co.A as a local company during routine plant inspections. Another key strategy used by most companies was to emphasize their superior knowledge and networks. These could be considered to be assets of foreignness (AOF) (Sethi & Judge, 2009). The companies we studied were more experienced in EP compliance than local actors and were recognized as such. The local companies/government responded to this expertise of foreign companies favorably and this undoubtedly reduced their LOF.

Although all firms were aware that local competitors were emerging and they needed to constantly upgrade their capacities to retain their advantage.

Conclusions, Shortcomings, and Proposals for Future Research

In conclusion, in this brief chapter we cannot explore all of the aspects of LOF which emerged from our research. We have focused on highlighting the clearest examples of LOF experienced by our case study companies and providing some examples of the strategies which they used to mitigate these difficulties. As expected, the institutional distance between the EU and China fostered quite extensive LOF across all of the categories identified by Eden and Miller (2004). In addition, as prior literature suggests, discriminatory hazards were often the most difficult to overcome. Strategies involved a complex combination of local networking, well-chosen local partnerships, and leveraging superior knowledge/experience. We see from Co.F's experience that LOF has the capacity to resurface despite years of local presence, experience, and relations with government. However, the case study companies consciously chose not to adopt a more confrontational, legalistic approach by challenging the discriminatory laws or practices. There was a general feeling that a more constructive strategy, based on increasing local embeddedness through partnerships and networking, together with leveraging superior performance and knowledge, would overcome discrimination in time. Hazards like delays in licensing and excessive vigor in inspections were irritants, but didn't undermine the business case for developing the Chinese market.

This study is based on only six cases and we are well aware of the shortcomings of studies based on relatively few actors. As explained in the methodology section, we believe that such work can complement more extensive quantitative studies, to provide a more multi-faceted view of the nature of LOF and the coping strategies of investors. In addition, all of the companies are rather important actors and have been in China for many years. Thus, they bring extensive knowledge of the context and difficulties to our research. Finally, in spite of operating in rather different sub-sectors, there was a lot of commonality, both in the LOF experienced by our case study companies and in the strategies they used to cope. This coherence helps to validate the legitimacy of our findings.

A wider range and depth of case studies would certainly help to confirm and extend our findings, as would more in-depth research on the institutional context with which these firms interact. The LOF faced by the companies could not be explored further with the relevant local institutions, due to difficulty in gaining access to them. This underlines the importance of having "guanxi" in the Chinese institution context, even for academics. Joint research with government institutions could facilitate better understanding of these relationships.

In addition, it is possible that the LOF identified in this study is specific to the EP sector – which is both highly regulated and highly dependent on the public sector as a key customer. Comparative studies of LOF faced by companies in other industries could provide useful insights into which issues are more generic, and therefore cross sectoral, and which are more likely to emerge in certain kinds of sectors. Further research could also explore a wider range of companies (from different home countries) operating in these two industries in China. This would help to establish whether companies from countries with greater or lesser institutional distance from China experience different types of LOF to those from the EU. If so, to what extent and how do their mitigating strategies differ?

References

Boeh, K. K., & Beamish, P. W. (2012). Travel time and the liability of distance in foreign direct investment: Location choice and entry mode. *Journal of International Business Studies*, *43*(5), 525.

Bonoma, T. V. (1985). Case research in marketing: opportunities, problems and a process. *Journal of Marketing Research*, *22*(2), 199−208.

CCICED. (2013). China Council for International Cooperation on Environment and Development (CCICED) Annual General Meeting 2013. Progress in environmental and development policies in China (2012−2013) and CCICED policy recommendations impact.

CEC. (2013). Memo. EU and China together explore the benefits of green growth. Commission of the European Communities, Brussels.

Curran, L., & Thorpe, M. (2015). Chinese FDI in the French and Australian wine industries: Liabilities of foreignness and country of origin effects. *Frontiers of Business Research in China*, *9*(3), 443−480.

Daamen, B., Hennart, J. F. K. D. J., & Park, Y. R. (2007). Sources of and responses to the liability of foreignness: The case of Korean companies in the Netherlands. *Global Economic Review*, *36*(1), 17−35.

Denk, N., Kaufmann, L., & Roesch, J.-F. (2012). Liabilities of foreignness revisited: A review of contemporary studies and recommendations for future research. *Journal of International Management*, 18(4), 322−334.

Eden, L., & Miller, S. (2004). Distance matters: Liability of foreignness, institutional distance and ownership strategy. In M. A. Hitt & J. L. C. Cheng (Eds.), *The evolving theory of the multinational firm. Advances in international management* (Vol. 16, pp. 187−221). Amsterdam: Elsevier.

Elango, B. (2009). Minimizing effects of 'liability of foreignness' response strategies of foreign firms in the United States. *Journal of World Business*, 44(1), 51−62.

Ghauri, P., & Gronhaug, K. (2002). *Research methods in business studies: A practical guide*. Harlow: Financial Times and Prentice Hall.

Hymer, S. (1976). *The international operations of national firms: A study of direct investment*. Cambridge, MA: MIT Press.

Klossek, A., Linke, B. M., & Nippa, M. (2012). Chinese enterprises in Germany: Establishment modes and strategies to mitigate the liability of foreignness. *Journal of World Business*, 47(1), 35−44.

Kostova, T. (1996). *Success of the transnational transfer of organizational practices within multinational companies*. Unpublished doctoral dissertation, University of Minnesota, Minneapolis.

Li, J. J., Poppo, L., & Zhou, K. Z. (2008). Do managerial ties in China always produce value? Competition, uncertainty, and domestic vs. foreign firms. *Strategic Management Journal*, 29(4), 383−400.

Li-Ying, J., Stucchi, T., Visholm, A., & Jansen, S. J. (2013). Chinese multinationals in Denmark. *Multinational Business Review*, 21(1), 65−86.

Luo, Y. D., & Mezias, J. (2002). Liabilities of foreignness: Concepts, constructs and consequences. *Journal of International Management*, 8(3), 217−221.

Miller, S. R., & Eden, L. (2006). Local density and foreign subsidiary performance. *The Academy of Management Journal*, 49(2), 341−355.

Pedersen, B., & Petersen, T. (2002). Coping with liability of foreignness: Different learning engagements of entrant firms. *Journal of International Management*, 8(3), 339−350.

Peterson, R. B. (2004). Empirical research in international management: A critique and future agenda. In R. Marschan-Piekkari & C. Welch (Eds.). *Handbook of qualitative research methods for international business* (pp. 25−40). Cheltenham: Edward Elgar.

Sethi, D., & Judge, W. (2009). Reappraising liabilities of foreignness within an integrated perspective of the costs and benefits of doing business abroad. *International Business Review*, 18(4), 404−416.

The Hofstede Center. (2015). *Cultural tools*. Country comparison. Retrieved from http://geert-hofstede.com. Accessed on February 16, 2015.

The World Bank. (2014). *Worldwide governance indicators 2014*. Retrieved from www.govindicators.org. Accessed on February 11, 2015.

Xu, D., & Shenkar, O. (2002). Institutional distance and the multi-national enterprise. *Academy of Management Review*, 27(4), 608−618.

Yin, R. K. (2002). *Case study research: Design and methods* (3rd ed.). Beverly Hills, CA: Sage.

Zaheer, S. (1995). Overcoming the liability of foreignness. *Academy of Management Journal, 38*(2), 341–363.

Zaheer, S., & Mosakowski, E. (1997). The dynamics of the liability of foreignness: A global study of survival in financial services. *Strategic Management Journal, 18*(6), 439–464.

5

The Renewable Energy Industry in Europe: Business and Internationalization Models. A Focus on the Chinese Market

Elena Cedrola and Loretta Battaglia

ABSTRACT

Purpose − The chapter aims to examine the number, type, and international presence of European companies (Italian, Spanish, French, German, Dutch, Rumanian, Bulgarian, and English) operating in the renewable energy industries, as well as Chinese companies. Through the analysis of two businesses that have established partnerships and a wholly foreign owned enterprise (WFOE) in China, the chapter identifies the main elements of their management strategies that led to successful operation in China.

Methodology/approach − To analyze the main characteristics and the internationalization of the European firms operating in the renewable energy industry, we collected information from secondary data. To identify the successful business models to operate successfully in China, we adopted a qualitative case study approach, based on direct interviews and information published on the company websites and articles found on the web.

Findings — European enterprises encounter difficulties in approaching the Chinese market, which is rapidly developing as a result of the latest five-year plan setting energy and climate change targets and policies. Indeed, the number of European firms investing in China is low. Through the analysis of two business cases (Asja and Caleffi) that have established partnerships and a WFOE in China, the chapter identifies the main elements of their management strategies that led to successful operation in China.

Research limitations — The relatively small number of cases (two) limits the generalizability of our findings. However, we are convinced that the size of our case companies and their experience in China mean our results are well grounded, although more research is needed.

Originality/value — To the best of our knowledge, this is the first study that has explored the business models adopted by European firms operating in the renewable energy industry in China.

Keywords: Renewable energy industry; case studies; business model; internationalization

Introduction

The European Union is currently a leader in technologies for renewable energy, providing employment for around 1.2 million people, holding 40% of worldwide patents and, in 2012, 44% of the global capacity of electricity production deriving from these sources, except hydropower (European Parliament, 2015). Since its establishment, the European Union has economically and geopolitically promoted and encouraged the use of renewable energies. The matter of the continuity, safety, and energy independence of developed countries goes beyond the environmental issue committing Europe to meeting its obligations under the Kyoto Protocol.

As for China, the energy sector has always been a thorny issue and despite having significant resources, the distribution, characteristics of the territory, and the inefficiency of systems make their use difficult and expensive. Nowadays, China is particularly interested in terms of renewable energies because the market will not only grow in terms of energy production but also in terms of manufacturing components for new plants (turbines, solar panels, dams, etc.) aided by low production costs, potential economies of scale, and the country's ability to attract large amounts of financial resources (The Economist Intelligence Unit, 2012). Moreover, the Chinese government, to further facilitate the expansion of the renewable energy sector, has defined subsidies, tax incentives, a reduction in customs duties, and the abolition of duty on importing wind and hydro technology equipment, a VAT reduction, a fund for the industrialization of equipment for wind power, preferential taxes for renewable energy, preferential rates for the purchase of onshore, biomass and photovoltaic solar energy, a solar photovoltaic subsidy program (Golden Sun program), a grant program for photovoltaic systems installed on roofs (Building-Integrated PV Solar Program).[1]

The objective of this chapter is to analyze the number, type, and presence of European companies – Italian, Spanish, French, German, Dutch, Rumanian, Bulgarian, and English – operating in the renewable energy industries in international markets.

Enterprises supplying energy from various sources and at different points in the supply chain have long faced the challenges that international and geographically distant markets such as China pose. Specifically, European enterprises appear to encounter difficulties in approaching the Chinese market, which is rapidly

---

[1]Details in the following documents: National Renewable Energy Laboratory, Renewable Energy Policy in China: Financial Incentives
http://www.nrel.gov/docs/fy04osti/36045.pdf
http://www.iea.org/policiesandmeasures/renewableenergy/?country=China
http://www.mof.gov.cn/index.htm
http://www.neiaap.org/Policy_show.asp?aid=2&bid=16&tid=1&id=65
https://sites.google.com/site/chinapolicyinfocus/china-s-solar-subsidy-programs/china-s-solar-industry/china-s-national-solar-subsidy-programs
http://en.ndrc.gov.cn/
http://www.gov.cn/english/
http://www.nea.gov.cn/2011-12/20/c_131316289.htm
http://jjs.mof.gov.cn/zhengwuxinxi/zhengcefagui/201203/t20120329_638930.html

developing as a result of the latest five-year plan setting energy and climate change targets and policies (China.Org.Cn, 2015; The National People's Congress of the People's Republic of China, 2007). Indeed, the number of European firms investing in China is low due their small size, high cultural distance, and inadequate management strategies. Through the analysis of two business cases (Asja and Caleffi) that have established partnerships and a wholly foreign owned enterprise (WFOE) in China, the chapter identifies the main elements of their management strategies that led to successful operation in China.

Companies in the Renewable Energy Sector and Internationalization

The energy market is a constantly changing reality characterized by globalization, the reduction of trade barriers, and technological development. In this context, the growing importance of multinational and transnational activities expose companies to the pressure of international competition, from which they can defend themselves only through internationalization, interpreted as the process that allows companies to seize new opportunities for growth and development while also presenting countless challenges. On one hand, market internationalization enables achieving economies of scale and scope and on the other requires gaining experience and knowledge of markets with a different language, cultural, political, and economic characteristic.

Businesses can make use of different internationalization strategies to adapt their activities to the trends and needs of foreign markets (Cedrola, 2005; Hollensen, 2014). In the policy development stage, companies need to identify two core elements: the target market and the entry mode. The choice of the target market is closely linked to two dimensions: market attractiveness and possible entry barriers. Both these variables influence the selection of the most appropriate input mode, namely export, cooperation or foreign direct investment (FDI). In taking the export path, firms can reduce the business risks arising from penetrating a new market. However, the degree of control is rather poor. A higher level of control is ensured by cooperation with other companies through the creation of joint ventures or licensing agreements, while in the case of FDIs, the level of control is complete as the company can adopt, for example, a Greenfield, international investment or acquisition strategy (Günter & Meckl, 2014).[2]

As part of the POREEN project, we examined the European markets including France, Spain, England, Italy, Bulgaria, and Romania, as well as China in an attempt to understand the characteristics of enterprises and the types of activities undertaken. In a second step, the authors analyzed their approach to international markets, considering collaborations between European and Chinese companies. The firms analyzed operate in the renewable energy sector, both directly (electricity supply chain-based activities) and indirectly (companies producing components or systems used in the field). Information gathering was undertaken through indirect means such as the Internet, articles in trade journals and case studies, and information obtained directly through collaboration with some of the leading authorities and industry associations. A database of firms operating in each market was then constructed, and some emblematic case studies were explored to understand further the approach to foreign markets, especially the Chinese.

Table 1 summarizes the number of the enterprises operating in the various countries studied (obtained from search engines and related keywords, and from ministries, associations, organizations and databases of different lists of firms).

Table 2 presents the energy sectors of specialization of the firms analyzed; the percentages indicate that many firms do not

---

[2]The German market provides some examples of valuable partnerships.

Trianel is a German cooperative of 45 small- and medium-sized enterprises and was designed to aggregate their strengths and investments. Around 40 companies in the group planned the construction of a 400 MW offshore wind power plant in the German North Sea. This project offers the members substantial added value as they can diversify their business portfolios with technologies that would otherwise not be available (Trianel Press Release, 2010).

Another example is the partnerships or joint ventures of project companies with electricity suppliers. Juwi is a German company and one of the leading project developers in the field of wind, solar, and biomass power in different countries around the world. The company has entered into joint ventures with energy suppliers to help generate energy capacity from renewable sources. Juwi offers the opportunity to co-finance joint-ventures with the aim of implementing combined renewable energy projects, offering its expertise in the development and operational management of projects. The energy companies instead manage the financial side of the projects and the related electricity use (Richter, 2012).

Table 1: Sources Used for the Construction of the Database of European and Chinese Firms in the Renewable Energy Sector.

Country of the Firm	Engines	Keywords	Ministries, Associations, Fairs, Databases	Number of Firms
Germany	Google	German renewable energy companies, German renewable energy associations of federations, German renewable energy industry, German wind/solar/bioenergy/geothermal associations	German Renewable Energy Federation – German Wind Energy Association	126
The Netherlands	Google	Dutch renewable energy companies, Dutch renewable energy associations of federations, Dutch renewable energy industry, Dutch wind/solar/bioenergy/geothermal associations		58
Spain	Google – Yahoo	Spanish renewable energy companies – renewable energy Spain	Ministerio de Industria, Energía y Turismo – l'Instituto para la diversificación y ahorro de la energía – IDAE – US Commercial Service – Agenzia ICE	103
France	Google – Yahoo	French renewable energy companies – renewable energy France	Ministère de l'écologie, du développement durable et de l'énergie – Agence de l'Environnement et de la Maîtrise de l'Energie – Syndicat des énergies renouvelables – U.S. Commercial Service – Agenzia ICE	71
Bulgaria	Google	Renewable energy companies Bulgaria – RES operators Bulgaria – RES producers Eastern Europe, Associations	South-East European Exhibition & Congress EE&RE – International Technical Fair – SunE – Agenzia ICE – Investbulgaria	96

Romania	Google	Renewable energy companies Romania – RES operators Romania – RES producers Eastern Europe, Associations	Romenvirotec e Enreg ENERGIA REGENERABILA – Agenzia ICE – OPCOM	91
The United Kingdom	Google	Renewable energy companies UK	Free Index	197
Italy	Google	Renewable energy companies Italy	Legambiente	191
China	–	–	Academic articles, Official Chinese government documents, List of participants in national and international exhibitions.	170

Table 2: Energy Sectors and % Composition of the Activities Carried Out by the Firms Analyzed.

Production Type	Germany	The Netherlands	Spain	France	Bulgaria	Romania	Italy	The United Kingdom	China
Wind energy	37.30	50.00	38.83	38.03	25.00	46.10	37.20	33.50	32.00
Biomass energy	28.50	50.01	41.75	39.44	19.70	36.20	37.70	38.10	9.00
Solar energy	23.81	34.48	63.11	63.38	83.30	75.80	83.80	81.70	76.00
Geothermal energy	15.87	10.34	3.88	15.49	4.10	8.70	35.10	45.70	6.00
Hydroelectric power	6.35	13.79	6.80	30.99	7.20	27.4	13.60	10.70	12.00
Marine energy	n.f.	n.f.	3.88	16.90	1.00	–	–	8.10	3.00

n.f.: data not found.

exclusively operate in one field, but operate in different energy sectors.

Table 3 shows the size of enterprises based on the number of employees. For the Chinese market, generally firms are medium and big size. The most important businesses in international markets have more than 1,000 employees. The firms were also analyzed by types of activities. As in the energy sector of specialization, many companies undertake more than one kind of activity.

Table 4 shows the position of companies in the supply chain. Beyond the specific specializations of each country and the widespread coverage of most activities in the energy value chain, a clear difference emerges in terms of size between European and Chinese companies. This difference may have an effect on the internationalization and cooperation activities particularly between Europe and China.

As for internationalization, the European players in the sector show a greater orientation toward western European markets as these are highly industrialized and geographically and culturally more proximate. Considerable importance is also attributed to the United States and Latin America, not only due to the significant potential of some markets but also with respect to business practices and cultural and linguistic affinities.[3] Asia and China, in particular, are high-potential markets but are difficult to penetrate due to the number of local enterprises

---

[3]Examples are the Spanish Iberdrola and Fundación Cartif.

Iberdrola is the first Spanish energy group that despite having originally based its activities on traditional energy sources, then dedicated a large part of investments to energy from renewable sources, especially wind power, in which the company is a global leader. From 2001 to 2006, the main investment concerned Spain and Latin America. The subsequent international consolidation strategy led the management to pursue integration with the Scottish Power, the US Energy East, and the Brazilian Elektro. Iberdrola is present with its plants in 40 countries and the company's desire to consolidate its presence in the United Kingdom, the United States, Brazil, and Mexico is evident. Future investments will be directed at the Middle East as a result of a collaboration with the Siemens smart grid division (http://www.iberdrola.es/inicio/).

Fundación Cartif, a technology center specialized in providing design solutions in the energy sector, was established in Latin America thanks to the Iberamericano de Ciencia y Tecnologia para el Desarrollo program (http://www.cartif.com/quienes-somos/centro-tecnologico.html).

Table 3: Size of Firms in the Database: Data in % on the Total Amount of Firms for Each Country Analyzed.

Size	Germany	The Netherlands	Spain	France	Bulgaria	Romania	Italy	The United Kingdom	China
Micro enterprises (0–9 emp.)	2.33	9.30	–	–	23.3	32.4	8.0	10.75	1.00
Small enterprises (10–49 emp.)	8.14	27.91	7.14	–	35.1	35.1	9.4	15.05	4.00
Medium enterprises (50–249 emp.)	31.4	23.26	19.05	14.29	18.9	18.9	6.8	11.82	27.00
Large enterprises (>250 emp.)	58.14	39.53	69.05	85.71	21.6	13.5	11.5	0.53	26.00
n.f.	–	–	–	–	–	–	63.8	61.82	41.00

n.f.: data not found.

Table 4: Position of Firms in the Supply Chain: Data in % on the Total Amount of Firms for Each Country Analyzed.

Supply Chain	Germany	The Netherlands	Spain	France	Bulgaria	Romania	Italy	The United Kingdom	China
Production of components	37.30	27.59	21.36	15.49	27.00	18.60	32.00	15.00	48.00
Plants (design, construction, installation, maintenance)	35.71	32.76	70.08	100.00	85.40	80.00	90.00	100.00	78.00
Energy production	13.49	13.79	28.16	28.17	31.20	38.40	42.00	100.00	32.00
Distribution and Services	34.92	37.95	18.45	18.32	32.20	29.60	63.00	30.00	24.00
R&D	1.59	8.62	33.98	25.35	2.00	7.60	40.00	7.00	35.00

growing at great speed and the fact that they are larger than most European companies.

In China, the large size of many companies and the negotiation characteristics based on personal (*guanxi*) and long-term relationships and reciprocity (also from a business standing perspective) (Cedrola & Battaglia, 2012; Fang, 2006; Pye, 1992; Salacuse, 1999; Weber, 2008) make "on par" business agreements difficult. This explains the considerable focus of Chinese enterprises on investing abroad, largely acquiring companies specializing in innovation, facilitating not only the penetration of foreign markets but also increasing the production standards of Chinese companies.[4]

As to entry mode, companies would seem to prefer direct and indirect export activities thereby reducing the business risks, albeit providing a lower degree of control in foreign markets. However, some firms are interested in international cooperation, establishing partnerships and joint ventures but the number of companies making use of FDIs is extremely low (NL EVD International Information, 2015).

The following sections present the emblematic cases of two Italian firms that have successfully penetrated the Chinese market: Asja Ambiente Italia and Caleffi. Their entry modes differed according to their products and target markets. Common to both companies and in part explaining their success in China is knowledge of the culture, the market and establishing local roots. Furthermore, their production specializations are a developing sector in China (biomass energy in the case of Asja) and manufacturing excellence regarding innovation and quality (components in the case of Caleffi).

Secondary data derived from their websites and financial statements. In addition, for detailed information on the Chinese market, interviews were conducted in May 2015 with Paolo Bazzoni, senior advisor for EU Markets at China Guodian Corporation and delegates of the Italian Chamber of Commerce in Chongqing, Catherine Cui, General Manager of Shenyang

---

[4]The Chinese Yingli Solar, world leader in the production of solar panels (60.3% market share in Europe, 23.3% in China, 14.1% in the United States), produces all products in China in the Baoding, Hainan, Tianjin, and Hengshui plants. R&D is mainly undertaken abroad in Madrid, Spain, and San Francisco in the United States (http://www.yinglisolar.com/en/).

Asja Renewables (April 2015), and Dario Shu, exclusive Caleffi agent for China (in April 2014 and 2015).

Asja Ambiente Italia S.p.A. – The Company Experience in China

Asja is an international group of companies working in the field of renewables. In particular, it operates in the biogas sector including landfill biogas, biogas from biomass and biomethane production, wind, photovoltaics, vegetable oils, and micro-cogeneration. It also offers an asset management service to assist customers in all their plant management aspects and a consultancy service related to carbon emission (Kyoto Protocol). Established in 1995 in Turin (Italy), Asja has grown exponentially ever since, building specialist know-how to manage all the issues related to clean energy generation using cutting-edge technologies, ensuring full compliance with domestic and international standards.

As a group, Asja generated total revenues from sales and services of 70.4 mil euros in 2014 (+4.1% on 2013). It operates 50 plants of which 47 in Italy, 2 in Brazil, and 1 in China, producing 550,000 MWh green energy (Bazzoni interview). As to international operations, Asja is active with two landfill gas plants in Brazil and one in China and holds a minority interest (10%) in Colombia in a company engaged in the cultivation of African palm for the production and sale of sustainable palm oil.

In China, Asja's activities comprise the implementation, construction and management of proprietary landfill biogas plants as well as third party and consultancy activities in the carbon market and auditing services for energy and greenhouse-effect gas emissions. The landfill biogas plant is located in Shenyang and in 2014 generated 13,100 MWh, for total revenues of 6.61 mil renminbi, thereby avoiding the release of 110,000 tons of CO_2 into the atmosphere.

Asja invested in China in 2006 through a greenfield investment in the Shenyang province. The choice of which Chinese province to invest in was favored by the twinning arrangement between the City of Turin and the Municipality of Shenyang. This enabled deepening the knowledge of the territory and developing relationships between the company and the municipality. These relationships granted investment opportunities and facilitated the strategic decision to invest in the country.

Asja's development in China was fostered by the following elements: the presence of a partner in the area, the city of Shenyang, access to the local market facilitated by the partner, and relationships and local connections. The "Country Localization" drives Asja Renewables from within by way of the local team that is committed and engaged as a result of being empowered and involved in the management of the Chinese subsidiary, while externally the relationship with the partner has been strengthened, particularly as Asja is seen as an international company that has invested and continues to invest in the country according to Chinese models. In line with this perspective, Asja has plans to expand investments in the biogas business in China and to develop innovative and new business areas. In biogas, landfill expansion with 70 new wells is in the pipeline. New development projects include bio-digestion and C-CERs (Chinese Certified Emission Reduction): bio-digestion is an under-developed sector where Asja is assessing new projects using the vast amounts of food waste deriving from the high number of restaurants in the country; C-CERs is a growing market for Asja Renewables, which has strengthened its consultancy team with five people in charge of Green Certificates. Likewise, the Chinese partner is more willing to invest in the company both directly and through expanding the facility and commercial support.

Caleffi — Hydronic Solutions — The Company Experience in China

Caleffi was founded in 1961 by Francesco Caleffi in Fontaneto D'Agogna, in the industrial district of valves in the province of Novara (Italy). Today, it is considered an Italian firm of excellence in the field of industrial equipment: production is entirely made in Italy. The company develops and produces components for heating, air conditioning and sanitary systems, heat metering systems, and specific components for renewable energy systems for private and industrial consumers. Today, Caleffi S.p.A. is the nucleus of an international group with subsidiaries and representative offices in Europe, America, China, Japan, and Australia. The group has 700 employees, 18 companies, 2 representative offices, and 3 production plants in Italy following a strategic management decision. The group owns several brands: Altecnic,

Allvalve, Pressco, RDZ, Tecsas, and Caleffi. One of the key factors underlying its success is the great emphasis on quality. Since its founding, the company has paid particular attention to meeting quality standards in all stages of the production process. A further key factor is an innovation aimed at building products and the corporate culture leading to the new Cuborosso Research Centre dedicated to improving the product portfolio and testing and monitoring standard components.

The company entered the EU15 market around 40 years ago followed by other European markets. Since 1995, Caleffi has pursued the penetration of new markets (North America, Asia and Oceania) and around 10 years ago the Middle Eastern, Central and South Central Asian markets. The weight of total foreign sales and the incidence of foreign customers to total customers is 54%. The company has operated in China for about 17 years through an exclusive agent, Dario Shu. Caleffi has a representative office in Beijing since 1998 although import and sales are handled by Mr. Shu and his company, the Tianjin Conferred HVAC Automatic Control Equipment. Sales offices are located in Tianjin, Shanghai, Guangzhou, Chengdu, Xi'an, Dalian, Qingdao, and Taiyuan (http://www.caleffi.com/international/en-int).

> Caleffi has adopted a strategy that provides for the retention of 100% of production in Italy, particularly to maintain quality standards. On the other hand, the figures do not enable considering production in China: the company could produce in a month what the Chinese market needs in a year. Despite the low cost of labour and the tax advantages, importing is still the best choice. The speed of transport, with products that can arrive in a week if necessary, and customs duties of between 5% and 7%, much lower with respect to other products such as radiators and boilers, allows the company to not increase prices too much, at least not to the point of making it uncompetitive. (Shu interview)

Caleffi primarily operates in the Chinese market with two types of customers: European manufacturers with a factory in China (including Vaillant and Viessmann) and construction companies commissioned to build luxury apartments and hotels. Both types of customers look for quality and a renowned brand in the industry. Of little importance in China instead is the market for private renovations since the large supply of new apartments induces people to buy new homes.

The company's main competitors are other international companies such as the German Oventrop, the Danish Danfoss, and the American Watts that manufacture in China, cutting prices and making the competition even fiercer, as well as Chinese producers. Given the known price propensity of Chinese customers, few understand and appreciate the value of "Made in Italy," at least in this sector where preference seems to prevail for the "Made in Germany." On the other hand, the lack of regulations governing the use of these products makes it difficult to accept and understand some of the most innovative features of the company's products (Shu interview). Despite this general propensity, the company's solutions have been used in major projects such as the skyscraper complex in the prestigious SOHO Chaoyang district of Beijing as well as the Beijing Huamao Centre, a skyscraper that houses important offices, famous restaurants and high fashion stores. The company participated in creating the famous National Aquatics Centre in Beijing, better known as the "Water Cube," built for the 2008 Olympics. It has been involved in providing solutions for some government buildings including the Central Military Commission and the headquarters of the State oil company (http://www.caleffi.com/international/en-int). The role of the "Made in Italy" for those companies operating in the mechanical sector is rather important for the company and based on the experience gained in the Chinese market, Caleffi believes that key aspects in evaluating the "Made in Italy" in the sector include attention to design, the aesthetic sense, and product creativity. The main problem in the Chinese market is conveying what is behind a "Made in Italy" product: design, quality control, research (Shu interview).

Conclusions

This work analyzes the situation of European companies in the renewable energy sector. From the regulatory contributions in specialist literature, we verified that the European market is particularly developed and internationalized. Many firms, including SMEs, have established and developed with an international approach focused on excellence, research, and development. Many of these companies, with different positions in the supply chain or supplying energy from various sources, have for a considerable time faced the challenge posed by international markets and countries with high geographic distance.

The Chinese market is in great development thanks to the latest five-year plan, yet European enterprises find it difficult to approach this market. In fact, the number of European firms investing in China is low as a result of their size, high cultural distance, and inadequate strategies. Due to the small size of firms, gaining bargaining power requires aggregations or establishing networks operating under an umbrella brand, flanked by expertise that meets specific non-technologically advanced niches in China. Two essential capabilities are knowledge of the culture and developing strong relationships at the local level. Cultural orientation, particularly in China, is a prerequisite to establishing strong business relationships and building trust, which in the Asian culture is considered an antecedent of relationship building (contrary to relationships between Westerners – Harris & Dibben, 1999). These relations, which are primarily personal but reflect business relations (Cedrola & Battaglia, 2012), are essential to building a business in China and must be accompanied by the deep understanding of the local culture and behaviors. Cultural understanding allows adopting forms of negotiation that are appropriate for the Chinese market (e.g., the importance of the relationship between hierarchical "peer-levels") and essential to successful outcomes. This reflects the importance of culture and trust not only in the early stages of market entry (Sigfusson & Harris, 2012) but especially in managing, maintaining, and developing relationships with the local market (Hall, 1976; Herbig, 2000; Fletcher & Fang, 2004; Usunier, 1996).

The results of the analysis of the two case studies (Asja and Caleffi) confirm the importance of collaborations between various actors located in China and their key role in the success of many activities along the value chain. This strong orientation toward understanding the local market enables entrepreneurs to exchange value with local partners and thus increase trust and *renqing* (Wang, Siu, & Barnes, 2008). Moreover, expertise, product quality, and innovativeness help entrepreneurs operate successfully in China, even when the companies are smaller in size. In particular, the case of Asja that established a WFOE confirms that the development opportunities in China can be seized through technology transfer accompanied by a complete localization of the business in China, even in a very competitive and changing market. In particular, the analysis points to the relevance of relationships (*guanxi*) at all levels of the enterprise: local partners in the territory such as the Chinese municipality and European institutions in China. Relationships also lead to the identification of business partners for new developments such as distribution, guaranteeing coverage, or service that completes the product offering. Alternatively, it leads to the identification of new provinces in which to establish businesses through examples of systems already operating successfully in other municipalities, such as Shenyang. According to Asja's management, today the obstacles related to the investment in China are largely commercial and in the perceived distance between Italy and China, albeit manageable through listening, continuous dialogue, and with an open mind.

References

Cedrola, E. (2005). *Il marketing internazionale per le piccole e medie imprese.* Milano, Italy: McGraw Hill.

Cedrola, E., & Battaglia, L. (2012). *Storia, economia, cultura, modelli di business e di marketing per operare con successo in Cina. La via verso la terra di mezzo.* Padova, Italy: CEDAM.

China.Org.Cn. (2015). *White paper on energy.* Retrieved from http://www. china.org.cn/english/environment/236955.htm

European Parliament. (2015). *Renewable energy.* Retrieved from http://www. europarl.europa.eu/atyourservice/en/displayFtu.html?ftuId=FTU_5.7.4.html

Fang, T. (2006). Negotiation: The Chinese style. *Journal of Business and Industrial Marketing, 21*(1), 50–60.

Fletcher, R., & Fang, T. (2004). Re-thinking culture's consequences on relationship creation and network formation in Asian markets. Paper presented at the annual meeting for the IMP Group, 20th IMP Conference, Copenhagen, September 2–4.

Günter, S. K., & Meckl, R. M. (2014). *Internationalization of renewable energy companies: In search of gestalts.* Bayreuth, Canada: Canadian Center of Science and Education.

Hall, E. (1976). *Beyond culture.* New York, NY: Doubleday.

Harris, S., & Dibben, M. R. (1999). Trust and co-operation in business relationship development: Exploring the influence of national values. *Journal of Marketing Management, 15*(3), 463–483.

Herbig, P. A. (2000). *Marketing interculturale.* Milano: Apogeo.

Hollensen, S. (2014). *Global marketing.* Edinburgh Gate, Harlow: Pearson.

NL EVD International Information. (2015). *Towards a sustainable, reliable and affordable energy system.* Retrieved from http://www.hollandtrade.com/sector-information/energy/?bstnum=4913

Pye, L. W. (1992). *Chinese negotiating style: Commercial approaches and cultural principles.* New York, NY: Quorum Books.

Richter, M. (2012). Utilities' business models for renewable energy: A review. *Renewable and Sustainable Energy Reviews, 16*(5), 2483–2493.

Salacuse, J. W. (1999). Intercultural negotiation in international business. *Group Decision and Negotiation, 8*(3), 217–236.

Sigfusson, T., & Harris, S. (2012). The relationship formation paths of international entrepreneurs. *Journal of International Entrepreneurship, 10*, 325–349.

The Economist Intelligence Unit. (2012). A greener shade of grey: A special report on renewable energy in China. Retrieved from http://www.eiu.com/public/topical_report.aspx?campaignid=ChinaGreenEnergy

The National People's Congress of the People's Republic of China. (2007). *Law on conserving energy.* Retrieved from http://www.npc.gov.cn/englishnpc/Law/2007-12/11/content_1383579.htm

Trianel Press Release. (2010). Retrieved from http://www.trianel.com/de/pressearchiv/details/article//way-cleared-for-trianel-offsho.html

Usunier, J. C. (1996). *Marketing across cultures* (2nd ed.). London: Prentice Hall.

Wang, C. L., Siu, N. Y. M., & Barnes, B. R. (2008). The significance of trust and renqing in the long-term orientation of Chinese business-to-business relationships. *Industrial Marketing Management, 37*(7), 819–824.

Weber, M. (2008). *In Due anni di Cina. Opportunità di business, scenari in evoluzione.* Milano: ETAS.

6 China's FDI in the EU's Environmental Protection Industries

Chunming Zhao, Mi Dai, Qun Zhang
and Lei Wen

ABSTRACT

Purpose – The objective of this chapter is to analyze China's outward foreign direct investment (OFDI) to the European Union in environmental industries.

Methodology/approach – We combine a narrative approach with statistical analysis. We first review the policy background concerning China's OFDI and environmental protection. Then, we provide statistics on China's OFDI to the EU in environmental industries, using firm-level data from one of China's major provinces: Jiangsu.

Findings – We find that the OFDI to the EU in environmental industries experienced a considerable growth in terms of number of investing firms and investment value. The OFDI in environmental industries to the EU was highly concentrated in a few countries, particularly Germany and Luxemburg, and a few industries, particularly new energy.

Research limitations – Using firm-level data from only one province may limit the generalizability of our findings. However, we believe the case of Jiangsu province sheds much light on the situation of entire China because Jiangsu is one of the most important Chinese provinces in terms of OFDI.

Practical implications – The detailed analysis of our Jiangsu's OFDI in EU's environmental industries in this chapter can help to inform the investment cooperation in environmental industries between China and EU in terms of both scope of investment partners and target industries.

Originality/value – This study is one of the first to provide a detailed summary statistics on China's OFDI to the EU in environmental industries. Given China's growing concerns regarding environmental protection and OFDI, we believe the question merits further analysis.

Keywords: FDI; environmental industries; EU; Jiangsu province

Introduction

In addition to trade in environmental goods and services (Zeng & Qu, 2016), another important channel for international cooperation in environmental protection is through foreign direct investment (FDI). Over the past two decades, China has been one of the world's largest receivers of FDI. This picture is changing recently. China is rapidly becoming an important source of outward foreign direct investment (OFDI). Starting from virtually no OFDI in 1979, the first year of China's open door policy, the stock of China's OFDI has accumulated over US$ 90 billion. China's OFDI flow and stock now stand as the 4th and 6th largest, respectively, among developing countries.[1] This opens the possibility of China-EU cooperation in the form of "green FDI" in the EU. In this chapter, we provide one of the first portrait of China's OFDI in the EU in environmental industries.

This chapter proceeds as follows. First, we review the existing literature on the potential relationship between FDI and environmental protection. Second, we introduce the policy background

---

[1]http://www.mofcom.gov.cn/

in China concerning OFDI and environmental protection. Lastly, drawing on a unique firm-level data set covering all OFDI firms in one of China's major province: Jiangsu, we analyze China's green OFDI in the EU.

Literature Review

The growing appreciation of the potential for "green FDI" (i.e., environmentally friendly[2] FDI) originates from the growing concerns regarding globally sustainable development. In addition to international trade in goods and services, foreign direct investment (FDI) is generally recognized as an important channel of transferring technology and know-how between countries. However, little attention has been paid to Green FDI because of the lack of clear definition and of available data on green FDI.

Existing studies on green FDI are mainly specific case studies. For example, Gentry (1999) studied the environmental performance of foreign firms in Brazilian soybean and pulp and paper industries and Costa Rican banana industry. It indicates that while the effects of FDI in the Brazilian soybean and pulp and paper industry are ambiguous, foreign firms in Costa Rican banana industry have positive effects on local environment by improving waste management and establishing their recycling and integrated waste management programs; Gallagher and Zarsky (2007) and Zarsky and Gallagher (2008) show that foreign firms that invest in Mexican manufacturing sectors are more environmentally friendly than domestic firms by using less energy and water. Lewis and Wiser (2007)'s case study on one of India's leading wind turbine manufacturers, Suzlon, indicates that FDI in the wind industry of Denmark was aimed to take advantage of knowledge spillovers. However, the spillover effects of foreign firms may be limited. Using firm-level data from a World Bank survey, Hale and Long (2006) find positive spillovers are captured by more technologically advanced domestic firms in the service market.

While the case studies show that the environment improving effect of FDI differs by firm, sector, and country; the empirical research on FDI and environment indicates the reasons why FDI

---

[2]Defining "green" as "Environmentally friendly" may be too vague. In the section "Data Selection and Methodology," we make a more specific definition.

improve host countries' environment and the determinants of the green effects of FDI. Based on a sample of 4,000 manufacturing firms, Johnstone (2007) finds that home country's stringent environmental policy regimes have an important impact on multinational firms' environmental performances because the regulations will affect firms' greening capacity. That is to say, standards tend to diffuse to countries with less stringent environmental regulation through MNE activity (Zarsky & Gallagher, 2008). However, Henna (2010) finds that the US Clean Air Act Amendments have led more firms to invest overseas. In this way, home countries' stringent policy may actually have negative effects on host countries' environment through so called "environmental dumping." In addition to regulations, home countries' specific policies may also influence firms' green FDI. As highlighted by Golub, Kauffmann, and Yeres (2011), the German government both provides direct subsidies for the construction of renewable energy plants and requires power companies to pay a fixed rate to third parties which feed power back into the grid, making location in Germany attractive to foreign firms (Golub et al., 2011).

All in all, existing studies on FDI and environment are mainly focused on the effect of FDI on host countries' environment, multinational firms' environmental performances, as well as the determinants of green effects of FDI. There has been little direct evidence on the FDI in environmental industries, that is, green FDI. The exception is Lv and Spigarelli (2015), who explore OFDI from China to the EU in the renewable energy sector. They find that location choices within the EU are affected by home and host country institutional factors as well as the development level of the industry. Most investments were primarily aimed at developing the local market. This chapter supplements this work, by looking at flows from a key Chinese province in a wider range of environmental industries.

China's Policy on OFDI

In order to understand the emergence and growth of China's OFDI in environmental industries, it is important to know the policy background in China regarding OFDI and environmental protection. In this section, we review policies and regulations related to China's OFDI and environmental protection. We first review the evolution of China's OFDI policies and then review the bilateral and multilateral treaties that China has signed with other countries. Since China's OFDI in environmental industries experienced significant growth during the *12th Five-Year Plan*, we review relevant policies and regulations issued in this period at the end of the section.

THE EVOLUTION OF CHINA'S OFDI POLICY

The scale and speed of China's OFDI are largely determined by China's OFDI policy. The evolution of China's OFDI policies experienced two stages.

THE FIRST STAGE: FROM1979 TO THE EARLY 1990S[3]

The basic guiding principle of OFDI policy system in this period was to limit Chinese enterprises' overseas investment. In 1991, *Strengthening of Overseas Investment Project Management Advice* submitted by the State Planning Commission argued that China does not have the conditions for a large-scale overseas investment and that the overseas investment by Chinese enterprises should focus on acquiring foreign technology, resources, and markets in order to supply domestic shortage. As a result, the size and amount of the China's OFDI were severely restricted. Though some OFDI related regulations were removed in the late 1990s, there is no fundamental change for restricting enterprises' OFDI and China's OFDI developed slowly in the following few years. In 2004, China's FDI only accounted for 0.9% of global flow and 0.55% of global stock, not representative of China's economic strength.

SECOND STAGE: FROM 2000 TO PRESENT

This period is characterized by the formation of systematic OFDI policies which are closer to international standards. In October 2000, China 10th Five-Year Plan proposed the "Going out" strategy for the first time, showing a significant change from restricting to encouraging OFDI. Under this background, China has issued a series of policies to support Chinese enterprises to invest overseas, including *Interim Management Measures about Approving Foreign Investment Projects, Policy on Giving Credit Support to China's OFDI in Key Industries, etc.*[4]

---

[3]Li (2008, pp, 4–6).
[4]http://www.sdpc.gov.cn/

BILATERAL AND MULTILATERAL TREATIES

Since 1982 China has signed investment protection agreements with more than 67 countries, including the United Kingdom, Germany, France, Japan, Australia, South Korea, and Malaysia. By 1994, China had also signed bilateral double taxation and prevention of tax evasion agreements with 40 countries. In addition, a series of international investment agreements, economic partnership agreements, and technology transfer agreements have been signed between China and foreign governments, which adjust China's OFDI from different perspectives.

Two main international multilateral treaties China currently has joined are *Paul Multilateral Investment Guarantee Agency Convention* and *the Washington Convention*. In addition, the *Code of conduct for transnational corporations* (established by the United Nations) and *Guidelines on the Treatment of Foreign Direct Investment* (developed under the auspices of the World Bank) are also important guides for China's FDI. Furthermore, after joining the WTO, China automatically became a member of the *Trade-Related Investment Measures Agreement*.

RELATED POLICIES DURING THE 12TH FIVE-YEAR PLAN PERIOD

The 12th Five-Year Plan gives great importance to environmental protection. Firstly, binding targets were established including reducing energy consumption, carbon dioxide emission, and greenhouse gas emission. Secondly, the government increased efforts to address pollution issues in drinking water, air, and soil and focus on strengthening the comprehensive management of environmental quality. Thirdly, enterprises were called upon to foster and develop the strategic emerging industries, strengthen research and development on key technologies, and promote breakthroughs in key areas. In addition, the government should actively and orderly adjust industrial structure, encourage the development in information technology, energy saving and environmental protection, new energy, biotechnology, new materials, and new energy vehicles. In addition, the government and some ministries also issued a series of regulations and provisions (Table 1) to support investment in environmental industries.

In terms of OFDI, the Five-Year Plan states that on one hand, in order to accelerate the implementation of the "going out" strategy, government should relax restrictions on enterprises, in accordance with the principles of a market-oriented economy and give enterprises autonomous decision-making rights. On the other hand, in certain areas, such as technical innovation and risk management, government should play a more active role. The government should guide enterprises to expand international cooperation in agriculture and deepen mutually beneficial international cooperation in energy resources. In order to prevent overseas risk, the government should help access the quality of investment projects and the overseas investment environment.

Table 1:   Related Support Policies in Environmental Industries during 12th Five-Year Plan Period.

Issuing Date	Issuing Authority	Document Name
2010	State Council	*Accelerating the Cultivation and Development of Strategic Emerging Industries*
2010	Ministry of Environmental Protection	*Notice on Strengthening of Sludge Pollution Prevention and Control Work in Municipal Wastewater Treatment Plant*
2010	Ministry of Environmental Protection	*Opinions on Further Strengthening the Supervision of Hazardous Waste and Medical Waste Work*
2011	Ministry of Environmental Protection	*Guidance on Environmentally Friendly Systems Further Promoting the Development of Environmental Industries*
2011	Ministry of Housing and Urban-Rural development, etc.	*Advices on Further Strengthening the Work of Municipal Solid Waste Disposal*
2011	National Development and Reform Commission and Ministry of Finance	*Programs on the Issuance of Special Funds Support to the Development of Recycling Economy for Kitchen Waste Recycling and Safe Disposal*
2015	National Development and Reform Commission	*2015 circular economy promoting plan*
2015	State Council	*Accelerating the construction of ecological civilization*

Source: Relevant official authorities' websites.

Data Selection and Methodology

In this section, we provide new statistics on China's green OFDI in the EU. There are two major challenges involved in this task. The first challenge is how to identify green FDI. Since there is no internationally accepted definition, we start this section with a discussion of the definition of green FDI and the methodology we used to identify green FDI in our data. The second challenge is data limitation. Although official data on China's OFDI reports the investment value by destination country or by industry, it does not report the investment value by both destination country and industry, preventing us from getting the information of China's OFDI to the EU in environmental industries. In addition, the industry category in the official data is only at the one-digit level (e.g., manufacturing, public facilities, finance, etc.), which is too aggregate for us to identify green industries. As a result, it is impossible to get the green OFDI information for the whole of China. However, we are able to get access to a unique data of OFDI firms in one of China's major provinces, Jiangsu. Thus, in the second part of this section, we provide facts on Jiangsu's total green OFDI flows into EU during 2004–2013.[5]

DATA

The OFDI data for Jiangsu province came from China Export & Credit Insurance Corporation (SINOSURE) and the List of Overseas Investment Enterprises on MOFCOM's website. It covers the universe of firms involved in OFDI during the period 2004–2013, and includes information such as certificate number, names of overseas investment enterprises both in China and in host countries, investment value, descriptions of the scope of business, license issuing authority, date of issue, and investment destination. The detailed description of the scope of business allows us to clearly identify green industries.

---

[5]The analysis on Jiangsu province is informative on China's OFDI to EU in environmental industries in several aspects. First, Jiangsu province is one of the most developed province in China. In 2011, its GDP per capita, comprehensive competitiveness, and Development and Life Index (DLI) rank 1st in China. Second, Jiangsu is a large province in terms of its size of OFDI. By the end of 2012, the outward FDI flows and stock of Jiangsu was 313.3 billion dollars and 783.2 billion dollars which ranked 4th and 5th in all China's provinces, respectively.

DEFINITION OF GREEN FDI

Defining green FDI (i.e., "FDI in environmental industries") is not a simple task. The efforts to define green FDI dates back to the 1980s when the OECD Development Assistance Committee (ODA) reported statistics on aid to environment according to a standard template which allows countries to specify when environmental sustainability, climate change, biodiversity, or desertification is a principal or a significant objective of aid (Golub et al., 2011). Subsequently, OECD and APEC created lists of environmental goods and services (EGS) for possible use in trade agreements.[6] While OECD list was intended to illustrate the scope of the environmental industry, the APEC list covers specific products in the environmental activities. However, the OECD and APEC list do not consider goods produced by environmentally friendly processes (Golub et al., 2011). That is to say, "green" is not only a matter of what you produce but also how you produce it. According to this definition, "green" means environmentally friendly. However, this definition is too vague. Therefore, in this report, we define a firm's OFDI as "green OFDI" if its target industry meets either of the two criterion: (1) the industry produces environmental goods and services ("EGS")[7] (2) the production of the industry adopts environmental-friendly technologies and practices defined as Golub et al. (2011).

Based on this definition, we select the green industries from the industry catalogue of Nomenclature of Economic Activities (NACE).[8] The selected industries are listed in Table A1. Then, we select out firms if the firm's investment target industry is a green industry.

To ensure a more comprehensive list of firms to be included in the analysis, we also identified a list of keywords that identifies green industries based on the EU SME Center definition (EU SME Center, 2011). These keywords are listed in Table A2. We then include firms whose description of scope of business includes at least one of these keywords. Overall, we identify Green FDI as firms whose scope of business include any green industries in the NACE list or include any keywords based on EU SME Center definition.

---

[6]Golub et al. (2011).

[7]OECD (2005) created a list of environmental goods (HS code) for possible use in trade agreements. See www.oecd.org/dataoecd/4/6/38025362.pdf

[8]*Source*:   http://ec.europa.eu/economy_finance/db_indicators/surveys/time_series/index_en.htm

Green OFDI Flows into EU: Micro Evidence from Jiangsu Province

TOTAL FLOWS

Jiangsu's green OFDI began in 2004 (Table 2). According to the statistics, there was only one firm which invested in Germany in that year. And in the following five years, there was a small increase of the number of firms engaging in green OFDI. In 2009, the total number of firms climbed to 11. However, during that time, the number of firms that invested in EU's environmental industries increased little. The number of firms had made a great breakthrough since 2010 and it continued to increase in subsequent years. In 2010, Jiangsu's OFDI in EU's environmental industries reached the peak. The number of firms and investment value was 11 and $217.67 million, accounting for 35.5% and 52.9% of the total OFDI in EU's environmental industries, respectively. After that, green OFDI in EU maintained a rapid growth rate. In 2013, the number of firms and investment value

Table 2: Jiangsu's Total OFDI in Environmental Industries and in EUs, 2004–2013.

Year/ OFDI	OFDI in Environmental Industries		OFDI in EU's Environmental Industries		EU's Proportion (%)	
	Number of firms	OFDI flows ($ million)	Number of firms	OFDI flows ($ million)	Number of firms	OFDI flows
2004	1	–	1	–	1	–
2005	1	0.6	0	0	0	0
2006	4	0.79	2	0.17	50	21.5
2007	9	10.69	3	0.692	33.3	6.5
2008	11	18.236	1	6.3	9.1	34.5
2009	11	79.63	2	1.29	18.2	1.6
2010	31	411.27	11	217.67	35.5	52.9
2011	40	548.55	12	203.78	30	37.1
2012	56	2,228.26	17	1,340.92	28.1	60.18
2013	63	1,258.56	16	566.15	25.4	44.98

Source: SINOSURE and List of Overseas Investment Enterprises on MOFCOM's website.

reached $16 and $566.15 million, increasing by 45% and 160%, respectively, compared with 2010.

In terms of investment value, with the exception of 2009, in which the sub-prime crisis in the United States had repercussions on China's outward investment, Jiangsu firms' engagement in green OFDI increased greatly from $0.17 million in 2006 to $566.15 million in 2013, an increase of more than 3,330 fold. Moreover, the EU's proportion of Jiangsu's investment value to the whole world had increased greatly since 2010 and maintained at about 40–50%.

GREEN OFDI TO INDIVIDUAL COUNTRIES

In Table 3, we report the distribution of Jiangsu's green OFDI in 2013 by destination country. Compared with 2004, when Germany was the only recipient country of Jiangsu's OFDI, in 2013, 16 firms with more than $566 million investment value invested in 7 EU countries. Though more EU countries became the recipient countries of Jiangsu's green OFDI, the distribution of the number of firms and investment value was uneven. From Table 3, we can immediately see that Germany, Luxembourg, and Holland were the top three countries of Jiangsu's OFDI in EU. Specifically, the 11 firms with an investment value of

Table 3: Distribution of Jiangsu's OFDI in Foreign Countries, 2013.

Country		Number of Firms	Investment Value ($ Million)	Share: Number of Firms (%)	Share: Investment Value (%)
EU countries	Italy	2	5.01	3.17	0.4
	Bulgaria	1	18.47	1.59	1.47
	Luxembourg	3	242.97	4.76	19.31
	Germany	5	171.5	7.94	13.63
	Romania	1	90	1.59	7.15
	Holland	3	22.2	4.76	1.76
	Spain	1	16	1.59	1.27
Non-EU countries		47	692.41	74.6	55.01
Total		63	1,258.56	100	100

Source: SINOSURE and List of Overseas Investment Enterprises on MOFCOM's website.

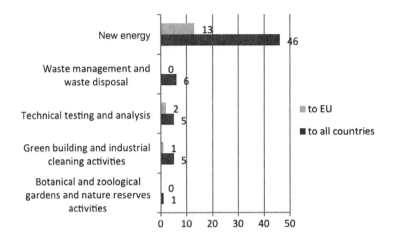

Figure 1: Distribution of Jiangsu's OFDI in Environmental Protection Industries, 2013 (Number of Firms). *Source:* SINOSURE and List of Overseas Investment Enterprises on MOFCOM's website.

$436.67 million invested in these three countries, representing 68.75% and 77.13% shares of the EU, respectively.

DISTRIBUTION BY INDUSTRY

Figures 1 and 2 report the industry distribution of Jiangsu's OFDI to all countries and to the EU in 2013. Compared with 2004 when Jiangsu began to invest in the solar industry (new energy industry)[9] in Germany, we can immediately see that Jiangsu's investment in environmental industries in 2013 experienced a considerable expansion in scope.

Figures 1 and 2 show that new energy was the main industry that absorbs Jiangsu's OFDI. For the investment to all countries,

---

[9]Note that we select firms engaged in green FDI according to Tables A1 and A2. Obviously, some industries or key words appear in both tables. Therefore, in order to analyze more clearly according to these tables, we reorganize the keywords and industries and reclassify them into the following eight categories: (1) green building (design, materials, appliances) and industrial cleaning activities; (2) technical testing and analysis; (3) waste management(collection, recycling, treatment) and waste disposal; (4) new energy (nuclear power, wind, solar, bioenergy, hydropower); (5) botanical and zoological gardens and nature reserve activities; (6) electric power (transmission, distribution, storage); (7) clean transportation (air, road, rail, waterway); (8) clean water (extraction, treatment, distribution).

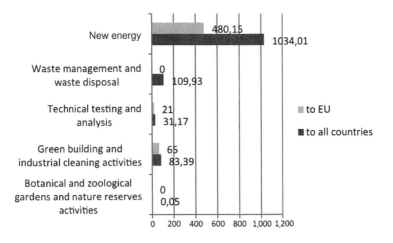

Figure 2: Distribution of Jiangsu's OFDI Flows in Environmental Protection Industries, 2013 ($million). *Source*: SINOSURE and List of Overseas Investment Enterprises on MOFCOM's website.

46 firms and 1.03 billion USD invested in new energy industries. Notably, firms that invested in EU's environmental industries mainly focused on energy industries (13 firms and 480.15 million USD). Obviously, with the issuing of *"Jiangsu's Twelfth Five-Year Plan in Cultivation and Development of Strategic Emerging Industries,"* new energy industries (especially, solar industry) have become the core environmental protection industries of investment of Jiangsu's enterprises.

Conclusions

With China's policies on OFDI shifting from restrictions to encouragement and its increasing awareness of environmental protection, more and more Chinese firms have started to invest in foreign countries' green industries. However, due to the lack of an internationally agreed definition of and relevant data on "green FDI," little is known about the magnitude of China's FDI in environmental industries, especially to the EU. Drawing upon a unique firm-level OFDI data for China's Jiangsu province, we analyze China's investment to the EU in environmental industries and highlight its key characteristics.

We find that the OFDI in environmental industries in EU experienced considerable growth between 2004 and 2013, both in terms of number of investing firms and investment value. From virtually no investment in 2004, the value of investment reached $566.15 million in 2013, accounting for 45% of China's total investment in environmental industries to the world. Despite the spectacular growth in total value, the OFDI in environmental industries to the EU are highly concentrated in a few countries, particularly Germany and Luxemburg, and a few industries, particularly new energy. Therefore, there is still a potential to deepen the investment cooperation in environmental industries between China and EU in terms of both the scope of investment partners and the scope of target industries.

Acknowledgments

We thank Francesca Spigarelli and the editor for their very helpful comments and constructive suggestions. Our research was funded from Marie Curie project on *Partnering opportunities between Europe and China in the Renewable energies and environmental industries-POREEN*. This publication does not necessarily reflect the opinion of the EU, all errors are ours.

References

EU SME Center. (2011). The green tech market in China.

Gallagher, K., & Zarsky, L. (2007). *The enclave economy*. Cambridge, MA: MIT Press.

Gentry, B. (1999). *Private capital flows and the environment: Lessons from Latin America*. Cheltenham: Edward Elgar Publishing.

Golub, S., Kauffmann, C., & Yeres, P. (2011). *Defining and measuring green FDI: An exploratory review of existing work and evidence*. OECD Working Papers on International Investment No.2011/2; OECD Investment Division. Retrieved from www.oecd.org/daf/investment/workingpapers.

Hale, G., & Long, C. (2006). *What determines technological spillovers of foreign direct investment: Evidence from China*. Economic Growth Center, Yale University. Retrieved from http://ideas.repec.org/p/egc/wpaper/934.html

Henna, R. (2010). US environmental regulation and FDI: Evidence from a panel of us-based multinational firms. *American Economic Journal: Applied Economics*, 2(3), 158–189.

Johnstone, N. (2007). *Environmental policy and corporate behaviour*. Cheltenham: Edward Elgar Publishing.

Lewis, J., & Wiser, R. (2007). Fostering a renewable energy technology industry: An international comparison of wind industry policy support mechanisms. *Energy Policy*, 35(3), 1844–1857.

Li, B. (2008). The evolution of China's foreign investment policy and outlook. International Trade Practice, 342(4), 4−7.

Lv, P., & Spigarelli, F. (2015). The integration of Chinese and European renewable energy markets: The role of Chinese foreign direct investments. *Energy Policy, 81*, 14−26.

OECD. (2005). *Trade that benefits the environment and development.* Paris: OECD Publishing.

Zarsky, L., & Gallagher, K. (2008). *FDI spillovers and sustainable industrial development: Evidence from U.S. firms in Mexico's silicon valley.* Discussion Paper. Working Group on Development and Environment in the Americas. Retrieved from http://ase.tufts.edu/gdae/Pubs/rp/DP18Zarsky_GallagherApr08.pdf

Zeng, Y., & Qu, R. (2016). The environmental goods trade between China and the EU: Development and influencing factors. In F. Spigarelli, L. Curran, & A. Arteconi (Eds.), *China and Europe's partnership for a more sustainable world: Challenges and opportunities.* Bingley, UK: Emerald Group Publishing Limited.

Appendix

Table A1: Selected Green Industries from the NACE List.

NACE Code	Industry Name
24.46	Processing of nuclear fuel
36	Water collection, treatment, and supply
37	Sewerage
38.11	Collection of non-hazardous waste
38.12	Collection of hazardous waste
38.21	Treatment and disposal of non-hazardous waste
38.21	Treatment and disposal of non-hazardous waste
38.22	Treatment and disposal of hazardous waste
39	Remediation activities and other waste management services
42.91	Construction of water projects
71.2	Technical testing and analysis
81.22	Other building and industrial cleaning activities
91.04	Botanical and zoological gardens and nature reserves activities

Source: http://ec.europa.eu/economy_finance/db_indicators/surveys/time_series/index_en.htm

Table A2: Keywords to Identify Green Industries Based on EU SME Center Definition.

Cleaner coal, Cleaner oil, Cleaner Gas, Nuclear power, Wind, Solar, Bioenergy, Hydropower, Green building (design, materials, appliances), Electric power (transmission, distribution, storage), Clean Water (extraction, treatment, distribution), Cleaner transportation (air, road, rail, waterway), Energy efficiency (monitory systems, design), Waste management (collection, re cycling, treatment) and waste disposal, Energy from waste recovery

Source: EU SME Center (2011, p. 1).

7

Chinese OFDI to Germany in the Environmental Industries: A Multiple Case Study

Katiuscia Vaccarini, Francesca Spigarelli, Christoph Lattemann, Federico Salvatelli and Ernesto Tavoletti

ABSTRACT

Purpose — Chinese foreign direct investments (FDI) to developed countries, such as Germany, seems to follow unique rules, which are different to traditional international business (IB) practices in terms of entry modes, speed of internationalization, and target countries. To shed light on these unique rules, we analyze motivation and location choices of FDI from China to Germany by describing a sample of five companies from the environmental industry.

Methodology/approach — A multiple case study research design is adopted. The study is based on five Chinese companies investing in Germany in the environmental industry through FDI (Greenfield Investment and Merger and Acquisition). Chinese managers were interviewed on the basis of semi-structured questionnaires.

Findings — According to the main findings from the interviews, when investing in Germany, managers take into account a series of factors. Chinese firms go global for traditional motives such as market-seeking purposes and with the aim of improving their production process through skills and know-how acquisition. Additional motives, such as labor cost and fiscal incentives are not considered relevant as factors for internationalizing. Entry mode choices are mainly driven by legal factors in the environmental industry.

Originality/value – The analysis is conducted at industry level with the aim to contextualize the results within the environmental sector. The case studies are focused on Chinese investments in Germany.

Keywords: Chinese outward foreign direct investment (OFDI); Greenfield; M&A; environmental industry; entry mode choice

Introduction

China is an increasingly important global player in OFDI (Athreye & Kapur, 2009). OFDI from emerging economies, such as China, has grown massively and has become an important engine for the global economic growth (Deng & Yang, 2015; Lattemann & Alon, 2015). Usually, emerging markets multinationals tend to enter developed economies with the aim to explore assets and acquire new technological capabilities that will allow them to be more competitive in the global scenario (Wright, Filatotchev, Hoskisson, & Peng, 2005).

In particular, China has been supporting the domestic growth and – later – the international expansion of firms in the environmental industries since the Sixth Five-Year Plan (Hu, 2014). As a result of combined mix of production supportive policies for renewable energies (RE) in China and internationalization promotion measures, Chinese foreign direct investments (FDI) flows to Europe have increased in the last decade in the environmental sector (Lv & Spigarelli, 2015, 2016). In addition, the economic recession in Europe has created a climate, which is increasingly conducive to Chinese OFDI, especially in key sectors such as energy industry (Rhodium Group, 2012).

According to recent studies on integration of European and Chinese environmental sectors (Curran, 2015; Lv & Spigarelli, 2015,

2016), Europe has become an important sales destination from Chinese global environmental firms. Germany, that is one of the world largest actors in the RE sector, is attracting an increasing number of Chinese investments (Clegg & Voss, 2012; Klossek, Linke, & Nippa, 2012; Lv & Spigarelli, 2015, 2016; Schütte & Chen, 2012).

In this chapter we provide a qualitative analysis of five cases on Chinese investments in the environmental and RE industries in Germany. The mode of entry is one of the most important decisions in the internationalization process because of its implications for performance and long-term consequences for the firm. Hence, key aspects under investigation are modes of entry in Germany as well as motivations for location choices. The motivation for location choices is a fundamental factor to be analyzed to grasp the nature and possible "consequences" of market entry. As an important contribution to the literature, we follow-up the call for more studies at the industry level (Wang, 2012).

The chapter is structured as follows. We firstly present the theoretical background that is linked to Chinese firms' global expansion within the international business literature. We then illustrate our cases in the methodology section and present the main results. This chapter ends with a discussion and conclusion.

Theoretical Background

Within the vast literature on Chinese firms international expansion (Alon, Fetscherin, & Gugler, 2012; Deng, 2012) scholars have typically focused their attention on antecedents of Chinese firms strategies, such as factors on firm-level, industry-level, institutional-level, and transaction-specific factors. Less attention has been devoted to the process of going global and factors affecting implementation of the strategy, such as corporate internal resources and capabilities (Deng, 2009; Oliver, 1997). Those factors include also motivation and strategic intent, as well as mode of entry.

Prevailing motivations underlying Chinese investments seem to depend on host locations. In the case of industrialized countries market-seeking motivations prevail (Buckley et al., 2007; Cheung & Qian, 2009; Hurst, 2011; Kolstad & Wiig, 2012), while resource-seeking motivations tend to be more important in emerging or developing economies (Buckley et al., 2007; Hurst, 2011; Kolstad & Wiig, 2012; Pradhan, 2011; Sanfilippo, 2010). Strategic asset-seeking motives to acquire technologies and intangible assets might be sector-specific (Amighini, Rabellotti, & Sanfilippo, 2011).

In the case of the environmental industry, recent studies show that market-seeking and technological asset-seeking motivations for Chinese firms prevail in Europe (Lv and Spigarelli, 2015).

Several scholars show that the entry mode choice is highly correlated with underlying motivations (Cui & Jiang, 2009; Voss, Buckley, & Cross, 2009). Cui and Jiang (2009) find out the entry mode choice is influenced by firm's strategic fit in the host industry and its strategic intent for FDI. Further, industry specificity also has an impact on mode of organizing transnational operations (Lv & Spigarelli, 2015). Chinese firms, for example, tend to prefer wholly owned subsidiaries, as an entry mode, when adopting global strategies and pursuing asset-seeking goals. Also, Chinese state-owned enterprises (SOE), which are subject to regulatory institutional barrier, usually choose Joint-Ventures (JV) to "exchange ownership for legitimacy" (Lin, 2010). Greenfield investments and merger and acquisitions (M&A) are the two typical organizational modes used by Chinese firms to go global (Child, Ng, & Wong, 2002; Child, Rodrigues, & Frynas, 2009). M&As have become increasingly common (Antkiewicz & Whalley, 2007; Globerman & Shapiro, 2003; MOFCOM, 2011) to quickly access brands, know-how, and other strategic assets overseas (Buckley et al., 2007; Deng, 2009; OECD, 2008, 2013; Rui & Yip, 2008; Yiu & Makino, 2002). However, in recent years a large number of Chinese firms have entered the European market through Greenfield investment.

Methods: Multiple Case Study

Motivation of global expansion and the mode of entry choices are examined in five case studies of Chinese companies operating in the environmental industry in Germany. We use a convenience sample of five companies headquartered in China. These Chinese firms have recently (within the past 10 years) entered the German environmental market through FDI. The Chinese Chamber of Commerce in Berlin, a private consultancy company and an exhibitors' database of the annual international RE fair held in Munich helped us to identify these companies. Data and methodology used in this study are built on a recent research about managers' perceptions of psychic distance in the context of Chinese OFDI to Germany (Vaccarini, Spigarelli, & Tavoletti, 2015).

We adopted a multiple case study research design based on Eisenhardt (1989, 2009) and Yin's (1984) methodology. A case study design is the most appropriate methodology because of the explorative nature of our research questions. For the purpose of this chapter we conducted a descriptive analysis of these five companies. This enables us to conduct a within-case analysis including (1) general information of the Chinese headquarters and of the acquired company in Germany, (2) the reasons for choosing Germany, (3) the FDI entry mode, and (4) the reasons behind the entry mode choices.

We collected data in the fieldwork by gathering information from interviews conducted during company visits and phone calls as well as from other resources, such as companies' internet websites, annual reports, public available information from newspapers and online media. Our data collection took place in Spring/Summer 2015 in Germany, based on a questionnaire composed of five sections (Vaccarini, 2015). For the purpose of this work we analyze the general information about the companies and the responses on the modes of entry, the motives of the entry mode choice, and the reasons for choosing Germany. The managers who were interviewed cover the following positions: Director of Global Sales, Chief Liaison Officer, Marketing Manager, General Manager, and Manager's Assistant. In the following, the profile of the companies, the reasons for choosing Germany, the FDI entry mode, and the reasons behind these choices are illustrated (see Table 1).

RISEN ENERGY CO., LTD.

Risen Energy Co., Ltd., headquartered in Ningbo, settled its wholly owned subsidiary in Nuremberg in 2011.

The Chinese company was founded in 1986 and accounts for a turnover of about 50,000,000 USD with about 3,000 employees (in 2015). In 2010 it launched an IPO in the Shenzhen Stock Exchange Market. The core business of the company is located in the RE sector. In particular, it is a hi-tech enterprise which is engaged in R&D, production, sales, and service of solar modules, products of photovoltaic technology, solar terminal application, and integration. In the field of solar energy, Risen is one of the most competitive and advanced firms; it received the China

Table 1: Five Cases of Chinese Companies Investing in Germany.

Company	Risen Energy Co., Ltd.	Wuxi Suntech Power Co., Ltd.	Sany Heavy Industry Co., Ltd.	Phono Solar Technology Co., Ltd.	Shenzhen Everbest Machinery Industry Co., Ltd.
Subsidiary in Germany	Risen Energy GmbH	SF Suntech Deutschland GmbH	Putzmeister Holding GmbH	Sumec Europe GmbH	CEM Instruments GmbH
Interviewee	Manager's assistant	Director of Global Sales	Chief Liaison Officer	Marketing Manager	General Manager
Entry mode	Greenfield	Greenfield	Acquisition	Greenfield	Greenfield
Value of investment (USD)	18,000,000	N/A	360,000,000	N/A	N/A
Turnover in China (USD)	50,000,000	22,000,000	280,000,000	28,000,000	55,000
Investment in R&D	N/A	N/A	5% of sales revenue per year	N/A	N/A
Motives	Market seeking	Market seeking	Key technologies, brand, skills and know-how	Market seeking	Market seeking/ key technologies and brand
Push/pull factors	Incentive and supportive policies/ existing connection	Public incentives and supportive policies	Previous experience/EXISTING connection Financial crisis	Existing connection/logistic reason	Previous experience/cultural and language factors
Government structure	Chinese CEO	Chinese CEO	Chinese CEO and 100% control, Germany board structure and managers kept in place	Chinese CEO	Chinese CEO

National Accreditation Service for Conformity Assessment (CNAS) certification in 2015. Products of the company are second rank for performance ratio (ratio of the useful energy fed back into the grid to the energy which would be generated an ideal PV module) in a Global Modules Test by PHOTON laboratory in 2013 and 2014.

Risen Energy is currently present with more than hundreds of solar projects around the world. The Photovoltaic projects area has been all over Inner Mongolia, Ningxia, Qinghai, Jiangsu, Zhejiang, Gansu, and other cities and also worldwide as Germany, Bulgaria, Italy, France, the United Kingdom, Spain, the Middle East, and others.

Risen Energy GmbH, the German subsidiary, was established in 2011 and operates in the RE business, in particular, in the field of solar technology, service, and distribution. Currently, there are seven employees in Germany.

The company chose Greenfield investment as the mode of entry. The interviewed manager considered political and economic factors as key factors for the entry choices. Also previous experience with Germany and legal factors were relevant. Cultural factors were not crucial for the entry strategy.

Access to the local market was a crucial motivation to enter Germany. Risen's manager declared that it was particularly convenient to invest in Germany because of incentives and supportive policies that were available for the business.

Also the presence of existing connection was considered a determinant factor. Previous connection with local partners granted the possibility to better understand the business practices in the new market and to facilitate the activities of Chinese expatriates in the subsidiary.

WUXI SUNTECH POWER CO., LTD.

Wuxi Suntech Power Co. Ltd. entered the German market in 2008 by establishing its wholly owned subsidiary, SF Suntech Deutschland GmbH, with two employees in Frankfurt/Main.

Wuxi Suntech Power Co. Ltd. is based in Wuxi and was founded in 2001. Wuxi is focused on RE and produces photovoltaic solution that are sold in more than 80 countries. In 2014 the company accounted for a turnover of 22,000,000 USD (in 2015). In December 2005 Wuxi launched an initial public offering (IPO) at the New York Stock Exchange.

The company has a global network; it invested not only in Germany but also in London, Johannesburg, Tokyo, and Sydney.

Suntech received awards from the United Nations Climate Change Conference, the United Nations Human Settlements Programme, The World Economic Forum, EuPD Research, and worldwide top media outlets for (among other reasons) their contribution to environment protection. The German branch, Wuxi Suntech Power Co. Ltd., operates in the RE sector to distribute photovoltaic panels and provide services to the market. According to our interviewee, the most relevant reasons for choosing Germany were accessing the local market and benefiting from public incentives and supportive policies. Existing connections and logistical reasons played a minor role for the location choice.

Existing contacts and previous experience in Germany were the main determinants the Greenfield investment (entry mode), although these factors were not considered as highly relevant by the interviewee. Culture as well as economic, legal, and political factors did not influence the choice.

SANY HEAVY INDUSTRY CO., LTD.

Sany Heavy Industry Co. Ltd. is a non-state-owned company, located in Changsha. In 2012, it acquired 100% of one of the biggest and most competitive European producers of machinery for constructions: Putzmeister Holding GmbH, located in Aichtal, Germany.

Sany was founded in 1994 as a subsidiary of the Sany Group, which began in 1989 as a small welding material factory. Sany Heavy Industries Co., Ltd. is involved in all aspects of construction machinery manufacturing, with products as diversified as construction equipment, road construction equipment, and crane. Sany's products are eco-friendly for the green building sector. Company has been certified for Environment Management System Certification. Sany went public on the Shanghai Stock Exchange in 2003. The turnover is about 280,000,000 USD (in 2013).

Innovation and control environment impact are core parts of Sany's competitive advantage. Every year 5% of sales revenue is invested in R&D. The firm has its own research centers, which have become one of Chinese top technological development centers, obtaining more than 536 authorized patents and developing hundreds key technologies.

Worldwide, the company has set up over 30 overseas affiliates, covering more than 150 countries. In 2009, the company signed an agreement to build a R&D center and machinery manufacturing base in Bedburg in Germany. Its products have been exported to more than 110 countries. Currently Sany has invested in India and the United States in manufacturing plants and R&D centers.

The number of employees is 1,000. The activities of the subsidiary are development, production, and distribution of machinery for building and construction industry, industrial project, sewage treatment plants, and waste incinerators.

After Sany's acquisition of Putzmeister, Sany-Putzmeister invested more than three million Euros in 2015 for a new R&D center in Aichtal. An increasing important business is related to the construction of pumped storage power plants for the use of RE.

In our case study interview with Sany's manager, we found out that previous experiences in Germany were the main driver for investing in the country, as well as the presence of existing contacts. On the contrary, cultural, political, economic, and legal factors were not considered relevant factors for the acquisition.

The most relevant reason for choosing Germany and the target company was the availability of key technologies and the brand. Sany was mainly interested in the skills and know-how offered by Putzmeister, as well as in its top quality products to complement the product range.

PHONO SOLAR TECHNOLOGY CO., LTD.

The Nanjing-based Phono Solar Technology Co. Ltd has a turnover of about 28,000,000 USD and established its wholly owned subsidiary in Willich, Germany in 2005. In 2012, the firm invested in Germany by starting the Sumec Europe GmbH. The purpose of the investment was to benefit from favorable legal conditions and easy access to the local market, as well as the presence of local business partners and existing connections.

Phono Solar Technology Co. Ltd. is a Chinese SOE founded in 1978 by Sumec Group Corporation, a member of the China National Machinery Industry Corporation (SINOMACH). The business of RE products started in 2004, driven by both innovations in technology and by an effective brand strategy.

The company is specialized in PV power plant investments and PV technology innovations and smart micro-grid systems. Working in the field of RE, Phono Solar promotes solutions for energy supply, energy management, energy saving, and energy storage.

According to our interview, the company entered Germany with the purpose to improve the quality of internal production processes. Phono Solar entered Germany through Greenfield investment aiming at acquiring know-how and technology. This is coherent with the general motives of emerging countries multinationals investing in Europe to explore assets and acquire new technological capabilities that will allow them to be more competitive in the global market.

According to the manager, the motives for choosing a Greenfield mode of entry were related to legal issue and institutional maturity of Germany. The entry strategy was easy to implement and did not require huge investments. The subsidiary had twenty employees in 2015. The core business of Sumec Europe GmbH in Germany is RE, in particular solar products and solutions, is R&D as well as marketing services.

The interviewed manager confirmed that the investment in Germany enabled the Chinese company to have access to the local market. The need to expand sales market abroad is strictly linked to overcapacity. The volumes of production in China are high. Overcapacity can bring economy of scale, but then requires finding outlet markets: Germany was considered a very important market to sell "Made in China" products.

Another interesting factor to choose Germany was the presence of a local business partner. Thanks to this type of connection, the Chinese managers were able to better understand the features of the local market and environment.

Finally, in the case of Sumec Europe GmbH, the location choice was driven by logistic reasons, as well as cultural and language factors. As for logistics, the manager considers Germany as a strategic country with good air quality and marine connections, which simplify trade. The quite high rate of Chinese expatriates in Europe and in particular Germany contributes to find a more familiar environment for the Chinese company.

SHENZHEN EVERBEST MACHINERY INDUSTRY CO., LTD.

Shenzhen Everbest Machinery Industry Co. Ltd., with a turnover of about 55,000,000 USD in 2014, entered the German market by a Greenfield investment. The new business started in 2014 with the subsidiary CEM Instruments GmbH. The international expansion aimed to improve the relationship with existing local business partners, as well as to have access to key technologies, relevant brands, and to benefit from logistics.

For over 25 years Shenzhen Everbest Machinery Industry Co. Ltd. has been a leading Chinese manufacturing firm with a diversified product range, including measuring and monitoring instruments.

The company is located in Shenzhen with two R&D centers. In 2014, the firm had 900 employees, operating in 5 production department. The company sells its products in Europe and America and in more than 90 other countries and regions.

A Greenfield entry mode choice has been adopted to enter in Germany. According the interviewed manager the Greenfield investment was preferred to M&A in order to maintain total control and reduce the cost for internal coordination. The general manager of CEM Instruments GmbH declared that the choice for Germany was influenced by cultural and language factors. Legal and economic factors affected the decision of entry mode. Greenfield was chosen because of simple and quick procedure to start the subsidiaries reduced costs. Also, previous experience in Germany played a role.

CEM Instruments GmbH works in the same core business of the parent company. The presence in Germany is relevant not only for sales distribution in Europe, but also to act as service center for worldwide clients. The manager we interviewed considered access to local market as one of the most important goals for investing in Germany, which is a particularly strategic country and a platform for international trading and for serving the Euro zone. Also, availability and acquisition of key technologies and brands is likewise important.

Discussion and Conclusions

This chapter aimed at exploring the case of five Chinese companies investing in Europe in the environmental industry, with Germany as a country focus. We conducted a descriptive within-case analysis by covering the following information: general information of the Chinese headquarters and of the acquired company in Germany, the reasons for choosing Germany as a host country, the FDI entry mode, and the reasons behind the entry mode choices.

Based on previous literature, motivations driving Chinese investments into industrialized countries are usually market-seeking (Buckley et al., 2007; Cheung & Qian, 2009; Hurst, 2011; Kolstad & Wiig, 2012) and strategic asset seeking (Amighini et al., 2011; Lv & Spigarelli, 2015). Our case studies on Chinese companies investing in the German environmental sector largely confirm these findings. Chinese companies enter Germany to have access to the market and to improve their production processes through skills and know-how acquisition.

In our case studies, the choice for the German market is motivated by a demand for environmental products, also as a consequence of subsidies and consumption policies for green products. The supremacy of Germany in the industry was also relevant, due to the high level of R&D and technology.

The presence of a local business partners as well as pre-existing connections play a role, even if minor, in the location choices. Labor cost and tax regime motives are not considered as relevant.

The literature on entry modes considers a prevalence for M&A. Our case studies are not supporting the prevalence of these entry modes as four out of five cases preferred Greenfield investment. The prevalence of market-seeking purposes seems to be a major motivation for entering the German market, as the initialized subsidiaries are fairly small for a sustainable relocation of R&D or production plants. Legal factors and previous experience in and with Germany seem to be the main motives for choosing Greenfield and Acquisition, while economic factors played a marginal role.

References

Alon, I., Fetscherin, M., & Gugler, P. (2012). *Chinese international investments*. New York, NY: Palgrave Macmillan.

Amighini, A., Rabellotti, R., & Sanfilippo, M. (2011). *China's outward FDI: An industry-level analysis of host country determinants*. CESifo Working Paper No. 3688. Empirical and Theoretical Methods.

Antkiewicz, A., & Whalley, J. (2007). Recent Chinese buyout activity and the implications for wider global investment rules. *Canadian Public Policy/Analyse de Politiques, 33*(2), 207–226.

Athreye, S., & Kapur, S. (2009). Introduction: The internationalization of Chinese and Indian firms – Trends, motivations and strategy. *Industrial and Corporate Change, 18*(2), 209–221.

Buckley, P. J., Clegg, L. J., Cross, A. R., Liu, X., Voss, H., & Zheng, P. (2007). The determinants of Chinese outward foreign direct investment. *Journal of International Business Studies, 38*(4), 499–518.

Cheung, Y. W., & Qian, X. (2009). Empirics of China's outward direct investment. *Pacific Economic Review, 14*(3), 312–341.

Child, J., Ng, S. H., & Wong, C. (2002). Psychic distance and internationalization: Evidence from Hong Kong firms. *International Studies of Management & Organization, 32,* 36−56.

Child, J., Rodrigues, S. B., & Frynas, J. G. (2009). Psychic distance, its impact and coping modes: Interpretations of SMEs decision-makers. *Management International Review, 49*(2), 199−224.

Clegg, J., & Voss, H. (2012). *Chinese overseas direct investment in the European union. Europe China Research and Advice Network.* Retrieved from https://www.chathamhouse.org/sites/files/chathamhouse/public/Research/Asia/0912ecran_cleggvoss.pdf. Accessed on September 19, 2015.

Cui, L., & Jiang, F. (2009). FDI entry mode choice of Chinese firms: A strategic behaviour perspective. *Journal of World Business, 44*(4), 434−444.

Curran, L. (2015). The impact of trade policy on global production networks: The solar panel case. *Review of International Political Economy.* Retrieved from http://dx.doi.org/10.1080/09692290.2015.1014927. Accessed on July 10, 2015.

Deng, P. (2009). Why do Chinese firms tend to acquire strategic assets in international expansion? *Journal of World Business, 44*(1), 74−84.

Deng, P. (2012). The internationalization of Chinese firms: A critical review and future research. *International Journal of Management Reviews, 14,* 408−427.

Deng, P., & Yang, M. (2015). Cross-border mergers and acquisition by emerging market firms: A comparative investigation. *International Business Review, 24,* 157−172.

Eisenhardt, K. M. (1989). Building theories from case study research. *Academy of Management Review, 14,* 532−550.

Eisenhardt, K. M. (2009). Origin of alliance portfolios: Entrepreneurs, network strategies, and firm performance. *Academy of Management Journal, 52*(2), 246−279.

Globerman, S., & Shapiro, D. (2003). Governance infrastructure and US foreign direct investment. *Journal of International Business Studies, 34*(1), 19−39.

Hanemann, T., Rosen, D. H., & Rhodium Group. (2012). *China invests in Europe patterns, impacts and policy implications.* Retrieved from http://rhg.com/wp-content/uploads/2012/06/RHG_ChinaInvestsInEurope_June2012.pdf. Accessed on May 15, 2015.

Hu, A. (2014). *China: Innovative green development.* Berlin: Heidelberg: Springer Verlag.

Hurst, L. (2011). Comparative analysis of the determinants of China's state-owned outward direct investment in OECD and Non-OECD countries. *China & World Economy, 19*(4), 74−91.

Klossek, A., Linke, B. M., & Nippa, M. (2012). Chinese enterprises in Germany: Establishment modes and strategies to mitigate the liability of foreignness. *Journal of World Business, 47*(1), 35−44.

Kolstad, I., & Wiig, A. (2012). What determines Chinese outward FDI? *Journal of World Business, 47*(1), 26−34.

Lattemann, C., & Alon, I. (2015). The rise of Chinese multinationals: A strategic threat or an economic opportunity? *Georgetown Journal of International Affairs,* Winter/Spring, 168−175.

Lin, J. Y. (2010). *New structural economics: A framework for rethinking development*. Policy Research Working Paper No. 5197, World Bank, Washington, DC.

Lv, P., & Spigarelli, F. (2015). The integration of Chinese and European renewable energy markets: The role of Chinese foreign direct investments. *Energy Policy, 81*, 14–26.

Lv, P., & Spigarelli, F. (2016). The determinants of location choice: Chinese foreign direct investments in the European renewable energy sector. *International Journal of Emerging Markets*, forthcoming.

MOFCOM. (2011). *2010 statistical bulletin of China's outward foreign direct investment*. Retrieved from http://images.mofcom.gov.cn/hzs/accessory/201109/1316069658609.pdf. Accessed on September 18, 2015.

OECD. (2008). *China: Encouraging responsible business conduct*. OECD Investment Policy Reviews.

OECD. (2013). *Urbanization and green growth in China*. OECD Regional Development Working Papers No. 2013/07, OECD Publishing. Retrieved from http://dx.doi.org/10.1787/5k49dv68n7jf-en

Oliver, C. (1997). Sustainable competitive advantage: Combining institutional and resource based views. *Strategic Management Journal, 18*(9), 697–713.

Pradhan, J. P. (2011). Emerging multinationals: A comparison of Chinese and Indian outward FDI. *International Journal of Institutions and Economies, 3*(1), 113–148.

Rui, H., & Yip, G. S. (2008). Foreign acquisitions by Chinese firms: A strategic intent perspective. *Journal of World Business, 43*, 213–226.

Sanfilippo, M. (2010). Chinese FDI to Africa: What is the Nexus with foreign economic cooperation? *African Development Review, 22*, 599–614.

Schütte, H., & Chen, S. (2012). *Reaching high: Sany's internationalization (A) and (B)*. China Europe International Business School. Case CC-312-019, case CC-312-020.

Vaccarini, K. (2015). *Questionnaire on Chinese OFDI to Germany*. Retrieved from https://docs.google.com/forms/d/1LCXei5edMbskRrlylFslGyi7M9PrGPnf HptlVgUkdZg/viewform?c=0&w=1

Vaccarini, K., Spigarelli, F., & Tavoletti, E. (2015). *European green tech FDI in China: The role of culture*. c.MET Working Papers No. 1507, c.MET-05. Centro Interuniversitario di Economia Applicata alle Politiche per L'industria, lo Sviluppo locale e l'Internazionalizzazione. Retrieved from https://socionet.ru/publication.xml?h=repec:cme:wpaper:1507&l=en. Accessed on August 21, 2015.

Voss, H., Buckley, P. J., & Cross, A. R. (2009). An assessment of the effects of institutional change on Chinese outward direct Foreign investment activity. In I. Alon, J. Chang, M. Fetscherin, C. Lattemann, & J. McIntyre (eds.), China rules: Globalization and political transformation. (pp. 135–165). London: Palgrave Macmillan.

Wang, A. (2012). The choice of market entry mode: Cross-Border M&A or greenfield investment. *International Journal of Business and Management, 4*(5), 239–245.

Wright, M., Filatotchev, I., Hoskisson, R. E., & Peng, M. W. (2005). Strategy research in emerging economies: Challenging the conventional wisdom. *Journal of Management Studies, 42*(1), 1–33.

Yin, R. (1984). *Case study research: Design and methods* (1st ed.). Beverly Hills, CA: Sage.

Yiu, D., & Makino, S. (2002). The choice between joint venture and wholly owned subsidiary: An institutional perspective. *Organization Science, 13*(6), 667–683.

Part II
Environment and Regulations

8

China: The Long March toward a Virtuous Environmental Legal Framework

Lihong Zhang

ABSTRACT

Purpose – This chapter presents a review about the history of how China's environmental legal framework was built up.

Methodology/approach – The chapter explores environmental legal framework development through two paths: political path and the associated judicial path. It tries to connect the political slogans of China, under each leadership since the "Opening Up" in 1978, to the legislative development on environmental issues.

Findings – Regardless of each leadership's political slogans, China's economic reform and legislative development had always revolved around the objective – "revive China and its economy in the world," which had been set by Deng Xiaoping. The "sustainable development," that as a guiding principle, has already been incorporated into Five-Year Plans as well as China's environmental legislation since economic reform.

Originality/value – Compared with previous research on this area, the pragmatical approach of this investigation confirms the originality of the research. Literature on this topic, in fact, hardly investigates China's environmental issue by combining the analysis of the political and the legal perspectives.

Keywords: China environmental protection; juridical legal framework; political and judicial paths; sustainable economy; sustainable economy

Introduction

For over more than three decades after China's "Opening Up" in 1978, China's economy has underwent an exceptional growth of nearly 10 percent annually, and only in recent years, did the economy growth begin to slow down. Yet, what's correlated with this intensive economic growth is an ever incessant and solid demand for energy consumption. In China's "extensive growth" case, without energy consumption such as electricity, petroleum oil, etc., it couldn't sustain itself at a high level of growth rate. However, with heavy reliance on coal and fossil resources like oil and gas, also creates a great deal of environmental problems and resource shortage issues, which eventually become a prominent constraint on economic development's sustainability.

To solve this social-economic conundrum, it wasn't really an only recent concern, but rather already partially existed in the Five-Year Plan, in the late 1970s. And thereafter, this concern for a sustainable development, in fact, has gradually assumed its connotations of greater impact on governmental priorities during 1990s and 2000s. On another side, these connotations of sustainable development that cumulated in a time span from late 1970s till today, also evinced a "continual" institutional change after President Deng Xiaoping took the leadership. Such institutional change, in its essence, was "continual," due to the fact that all Chinese leaderships since the end of Maoist period are in accord with the primary objective that was launched by Deng, which aimed to revive China and its economy in the world. Although each leadership is remembered for their own slogans, as if they were mantras, the primary objective hasn't been changed.

Truly, China's system reform is an institutional reform of its political economy as well as the corresponded legal framework. As the major roles of institutions are to reduce uncertainty by establishing a stable structure for human interaction (North, 1990, p. 6), and its change is rather a very complicated process, we ought to understand China's environmental legal framework through a historical perspective rather than merely considering it as an "autonomous" establishment (Li & Trautwein, 2013, pp. 250–252). This chapter will investigate the gradual Chinese political and juridical path in the construction of a more strict and incisive legal framework in consideration of environment both with reference to domestic and foreign direct investments.

Political Path in the Construction of a Virtuous Environmental Legal Framework

THE DAWN OF REFORM: "PRACTICE IS THE SOLE CRITERION OF TRUTH," AND THE DENG XIAOPING'S LEADERSHIP FROM LATE 1970S TO EARLY 1990S

China's reform is unveiled with the Third Plenum of the Eleventh Central Committee of the Communist Party of China (CPC) in December 1978. The Third Plenum decided to move CPC's whole work focus onto the construction of socialist modernization. But there occurred some theoretical dispute in the period after Mao Zedong's death and before the reform, which was mainly about *truth criterion* and the debate over rural reform in terms of the household responsibility system (Guo & Zhang, 2013). In May 1978, the article *Practice is the sole criterion of truth* in *Guangming Daily*, was a strong blow, that time, to the rigid obedience of Mao Zedong's thoughts, which was known as *Two All*, which literally means that "we must safeguard firmly all of the decisions made by Chairman Mao; and we must follow consistently, all of the instructions made by Chairman Mao" (Guo & Zhang, 2013, pp. 218-219). Then afterwards, the "thought emancipation movement" that initiated, freed people from major theoretical constraints (such as "class struggle" and "dictatorship over bourgeoisie") for China's economic reform (Wu, 2013, pp. 34–35).

Soon after the reforms began, "household responsibility system" was the first eminent institutional reform over China's agricultural production. In the beginning, central authorities didn't intend to change the rural collective institutions. They only allowed the household responsibility system to be applied to poor agricultural regions and poor collectives. But the regulation was ignored in most regions. One reason was that People's Commune was not efficient in production; it had created a massive famine that happened across the country during the years 1958–1962. And the other reason was that the People's Commune model of agricultural production wasn't really a sustainable development in terms of satisfying China's modernization needs.

Under the Deng Xiaoping's leadership, several slogans were proposed, such as *crossing the river by groping for stepping stones* and *it doesn't matter if a cat is black or white, as long as it can catch mice*, as well as *open and reform: centered on economic construction*, etc. However, due to struggles within China relating to political and economic leadership, it was somehow later that the nation began to tackle its environmental problems (Imura, 2007, p. 17). During 1980s and 1990s, China began to face more environmental problems, and especially almost during these two decades, legal institutions were started to be established to formalize the environmental protection and energy utilization instead of mainly relying on a few regulations and political efforts such as cooperations with other neighborhood countries like Japan, Singapore, etc. An epitome would be the "Sixth Five-Year Plan" for 1981–1985. It started to craft a special chapter on environmental protection ("Chapter 35: Environmental Protection") that called for environmental legislation and a section of the energy chapter upon energy use, particularly means to save the use of 70–90 million tons of coal. While, energy conservation not provided in the Plan means that the government remains not having much knowledge of energy utilization, and its governance strategy was *crossing the river by groping for stepping stones.* In Sixth Five-Year Plan's Chapter 19: Foreign Trade, regards foreign direct investments, the Plan set out that, *focus on using foreign capital at energy and transportation sector.* This period of domestic investments was still centered upon basic infrastructure.

When it comes to the "Seventh Five-Year Plan" for 1986–1990, it continued to put emphasis on economic reform, as well as on environmental legislation work. It also went specifically to require that foreign investments ought to be mainly used in telecommunications, raw materials (especially, electricity, harbor, and oil) unlike the Sixth Five-Year Plan's emphasis on energy and transportation. Besides, the Seventh Five-Year Plan, contrary to the Sixth Five-Year Plan, emphasized on the legislations' crafting regards foreign direct investment. Another fact that cannot be ignored is, the Sixth Five-Year Plan mentioned eliminating the pollution sources, while in the Seventh Five-Year Plan, it is mostly about controlling environmental pollutions. This rhetoric change represents an attitude of China's authorities toward environmental pollutions, which had became an inevitable byproduct of China's growth, yet still needed to be dealt with rationally. Overall, this period under Deng's leadership, domestic investment was channeling mainly into infrastructure and dominate industrial sectors as China was still one of the developing countries.

"SOCIALIST MARKET ECONOMY" AND ECONOMIC DEVELOPMENT FROM MID-1990S TO 2003

There was already a decade-long debate between plan and market's relation, and which is primary, before "Socialist market economy" was accepted by the Fourteenth National Congress meeting in 1992. Such doubt was also reflected in political disputes, particularly after 1989 Tiananmen square event. However, Deng Xiaoping's argument that *a socialist country can also have a market economy*, during his tour to south China in the springtime of 1992, had aided much to the wave of pro-market reformists' political views. Under the umbrella of the general principle "Socialist market economy," China has undertaken a series of very important institutional reforms during President Jiang Zemin and Premier Zhu Rongji's leaderships. Notably, the taxation systemic reform, price marketization reform, stock markets, and also fiscal reforms, as well as State Own Enterprises (SOEs)' structural reform which leads to effective corporations. All these reforms could also be traced in the Eighth Five-Year Plan for 1991–1995.

Probably, much worthy to tell is that, in the Ninth Five-Year Plan for 1996–2000, *sustainable development* had been addressed for the first time in the plan explicitly, and had been treated as an important national strategy for the country's primary objective. One of the prominent features of the Ninth Five-Year Plan is the government's environmental governance shift, which aimed to shift from "*the governance at the end model to the governance over whole production process*" in terms of industrial pollution control. This represents a big change for governance rules and methods, which means the governance would not be like before, that is with having emphasis only at the end, that usually exampled in taxation or administrative injunctions; however, it often went less effective at local level.

SLOGANS – "BUILDING A HARMONIOUS SOCIALIST SOCIETY" AND "SCIENTIFIC OUTLOOK ON DEVELOPMENT" UNDER HU JINTAO'S LEADERSHIP

"Building a harmonious socialist society" was first introduced in the Fourth Plenum of the Sixteenth Committee of CPC in September 2004. "Scientific Outlook on Development" was a little earlier as proposed by Hu Jintao in July 2003. One of the latter notion's main content is sustainable development, that encourages cyclic economy and green production and also civilized consumption. The "Scientific Outlook On Development," albeit concerns a new model of production, and environmental protection, its emphasis is centered upon economic growth's efficiency. Well, "building a harmonious socialist society" can be called as a mantra; that is, human living in harmony with nature. It also incorporated in the notion of "Scientific Outlook on Development." This was the period that environmental consideration began to enter into the core of China's political context, in part also due to the fact that after joining with WTO, China's environmental problems have created more international frictions especially regards to GHG emission and climate change, as well as emission cut responsibilities.

In 2007, the State Council issued the "Eleventh Five-Year Plan." The plan takes "Scientific Outlook on Development" as its main clue threading through the plan's guiding principle, development objectives, policies, etc. And indeed, one of the plan's objectives is to strengthen the country's development sustainability. Besides this, the Eleventh Five-Year Plan also contributed a single part (Part Six) on constructing a society that saves energy use and also environmental friendly. In line with the slogan "Scientific Outlook on Development" that encourages cyclic economy, the Plan also incorporated it, and later the Law on Promoting Cyclic Economy was promulgated in 2009. Such a trilogy well reflects the leadership's political thought that evolves from mantras to real economic plans and later legal documents in China.

"CHINA DREAM," UNDER CURRENT LEADERSHIP OF XI JINPING

"China Dream" proposed by Xi Jinping, could be seen as a restatement of the primary objective that Deng Xiaoping launched for China's economic reform. It is to revive China and its economy or to use Xi's words, that is, the rejuvenation of China's prosperity. And like other slogans, this slogan also has many official annotations by the central authorities of China. And one of the official annotations is about the construction of ecological civilization, which has also been brought into the Thirteenth Five-Year Plan for 2016–2020.

This China's new political administration is continuously striving to develop the sustainable economy and reduce dramatically the environmental pollution. In particular, China actively participated in the negotiation of *Paris Agreement of Framework Convention of Climate Change of United Union* (FCCC) in December 2015. By entering into this treaty on April 22, 2016 as one of the main promoters and strengthening the development of sustainable economy in its Thirteenth Five-Year Plan, China committed to adopt more green energy and supervise, control, and significantly reduce the GHG emission.

The main measures adopted in this direction are as follows: (a) to draw up a national carbon emission inventory; (b) to regulate carbon emission price and set up its related trading market; (c) to intensively provide preferential tax benefit policies and energy subsidies; (d) to apply largely the high technologies on green energy; (e) to encourage the domestic and foreign investments in the field of the reduction and trading of carbon emission and the application of green-energy technologies; (f) to strengthen the local government responsibility on the reduction of carbon emission; and (g) to stimulate the consumption of green products and services.

Legal Path in the Construction of a Virtuous Environmental Framework

EARLY ENVIRONMENTAL CONSIDERATION IN CHINA'S LEGISLATION FROM LATE 1970S TO 1980S

Environment wasn't a political and legislation consideration in the late 1970s, since the reform was just started, and much of the political considerations were resolved around theoretical debates and economic production, particularly agricultural production. China wasn't an industrialized society; it was still an agrarian country, but it was about to be industrialized. Therefore, environmental pollutions were like a nightmare for developing countries' economy development, would gradually become a real concern. Starting from the 1980s, there were some laws taking environment into account, albeit, in retrospective, the rules of this period concerning environment still lack incisiveness and strong deterrence effects. The pioneer is China's Constitution (1982). In its Article 26, it expresses that,

> The State protects and improves the living environment and the ecological environment, and prevents and controls pollution and other public hazards. The State organises and encourages afforestations and the protection of forests.

As Constitutional Law didn't have substantial enforcement in China, the rules above couldn't be employed in judicial reasoning, yet it contains "natural law" elements. In 1987, the Civil Law ("General Principles of the Civil Law of the People's Republic of China") was promulgated. Its Article 124 States that,

> Any person who pollutes the environment and causes damages to others in violation of State provisions for environmental protection and the prevention of pollution shall bear civil liability in accordance with the law.

This civil liability stipulation was a progress, as liability rules have clear deterrence effects. Although this single liability rule couldn't perform well that time due to the non-existence of procedure laws, and high costs of proof burdens, as well as people's reluctance toward lawsuits, it was perceived as for accommodating in future that environmental tort compensation claims would certainly grow.

Two years later, the Environmental Protection Law (1989, amended in 2014) became the basic law on environmental protection in China, establishing the framework and legal basis for environmental protection (Deng, 2012, p. 118). The law also for the first time rendered the "environment" definition in its Article 2, as *refers to the total body of all natural elements and artificially transformed natural elements affecting human existence and development, which includes the atmosphere, water, seas, land, minerals, forests, grasslands, wildlife, natural and human remains, nature reserves, historic sites and scenic spots, and urban and rural areas.* Besides, it also specifies management and supervision rules over environment, as well as legal liabilities. What's progressing is the newly amended version of the Environmental Protection Law (2014, promulgated on January 1, 2015). The amended Environmental Protection Law has 70 articles, while the older law (1989) has only 47 rules. This new law well presents not only the legislative technique progress in environmental laws but also much strict and incisive attitude toward environment pollutions that will be discussed later.

Throughout the 1980s, China began to face more pollution problems after its economic reform process that pushes industrialization. There were other environmental laws under the legislation process from late 1970s to 1980s as well, such as the Law on Prevention and Control of Water Pollution (1984, amended in 1996, amended again in 2008), Grassland Law (1985, amended in 2002, and 2013), Forest Law (1984, amended in 1998), Law on Wildlife Protection (1988, amended in 2004 and 2009), and Marine Environment Protection Law (1999, amended in 2013).

ENVIRONMENTAL LAWS AND LIABILITY RULES IN A CONTINUUM SINCE 1980S

More specific laws on environmental protection began to appear since 1980s, also legislation amending projects. After almost three decades' legislation work since the 1980s, there were already over 16 specific laws that directly set their themes on the environment and already over 33 laws concerning environmental protection. There are examples like China's law on Soil and Water Conservation (1991, amended in 2010) ("Soil and Water Conservation Law"), Prevention and Control of Solid Waste Law (2004), etc.

What's more important is these laws' correlation and liabilities containment that gradually offered a well-rounded legal framework for environment issues. For instance, for a big construction project in a city, it then will be first related to the Urban and Rural Planning Law (2007, amended 2015) which requires that urban and rural planning shall be conducted with obedience to laws and regulations governing land management, natural resources conservation, and environmental protection. Then, undoubtedly, the construction project shall not be implemented without evaluation of the Environmental Effects, according to China's Law on Evaluation of Environmental Effects (2003). If there is any environmental pollution after the project has been started or finalized, then other specific laws like Prevention and Control of Solid Waste Law or Prevention and Control of Environmental Noise Pollution Law (1997) may also come into force. Regards construction project, Prevention and Control of Environmental Noise Pollution Law specifically has its fourth chapter on the prevention of construction noise pollution, as well as very incisive liability rules that deal with construction misconducts while disobeying the law. Such a case of a construction project, clearly illustrates that China has gradually established a comprehensive legal framework addressing the different environmental concerns.

Legal liabilities and environmental laws are in a continuum. Not only that environmental laws specified clear liability rules in their legislation texts, but there are also other basic laws like criminal law, civil laws, and procedure laws as well as their judicial interpretations, altogether they also provide stringent rules, that is, either punishing for environmental misbehaviors or facilitating lawsuits by reducing environmental pollution victims' difficulties in requesting for compensations. For example, for factories' environmental pollution liabilities, apart from the fact that the factory might have to pay the administrative fines and accept administrative injunctions or its chief employees bearing criminal penalties according to related laws, when it comes to a private lawsuit, it is of interest to observe law's presumptions while helping environmental victims. As we already know, the burdens of proof, is always essential to both parties in private lawsuits. Legal presumptions is a way often used to allocate the burdens of proof, which requires a party to prove something, by virtue of which something else will be presumed (Shauer, 2009, p. 226). In environmental pollution tort case, according to Several Provisions of Supreme People's Court on Evidence in Civil Procedure (2001)'s §3, Article 4, that in suing for damage compensation, *the infringing party shall be responsible for producing evidence to prove the existence of exemptions of liabilities as provided in laws or that there is no causal relationship between his act and the harmful consequences.*

Almost 165 cities amounting to 367 cities in the whole nation suffered from different degrees of air pollution (Environmental Protection Ministry, 2016), and as China's environmental pollution problems deepens, the newly amended Environmental Protection Law (amended in 2014, promulgated in 2015) also adopted stringent liability rules toward environmental pollution. Its Article 59 allows environmental protection authorities to punish violators by imposing fine consecutively on a daily basis according to the original amount of the fine, in case that the violators refuse to make the correction the authorities required. Compared with the old 1989 Environmental Protection Law the rule of imposing fines on a daily basis in the amended Environmental Protection Law is much easier for authorities to enforce and is much efficient concerning the enforcement cost.

ENERGY LAWS AND ITS INCREASING COHESION WITH ENVIRONMENTAL LAWS

An important feature of the judicial path in the construction of a virtuous environmental legal framework is the increasing cohesion between energy laws and environmental laws. All economic development is based to some extent on the exploitation of natural resources (Cleaver, 2011, p. 242). And energy resource consumption is undeniably a prime engine for a nation's economic growth. Therefore, energy laws, policies, and regulations as institutions are essential for energy sector utilizations and energy developments, particularly in green energy development.

It's suffice to say, China still doesn't have basic energy law, although energy sector has always been a key to the country's industrialization. And the construction of the legal framework for energy, could be traced back to 1995 when China began to implement its first energy law – "Electricities Law" (amended in 2002, 2015). Then one year later, Coal Law (amended in 1996, 2011). These two laws are much emphasized on energy utilization. Later, Energy Conservation Law in 1997 (amended in 2005), the Renewable Energy Law in 2005 (amended in 2009) offered general principles on renewable energy and energy conservation (Qiu & Li, 2012, pp. 10678–10682). And China's Law on Promotion of Cleaner Production (2002), focuses on increasing the utilization ratio of resources as well. These laws provided a system of rules encouraging green energy practice, as well as refraining from GHG emissions and other environmental pollutants. For example, China's Law on Promotion of Cleaner Production, explicitly states:

> This Law is enacted for the purpose of promoting cleaner production, increasing the utilization ratio of resources, reducing and preventing pollutant-generating, protecting and improving the environment, protecting human health, and promoting the sustainable development of the economy and society.

The utilization of resource uses, and reducing/preventing pollutant-generating, and sustainable development, obviously, also fit into essence of environmental laws' primary objectives. In 2009, the amended Renewable Energy Law also has its objective, as expressed in its Article 1, as "promoting the development and utilization of renewable energy, increasing the supply of energy, improving the structure of energy, safeguarding the safety of energy, protecting environment and realizing a sustainable development." On another side, promoting sustainable development is not the explicit goal of energy laws. It is also present in specific environmental laws such as Prevention and Control of Atmospheric Pollution Law (2000); it also focuses on the development and utilization of clean energies that help to control air pollutants and reduce GHG emission. All these laws cannot be viewed as isolated; they are all within a big, broad, and virtuous environmental legal framework, which aimed to promote sustainable social-economic development.

Conclusion

In the latest years, politically and legislatively, to realize a sustainable economy, China has been attaching more and more importance to the environmental protection. Even if it is still fragmentized and uncompleted, an environmental legal framework, whose center is the 1989 *Environmental Protection Law*, has already been established. With its recent entry into *Paris Agreement of FCCC*, again Chinese government commits to actively contribute to the improvement of global environment, by adopting many important policies and legal measures related to the energy conservation and GHG emission reduction. However, it is early to say that China has achieved its success in fighting against environmental pollution. Such triumph depends more on the implementation of those laws and policies than their enactment. Till now, due to the inefficiency of the implementation of its law and the insufficiency of environment-protection education for its citizens, it seems that China has a long and rough road to go for the improvement of its environment and the realization of a sustainable economy.

References

Cleaver, T. (2011). *Economics: The basics* (2nd ed.). London: Routledge.

Deng, F. (2012). China. In R. Lord, S. Goldberg, L. Rajamani, & J. Brunée (Eds.), *Climate change liability*. Cambridge: Cambridge University Press.

Environmental Protection Ministry. (2016, January 19). *Air quality index daily report*. Retrieved from http://datacenter.mep.gov.cn

Guo, X., & Zhang, P. (2013). Thirty years of disputes on China's economic reform. In Y. Ma & H. Trautwein (Eds.), (2013), *Thought on economic development in China*. New York, NY: Springer.

Imura, H. (2007). *Environmental issues in China today: A view from Japan*. New York, NY: Springer.

Li, W., & Trautwein, H. M. (2013). Northian perspectives on China's economic reform. In Y. Ma & H. Trautwein (Eds.), *Thought on economic development in China*. New York, NY: Springer.

North, D. (1990). *Institutions, institutional change and economic performance*. Cambridge: Cambridge University Press.

Qiu, X., & Li, H. (2012). Energy regulation and legislation in China. *Environmental Law Reporter, 40*, 10678–10682.

Shauer, F. (2009). *Thinking like a lawyer*. Cambridge, MA: Harvard University Press.

Wu, J. (2013). Thinking though China's thirty-year economic reform process from an institutional perspective. In B. Naughton (Ed. & Trans.), *Wu Jinglian: Voice of reform in China*. Cambridge, MA: MIT Press.

9 Chinese Environmental Protection: Between National Laws and Governance System

Federica Monti

ABSTRACT

Purpose – This chapter investigates and explores the array of political and social factors which influence the Chinese system of environmental protection, shedding light on the Chinese political and juridical process in constructing a stricter and more incisive legal framework.

Methodology/approach – Starting by observing national macroeconomic data, this chapter explores how the Chinese governance system affects the implementation of the legal framework of environmental protection. In addition, it also traces a brief panorama of the most important laws framing environmental protection in China.

Findings – Over the years, the Chinese environmental protection system has been strongly affected by the national multilayered governance system. Nevertheless, the initiative launched by China (more intensively starting from the 11th five-year plan) to build a more virtuous environmental protection system now seems to be returning positive results, in both the renewed legal framework and – even more so — in the attempt (through addressing environmental issues) to reform the entire apparatus of national governance.

Practical implications — The multi-structured national system, which hides conflicting political and economic interests at central and local levels, represents one of the biggest problems for China. This chapter argues that only through a deep reform of the national management scheme can China really guarantee a better future for its environment.

Originality/value — Literature on Chinese environmental protection tends more often to investigate the legal aspect when edifying its environmental legal framework. Very few studies combine economic data and political analysis when studying the Chinese legal framework and its implementation.

Keywords: Chinese environmental protection; national governance; implementation of national laws; legal framework edification

Introduction

China's economy has performed exceptionally in recent years, particularly since joining the World Trade Organization in 2001. But the country demonstrates an immature juridical scenario in the full phase of edification and modernization (Moccia, 2009), and both citizens and entrepreneurs lack awareness (Li, 2001; Zhang, 2013) of 环保 (huanbao, which means at the same time "to be eco-friendly" and "environment protection"). Despite its success, the economy has suffered some dramatic consequences, driving the country toward serious environmental problems (Yok-Shiu, 2005).

Probably, the most important step the Chinese government took after the Maoist era was returning to citizens the freedom to privately initiate an economic activity, with the consensus of the political leadership.

Previously, the management of private activities was deemed a synonym of capitalism[1] (Chen, 2000; Prybyla, 1970). Then,

---

[1] With the progressive Maoist nationalization policies, before the 1990s, all economic initiatives by private citizen were considered a clear sign of capitalism and for this reason an extremely detrimental to the country's economy is considered.

starting from mid-1980s with the new policy promoted by Deng Xiaoping and prosecuted by other Chinese leaders, private economic activities became the perfect engine for China's economic development.

The Communist Party of China (CPC) well understood that the key to the country's successful rebirth was not to be found in a monopolistic-centralized economy completely controlled by the government and mostly made of state business activities (a situation that was strongly desired by policy makers until that period) operating in the nonpublic sector.

Leveraging on the complementary nonpublic sector[2] from that age onward, the maximization of profit, preached by Deng Xiaoping and firmly confirmed by Jiang Zemin (often both referenced as the leaders of the *"GDP first and Welfare Second"* policies) and by further Chinese leaders, has helped to negate many of the negative consequences of the Mao period. But at the same time, this has generated new problems, limiting the ability of the population to fully enjoy the benefits of economic growth.

Beginning only in urban areas, the government allowed private citizens to employ themselves in private business (Krauss, 1991). The immediate consequence was a massive population transfer to urban centers, where labor conditions were better and possibilities were greater (Gold, 1980; Qin, 2010; Tuñón, 2006; Zhu, 2003).

As a result, in recent years, a higher level of environmental pollution has affected mostly first-tier big cities (Greenpeace East Asia, 2015), where China has embraced more industrialization.[3] In addition, the wealthier the citizens are (in monetary terms), the more they move toward urban areas or settle there. Residents in

---

[2]Up to the end of the 1990s, the Chinese economic private sector didn't received any recognition, including at Constitutional level. The recognition of the nonpublic sector (within which you can find the private subsector) as an important component of the socialist Chinese economy, for the first time was provided in Article 11 of the Constitution Chart of the People's Republic of China of 1999.

[3]The first region of interest to private business and industrialization was undoubtedly the Wenzhou area, where private sector even predominates over both the state and collective sectors even though, in early 1980s, it was deemed as a mere supplementary sector of the State economy. For further details see Hua and Chen (2015, p. 57) and Liu (1992, p. 294).

urban areas use an average of up to four times more energy than residents in rural areas (Lin, 2012).

An unprecedented government disclosure of air pollution information,[4] conducted on economy-key regions and 74 cities including Beijing,[5] seems to reveal the situation has now partially changed.

The air quality standard, measured by the mean annual reading of six pollutants (such as particulate matters $PM_{2.5}$, inhalable particulate matters PM_{10}, nitrogen dioxide NO_2, sulfur dioxide SO_2, carbon monoxide CO, and ozone O_3), reports a small decrease in air pollution in some eastern and coastal areas over the past 12 months.

Contrary to what was observed in past years, China's central and western provinces have been demonstrating the worst levels of air pollutants. According to Ministry of Environment Protection (MEP) officials, the top 10 worst cities in terms of air condition in 2014 were Baoding, Xingtai, Shijiazhuang, Tangshan, Handan, Hengshui, Jinan, Langfang, Zhengzhou, and Tianjin. Seven out of ten are in the northern part of China, in Heinan province beside to Shanxi and Inner Mongolia (Herrias, Joyeux, & Girardin, 2013).

Conversely, cities with the best air condition, in the same period, were Haikou, Lhasa, Zhoushan, Shenzhen, Zhuhai, Fuzhou, Huizhou, and Kunming.

One question springs to mind: *what could have caused this new scenario?*

The Chinese Environmental Governance: An Important Obstacle

The answer to the above question is actually just around the corner. Since governmental bureaucratic divisions denote bureaucrats'

---

[4]Ministry of Environmental Protection of People's Republic of China (2015).
[5]With particular reference to Beijing municipality, data on the Beijing Statistical Yearbook 1998 and 2011 reveal an increase of the permanent population of up to 19.6 million in 2010, with an annual growth rate of 3.6% since 1997 and a corresponding increase in energy consumption and air pollutants emissions during the same years (1997–2010). A Greenpeace East Asia analysis reports that even if PM2.5 concentration is improved more than 13% compared to the first quarter of 2014, however it still ranks in the top five worst polluted provinces in China.

perceptions[6] about the environment and natural resources, areas where environmental pollution have recently registered better air quality conditions are, in fact, those under direct and strict control of the State. Indeed provinces like Henan, Hubei, Hunan, and Sichuan, situated in central or western China, where rigid forms of pollution controls have never been enacted, were among the 10 worst polluted provinces in 2014, confirming similar levels of pollutants in the first quarter of 2015 as well.

Trying to give structured argumentation to that question, we should remember that starting from the last 1970s and the early 1980s, inspired by the Soviet Union experience, China adopted a decentralized structure of its political system, distinguishing its system as one with a high level of politicization and hierarchical division, rarely found in other countries.

Despite the fact decentralization seemed to represent, in the beginning, the key factor for a deeper control over the country, on the contrary, today represents one of the biggest limits (Jahiel, 1998) to China in solving social issues (like the environmental pollution). This is firstly due to the weak relationship between central and local governments, and secondly due to the deep influence generated by the *Target Responsibility System* (TRS)[7] since its implementation, which strictly determines local officials' career advancement.

Environmental policy-making in China perfectly reflects the multilayered institutional management that governs the formulation of Chinese national economic policy. Thus, the growing power left over the years to local authorities to foster the development of China's economy at all levels gave them rising stature in the Chinese Party state. This caused recurring contrasts between locally implemented and enforced policies, and those enacted at central level.

---

[6]The level of environment pollution is undoubtedly perceived by Chinese government, at central level as a real problem, while at local level officials seem to continue perceiving environment as *resources* to be exploited for the achievements of economic goals. For further analysis see Jin and Qin (1999, pp. 8–13).

[7]The TRS is a method of collecting, monitoring, and misusing the performance of local governments and enterprises. It was promoted by China as a result of a regulatory scheme published by State Council in 2007 and developed by National Development and Reform Commission (NDRC). The TRS ensures the effective implementation of central policies by linking the status of target achievement of targets with a personnel evaluation system. For more information on this topic see Wang (2013, pp. 365–440).

A clear example is the conflicting response of local governments to the *Green GDP Campaign*, launched in 2005 by the former State Environmental Protection Administration (SEPA[8]) with the aim to rebalance economic growth and environmental degradation. It should have been an initiative to evaluate costs supported by local authorities, in facing problems linked to environmental degradation and pollution, serving, in the meanwhile, as a parameter for evaluating the performance of local officials, for both economic and environmental stewardship.

Despite the *Campaign* being launched at central level with the overall call to implement it, very few local authorities embraced the process; many more even reject the *Campaign*, fearing that adopting the suggested evaluation metric would have undermined the economic growth statistics in their own jurisdiction, with a consequent "negative mark" to the officials' performance evaluation on the basis of the TRS.[9]

This highlights that Chinese environmental management, like country management on the whole, reflects negatively on the empirical control and implementation of central policies.

In exacerbating relationships between governments, financial dependance among authorities at all levels should be considered as well as the natural administrative hierarchy. Considering financial dependence reveals different counterposed political and economical interests at central and local levels.

The current Chinese environmental protection governance and implementation model could be described as shown in Figure 1 (Liu, Zhang, & Bi, 2012).

Practical Implications

This context inevitably led to an environmental protection legal framework that reveals its weakness not much in contents or

---

[8]In 2008 renamed as MEP.
[9]An article on China Daily issued in 2013 titled "Green GDP Needed," noted: *"The government has developed its own methodology to calculate green GDP. [...] It is regrettable that the government has stopped releasing such data since then. [...] It is generally believed that it is not technical limits but local governments that have prevented such data from being released. Such data releases might affect the promotion prospects of local officials."* Retrieved from http://www.chinadaily.com.cn/opinion/2013-02/27/content_16259196.htm

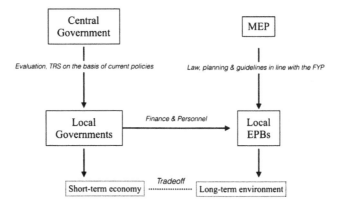

Figure 1: Vertical and Horizontal Relationship in China's Multilayered Environmental Governance. *Source*: Liu et al. (2012).

provisions, but rather in the institutional system which should enforce them and which then assumes a more relevant part in the path toward the edification of a virtuous environmental legal framework.

At central level, the policy and law making system is quite rigid, since all environmental policies must pass the consensus of several authorities such as Politburo, the State Planning Commission, the National People's Congress Environment Protection and Resources Conservation Committee, the MEP, and others (Jeon & Yoon, 2006). Despite this, local level officials involved in Environmental Protection Bureaus (EPBs, which are local branches of MEP) are free, and in some cases encouraged, to experiment with different implementation models (also inspired by international experiences). But in reality, they more often yield to the financial pressure and dependance of local governments (Figure 1).

In this way when some "conflicts" arise between the implementation of central policies and policies at local level (which aim to promote officials' goals), EPBs are more inclined to resolve problems in favor of local governments.

As seen at a local level, most institutions are subject to financial and personnel provision and supervision by local governments and the power of decision making is still largely wielded by the same local governments, instead of the EPBs (Figure 2) (OECD, 2006).

It is quite clear that the scenario in which China is moving with great effort to develop a comprehensive framework of

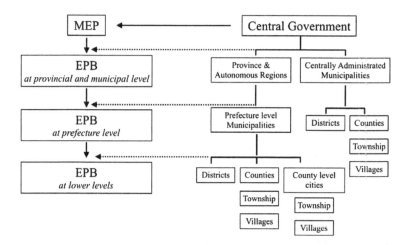

Figure 2: The Sub-National Institutional Structure for Implementing Environmental Policies Ex art. 30 of the Constitution of P.R.C. *Source:* OECD (2006).

reforms to benefit the environment is so complex and it is becoming even more convoluted, compared to the central government legislative activity itself.

The Chinese Efforts to Move Toward a Virtuous Environmental Legal Framework

The history of the environmental legal framework is much shorter than the economic path and this clearly confirms that over the years the Chinese central government gave its primary attention to economic development, rather than the environment.

The year 1972 is probably the most definitive starting point for the environmental protection legal framework in China. This year saw the first National Environmental Protection Conference, held in Peking, when China issued the first environmental set rules as a result of the Conference.

Later, with the amendment of the Constitution of the People's Republic of China of 1978, the National People's Congress added the art. 26 which declares "*The state protects and improves the living environment and the ecological environment, and prevents and remedies pollution and other public hazards,*" which represents the highest expression of China's will to solve the environment issue, other than the real starting point and the real legal basis for an environmental protection legal framework.

Actually, the first Environmental Protection Law (EPL) of the People's Republic of China came in 1979, in concomitance with the launch of the *Open Door Policy*. Nevertheless it was only a trial implementation version, and mostly remained ineffective until the enactment of the new Environmental Law in 1989 confirming the greater intention of China to face the environmental issue.

In the meantime, a huge set of new rules had been issued by China:[10] the Marine Environmental Law (1982, then revised in 1999); the Law on Prevention and Control of Water Pollution (1984, then revised twice, once in 1996 then in 2008); the Forestry Law (1984, then revised in 1998); the Grassland law (1995, then revised in 2002); the Mineral Resources Law (1986, revised in 1996); the Law on Prevention and Control of Atmospheric Pollution (1987, revised twice, once in 1995 and 2000); the Water Law (1988, revised in 2002).

Doing a brief check of current events, one can see at the beginning of 2016 the Standing Committee of the National People's Congress approved more than 30 laws about environmental protection, as well as further legal interventions in relevant laws and regulations (such as in Criminal Law[11]) which also provide new contents strictly linked to environmental protection.

Despite these efforts, the system on the whole still remains weak and this is confirmed by facts, given the poor effects and poor results achieved.

Even though China's first concerns, in providing an environment legal framework, date back to the years of the economic reforms, the country seems to have never taken the real "great step forward."

After the first and the second versions (respectively issued in 1978 and 1989), with the enactment of the new Environmental Protection Law (EPL, on April 24, 2014, in force since January 1, 2015), the legal scenario has radically changed.

---

[10]The list provided is not exhaustive. It includes only law issued up to 1989 with their related amendments.
[11]In 1997, the amendment of China Criminal Law introduced, for the first time, environmental crimes, confirming the growing importance, reserved at central level, attached to the environment.

Compared to the 1989 text, the new EPL appears definitely more rigid. It provides a strong increase of penalties against entrepreneurs who don't abide by the regulations, even stating daily sanctions throughout the entire period of the unlawful behavior. On the other hand, it provides tax incentives and benefits for companies that develop environmental technologies.

Before the enactment of the new EPL, there weren't any provisions for the accountability of polluters. As a result, in the past, entrepreneurs more often preferred to pay sanctions stated by the previous regulations than to support the higher costs requested by the system to abide by the law.

The new art. 59 of the new EPL, has been outlined above, states now: "*Where any enterprise, public institution, or other business is fined and ordered to make correction for illegally discharging pollutants but refuses to make correction, the administrative agency legally making the punishment decision may impose continuous fines on it in the amount of the original fine for each day from the next day after it is ordered to make correction. [...].*" Moreover, in the light of the combined provisions of art. 56, it is now certainly more difficult for companies to break law, due to the greater transparency requested through the Environmental Impact Assessment[12] (EIA) for construction projects which may damage environment.

The greater transparency should now worry entrepreneurs much more, not only for the deeper information required by EIA, but also for a publicity system that will overwhelm any guilty

---

[12]The Environmental Impact Assessment is defined by the EIA Law (promulgated by the Standing Committee of the People's Congress on March 15, 1999, and became effective as of October 1, 1999) as a system for analyzing, forecasting, and assessing the potential impact on the environment of the implementation of planning and construction projects. It also requires the definition of strategies and establishment of measures to prevent as well as to alleviate adverse impacts on the environment, implementing follow-up reviews and monitoring. The EIA Law requires the investor, as a sine qua non-requirement for its own investment project realization, to submit for the EIA document in front of the MEP, or its local branches before to start any activities which may damage the environment. The new EPL requires to give publicity to all projects requiring environmental impact assessment, in order to allow the local entities to object the development of the project or to require adequate warranties about their potential environmental impact.

party, ruining its public reputation to which should be add the legitimacy granted now to Non-governmental Organizations (NGOs) to fosters legal suits, on behalf of public interest, against those responsible for environmental damages (Wang, 2014).

This represents without a doubt an important progress achieved by China through the new EPL: under the previous version of the law, there was no possibility to bring lawsuits against polluters in front of courts simply because the old formulation of the law didn't provide anything in this sense. In this way, NGOs[13] were completely left on the borders.

Nevertheless, even if the new EPL has only partially solved this deficiency, it should be deemed a good signal of modernization of the environmental legal framework.

In line with the anticorruption policy launched by current President Xi Jinping, as well as the rigid control over entrepreneurs and companies, the new EPL prescribes much heavier penalties for local government officials who do not properly enforce the law or permit projects not in line with the environmental parameters to be developed. Over the years, the weakness of China's environmental governance and management has represented probably the biggest limit in the implementation of central policies (McElewee, 2011). For this reason, the increased accountability of local governments, bureaus, and officials may help to reduce the officials' conflicting and defiant behaviors.

Further, the new EPL seems also to give a new reading of the TRS. Before 2015, only performance evaluations based on economic targets and goals achieves were considered when advancing officials in the governmental hierarchy. Under the new EPL, officials receive feedback on their efficiency, on the basis of the environmental protection target they have gained (Chen, Ebenstein, Greenstone, & Li, 2013).

The above confirms China's efforts toward a virtuous environmental legal framework and a growing concern for the national environment conditions. Another confirmation came in late August 2015 with the reform of the Air Pollution Law, which seems to have the same strict features of the new EPL.

---

[13]Although the virtuous possibility is reserved by the new EPL to all NGOs, it needs to be kept in mind that actually only NGOs which have specific requirements, provided under Article 58 of the new EPL, can actually take action. Currently, there are only about 300 NGOs conform to those requirements.

Conclusions

The Chinese environmental issue is extremely complex. Although the statistics seem to confirm small improvements, the situation remains seriously worrying.

But the country's awareness of environmental matters is definitely greater than in the past and this is confirmed by the multi-year environmental reform and the legal advancements.

From what emerges, one can affirm that signs of optimism come not so much from the renewed content of legislation, but rather from the attempt – through the environment issue – to reform the entire apparatus of governance. This, for many years, has been the real limit to the implementation of a legal framework on the environment, which in the last 30 years has been slow to emerge.

Nevertheless, the new EPL suggests positive hopes for at least two reasons: the increasing system of accountability for both polluters and officials, and for the legitimacy given to NGOs and civil society to intervene in behalf and in defense of the environment.

Since only one year has passed since the implementation of the new EPL, it is not yet time to take stock. But through constant observation, it is surely time to question if the current legal framework can enhance the effectiveness of China's environmental governance system and improve environmental quality.

References

Chen, H. (2000). *The institutional transition of China's township and village enterprise*. Aldershot, Hampshire: Ashgate Publishing Limited.

Chen, Y., Ebenstein, A., Greenstone, M., & Li, H. (2013). Evidence on the impact of sustained exposure to air pollution on life expectancy from China's Huai River policy. *PNAS, 110*(32), 12936–12941. Retrieved from http://www.pnas.org/content/110/32/12936.abstract

Environmental Protection Law of People's Republic of China. (2014). Retrieved from https://www.chinadialogue.net/Environmental-Protection-Law-2014-ever-sion.pdf

Gold, T. B. (1980). Back to the city: The return of Shanghai's educated youth. *The China Quarterly, 84*, 755–770. Retrieved from http://www.jstor.org/stable/653180

Greenpeace East Asia. (2015). *En-greenpeace ranks 360 Chinese cities by PM 2.5 air pollution (Q1 2015)*. Retrieved from http://www.greenpeace.org/eastasia/press/releases/climate-energy/2015/air-ranking-2015-Q1/

Herrerias, M. J., Joyeux, R., & Girardin, E. (2013). Short- and long-run causality between energy consumption and economic growth: Evidence across regions in China. *Applied energy*, *112*, 1483−1492.

Hua, X., & Chen, Y. (2015). Institutional logics and financing mechanisms: A comparative study of Ningbo and Wenzhou entrepreneurs. In D. Cumming, M. Firth, W. Hou, & E. Lee (Eds.), *Sustainable entrepreneurship in China. Ethics, corporate governance, and institutional change*. New York, NY: Palgrave Macmillan.

Jahiel, A. R. (1998). The organization of environmental protection in China. *The China Quarterly*, *156*, 757−787.

Jeon, H., & Yoon, S. (2006). From international linkages to internal divisions in China: The political response to climate change negotiations. *Asian Survey*, *46*, 846−866.

Jin, L., & Qin, W. (1999). *A study on some problems in legislations about Chinese environment and natural resource*. [中国环境与自然资源立法若干问题研究]. Beijing: Beijing University Press.

Krauss, W. (1991). *Private business in China. Revival between ideology and pragmatism*. Honolulu, Hawaii: University of Hawaii Press.

Li, N. (2001). Environmental consciousness and environmental behavior [环保意识与环保行为]. *XueHai* [学海] *1*, 120−124.

Lin, B. (2012). Power future development. *USA China Daily*. January 20, Retrieved from http://usa.chinadaily.com.cn/business/2012-01/20/content_14480632.htm

Liu, L., Zhang, B., & Bi, J. (2012). Reforming China's multi-level environmental governance: Lessons from the 11th five-year plan. *Environmental Science & Policy*, *21*, 106−111.

Liu, Y. L. (1992). Reform from below: The private economy and local politics in the rural industrialization of Wenzhou. *The China Quarterly*, *130*, 293−316. Retrieved from http://www.jstor.org/stable/654402

McElewee, C. R. (2011). *The environmental law in China. Mitigating risk and ensuring compliance*. New York, NY: Oxford University Press.

Ministry of Environmental Protection of People's Republic of China. (2015). Retrieved from http://english.mep.gov.cn/News_service/news_release/201308/t20130822_257910.htm

Moccia, L. (2009). *Tra ritualismo e modernizzazione*. Torino, Italia: Bollati Boringhieri.

Organization for Economic Co-operation and Development. (2006). *Environmental Compliance and Enforcement in China. An assessment of current practices and ways forward*. Retrieved from http://www.oecd.org/env/outreach/37867511.pdf

Prybyla, J. S. (1970). *The political economy of communist China*. Scranton, PA: International Textbook Co.

Qin, H. (2010). Rural-to-Urban labor migration, household livelihoods, and the rural environment in Chongqing municipality, Southwest China. *Human Ecology*, *38*, 675−690. Retrieved from http://www.jstor.org/stable/40928156

The Constitution of the People's Republic of China. (2004). Retrieved from http://www.npc.gov.cn/englishnpc/Constitution/node_2825.htm

Tuñón, M. (2006). *Internal labour migration in China: Features and responses.* Beijing: ILO Office. Retrieved from http://ilo.int/wcmsp5/groups/public/—asia/—ro-bangkok/—ilo-beijing/documents/publication/wcms_158634.pdf

Wang, A. L. (2013). The search for sustainable legitimacy: Environmental law and bureaucracy in China. *Harvard Environmental Law Review, 37,* 365–440. Retrieved from https://www.law.ucla.edu/~/media/Files/UCLA/Law/Pages/Publications/CEN_EMM_PUB%20Search%20Sustainable%20Legitimacy.ashx

Wang, L. (2014). *Poverty alleviation investment and private economy in China. An exploration of the Guangcai programme.* Berlin, Heidelberg: Springer-Verlag.

Yok-Shiu, F. L. (2005). Public environmental consciousness in China. Early empirical evidence. In *China's environment and the challenge of sustainable development.* New York, NY: M.E. Sharpe Inc.

Zhang, S. (2013, August 27). *What Chinese factory bosses really think about environmental protection.* Retrieved from https://www.chinadialogue.net/article/show/single/en/6317-What-Chinese-factory-bosses-really-think-about-environmental-protection

Zhu, Y. (2003). The floating population's household strategies and the role of migration in China's regional development and integration. *International Journal of Population Geography, 9,* 485–502.

10 Efficient Energy Systems in the Chinese Electricity Sector: Some Legal Issues

Fabio Lorusso

ABSTRACT

Purpose – The Chinese electricity sector is in the midst of a transition from a state-owned monopoly to a market-oriented structural unbundling. In the process of restructuring, the power system is facing significant deficiencies which hinder integration of sustainable solutions and dramatically impact the environment.

Methodology/approach – The chapter provides a qualitative analysis of the legislative, regulatory, and administrative provisions that have been recently implemented in the Chinese electricity sector, in order to identify the barriers that limit implementation of sustainable solutions and suggest prospects of change.

Findings – Despite a strong commitment to renewable energy, integration of sustainable solutions in the Chinese power system is hampered by an inefficient coordination between the players variously operating in the electricity sector and a lack of consistency at the regulatory design stage.

Practical implications – A clear picture of the legislative, regulatory, and administrative inconsistencies that characterize

159

the Chinese electricity sector may help Chinese policy makers to overcome issues that hinder efficiency and hence develop a systemic approach useful to make the economic growth sustainable.

Originality/value – The chapter considers integration of sustainable solutions as related to the policy makers' ability to conceptualize systemic efficiency in relation to an original understanding of proximity between efficient energy systems to be developed on a regional basis.

Keywords: Energy efficiency; electric regulation; efficient systems; Energy Law

Introduction

An inefficient management of the electricity supply chain could hinder integration of renewable sources in the power system and dramatically impact the environment. This is even more evident in China, where the installed power capacity has ranked second in the world since 1996 and the greater percentage of power generation comes from fossil fuels.[1] The progressive increase of greenhouse gas emissions, depletion of natural resources, air and water pollution force Chinese regulators to seek out sustainable solutions to increase efficiency of the power system in a way that could even facilitate integration of renewable sources.

The main obstacle to implementation of energy efficiency measures is related to the fact that China has never built a nationwide electricity grid, focusing instead on a policy of geographical closeness between power plants and final users. The Chinese electricity infrastructure has been traditionally developed in relation to economic growth, with the installation of transmission power lines near to industrial districts (Song & Zhang, 2007). Due to the logistics of coal mining and transportation,

---

[1]In 2011, the global installed electricity capacity was about 962 GW and the net generation 4,228 TW. China's electric power comes from a variety of resources. Thermal generation makes up about 81 per cent of power generation and over 77 per cent of installed capacity, coal comprises the majority of this amount. Despite this large reliance on fossil fuels, a growing amount of China's electricity is generated from renewable resources, principally hydro and wind (*Sources*: GWC, 2012; IEA, 2011).

road and rail transport have therefore concentrated in the regions of the country where transmission lines have been built, with no connection to peripheral areas.

Electric Power Infrastructure in China

Provision of electricity in China has been traditionally under the exclusive control of a governmental authority which vertically integrated generation, transmission, and distribution services. Only in the late 1990s, when the vertically integrated governmental authority is converted into a corporation, the State Power Corporation, a restructuring process started. As of today, the Chinese power sector is in the midst of a transition from a state-owned monopoly to a market-oriented structural unbundling.

In 2002, generation assets originally owned by the State Power Corporation were allocated to five different companies, still under the direct control of the government. Each company was expected to be responsible of no more than 20 per cent of the generating capacity of the country. The remaining generation capacity was expected to be covered by independent industrial and financial enterprises which at regional or provincial level often operated with the involvement of the state-owned generating companies.

Contextually, in 2002, transmission and distribution services were allocated to two companies: the State Grid Corporation and the China Southern Power Grid Corporation. Six regional grids were identified: north, northwest, northeast, central, south, and east. Each regional grid was operated by a state-owned company, respectively subsidiary of the State Grid Corporation or the China Southern Power Grid Corporation. The former was the parent company of the companies operating in the north, northwest, northeast, central, and east, therefore controlling approximately 80 per cent of the overall transmission regional grids, whereas the latter controlled the remaining 20 per cent basically corresponding to the southernmost five provinces of the country.

While China is planning to strengthen the interconnections between regional grids, at present, the infrastructure is still underdeveloped. As a consequence, power flow between regions, as well as between provinces within regions, remains limited and in any case not sufficient to allow an efficient balance between surpluses and shortages occurring in different regions of the country (Cheung, 2011; Pittman & Zhang, 2008).

Electricity Regulation in China

The Electricity Law 1995, no. 74, adopted in 1995 and entered into force in 1996, is the fundamental law in the Chinese electricity sector. Since that time, China has been examining several revisions to its electricity regulation, though no revised law has been adopted yet. The main reason is that regulatory authority has been split between various offices, with no effective coordination. To overcome institutional fragmentation and to make it possible to boost the implementation of efficient measures in the management of electricity supply chain, Chinese government has eventually established a high-level energy policy coordinating group, the so called "Leading Group," with the task to work on the design of an overarching Energy Law (Cheung, 2011; Ciwei & Yang, 2010; Li, Shi, & Gao, 2010; Tawney, Bell, & Ziegler, 2011).

As per recent reforms, regulatory authority in the Chinese electricity sector is divided into two key institutions: the National Development and Reform Commission (NDRC) and the State Electricity Regulatory Commission (SERC). NDRC is primarily responsible for formulating regulatory targets, policies, and measures concerning the total size and structure of fixed asset investment and, in relation to this, even for pricing and power plants authorization procedure. Responsibility of SERC is instead that to implement the targets, policies, and measures adopted by NDRC and to supervise the integration of independent industrial and financial enterprises into the generation markets. On the basis of the operation of the generation markets, SERC is expected to highlight issues that thwart the implementation of market reforms and to provide inputs to achieve more cost reflective and efficient pricing.

While such a division of responsibilities between NDRC and SERC has no parallel in the world, it is undeniable that in practice policy and regulatory functions remain muddled between the two institutions, eventually compromising the distinction originally conceived at the regulatory design stage. The independence of SERC from NDRC is not that clear, also because the transition from state-owned monopoly to market-oriented structural unbundling is still a work in progress. China's electricity market keeps to be based on a single buyer model pursuant to which subsidiaries of the State Grid Corporation and the China Southern Power Grid Corporation continue to buy power from generators operating at provincial and municipal level and directly sell it to local distribution operators or even to final users. Apart from pilot experiments aimed at testing free market pricing in some regions of the country, NDRC still determines both wholesale and retail electricity prices on a price-cap regulation basis, including in the quantification of the retail prices also the costs of the transmission and distribution services. The wholesale prices are capped in order to allow generators to gain 12–15 per cent return, though margins really depend on costs of fuel. That means that significant rises in costs of fuel could put unsustainable pressure on generators because of price inflexibility.

With regards to a regulatory framework like the one above outlined, the support schemes that Chinese government has defined to boost integration of renewable sources into the power system could represent an extremely profitable opportunity for generators. As per the Renewable Energy Law which China adopted on February 28, 2005, in fact, grid operators are obliged to purchase all the electricity that renewable plants produce in their territory of reference at an incentivized price.

Commitment to renewable energy has been afterward restated both in the 11th and the 12th Five Year Plans. Pursuant to the principles therein conceptualized, in 2007, China launched a pilot program in five provinces of the country, requiring power generated from renewable sources to be dispatched first.

Despite a strong commitment to renewable energy, however, integration of renewable generation in the Chinese power system remains complicated.

Main Barriers to Energy Efficiency in China

Chinese electricity system is going through a deep regulatory transition. In the middle of such a structural change, regulatory contradictions are more evident at the level of implementation than at the stage of regulatory design.

The main barrier to implementation of efficiency measures is represented by a lack of alignment between the various players that operate in the electricity industry. Restructuring process launched in 2002 has resulted in provincial power companies owning significant portions of generation and provincial grid company subsidiaries taking control of the day-to-day grid operations and short-term planning. Central government agencies keep instead control on planning for larger scale projects and ratemaking (Cheung, 2011).

The lack of cooperation between the players operating in the electricity industry is already clear at the stage of project development, where the misalignment between developers and grid operators eventually causes projects not being connected to the grid in a timely manner. While that might depend on bad practices, a regulatory analysis could help to clarify that the reason why grid companies have little incentive to cooperate in devising solutions to inter-grid power flow and trading is related to the fact that in China, fiscal revenues are collected at the generation level. As a consequence of that, provinces, municipalities, and other government entities are incentivized to foster construction of generation units within their administrative boundaries so that to maximize their fiscal revenues, to the detriment of the development of interconnections and inter-provincial trading. Most of the trade that does happen is governed by long-term contracts, the terms of which are negotiated by the central government, provincial governments, and the grid companies. The cumulative effect of such a structural organization is that the power system does not provide clear market signals or incentives to grid operators to engage in efficient cross-grid trading.

Another significant barrier to energy efficiency, which particularly hampers the integration of renewable sources into the power system, concerns the lack of nationwide technology standards for connection of renewable generators to the grid. As an example, in 2005, the Chinese government issued Technical Regulations on Connecting Wind Power to Power Grids, but such regulations were not converted into laws afterward, therefore, expiring in 2008. Lack of nationwide technology standards limits integration of renewables into the power system as long as renewable developers and grid developers could not have same understanding of the connection procedure. As deducible, that might cause renewable plants being perfectly projected but remaining disconnected. What is worse, even when connected to the grid, integration of renewables into the power system is not automatic. Reason is that, although grid operators are partially reimbursed for costs of transmission through a government subsidy based on the distance between the renewable generation site and the main grid infrastructure, in most cases this subsidy is not sufficient to cover the costs of the transmission infrastructure. As a consequence, integration of renewables might result not to be sustainable for grid operators.

Main Barriers to Integration of Renewables in China

Integrating renewables into a power system traditionally relying on thermal plants could be challenging as long as generation of energy from renewable sources is less predictable than production of energy from fossil fuels.

While that could be valid for any power system, the variability nature of renewables sources results to be even more challenging with respect to a system, like the Chinese one, in which a nationwide transmission grid has never been developed. The country is geographically vast and it is extremely expensive and time consuming, to build a grid capable to transmit power from remote sources to distant load centers. That dramatically reduces the possibilities to integrate renewables into the power system, since they are abundant in the north and west, while most of the energy demand is in the south and east. As of today, interregional connections are weak and cross-regional trading accounts for only a little part of the total electricity produced.

First barrier to integration of renewables into the Chinese power system is then represented by segmentation of the transmission grid and weak interconnections between different regions of the country, though this is not the only one. The impact of renewables variability is even intensified by the lack of sufficient balancing options. In consideration of the historical development of the transmission lines near to industrial districts and the high level of industrial consumption of electricity in the country, Chinese power system has rather little experience in dealing with load following and peaking generation.

China's existing fleet is indeed largely comprised of coal-fired plants, mostly big since the smaller ones have been progressively replaced by more efficient ones specifically designed to serve industrial districts. Due to technical reasons, this kind of plants is particularly unsuited to quick response, as it takes quite a long time to ramp them up and rump them down. What is more, coal-fired plants frequently combine heat and power generation in industrial districts, but they do not usually have bypass technology allowing them to generate heat without electricity. Hence, they cannot be cycled as a balancing option.

Given the difficulty to further develop nationwide interconnections and the lack of sufficient balancing options that specifically characterizes the Chinese power system, the integration of renewables would depend more on the design of a national planning and a regulatory framework that could facilitate implementation and coordination of efficient models of consumption and production on a regional basis.

Prospects of Change in the Chinese Electricity Sector

Despite the various structural challenges that it faces, China is making admirable efforts to foster integration of renewable energy sources in the power system. Recently, Chinese central government has launched a program aimed at creating a more efficient and less carbon-intensive energy sector. The key targets stated in such program include, *inter alia*, promotion of renewable energy, introduction of demand side management, improvement of power plants efficiency and investments in ultra-high voltage transmission corridors, so called "west-to-east," designed to increase electricity transfer between different regions of the country. In parallel, China continues to look for ways to integrate more market-based mechanisms to encourage inter-grid trading.

The purposes above outlined shall be viewed also in light of great societal demand for electricity consumption which is expected in consideration of the continuous Chinese economic growth. The future directions of the Chinese electricity sector would be mainly related to the adoption of effective policies in terms of technology innovation stimulus, economic and social acceptability of energy costs, and environmental concerns.

There is a need to conceptualize the transition from a centralized to a market-oriented approach to energy distribution by questioning the value that proximity would progressively assume in the network of contractual arrangements that eventually lead users to be part of an energy community. To this

purpose, it becomes necessary to explore whether the interme-
diation of renewable energy sources in the dynamics of social
organization is anyhow likely to shift the relational value that
transversely interlink the players operating in the energy
industry.

In the process of designing policies aimed at making the
power system more efficient and less carbon intensive, Chinese
regulators might consider how other countries, especially
European, have managed to integrate renewable sources in small
islands or remote territories and how the same countries are trying to include such systems into a national planning. The focus
has to be primarily on the peculiarities and the limits that characterize these systems, both with respect to regulatory framework
and to market structure as well. The analysis of the intrinsic inef-
ficiencies and externalities of small islands and isolated off-grid
energy systems could constitute the initial reference from which
developing a transversal reflection upon the reasons that determine the autonomy of a system and the possibilities to coordinate
systems apparently self-sufficient. While to all appearances the
extremity of similar situations could suggest to ascribe the autonomy of such systems to borderline environmental features, in
reality, the autonomy of a system depends on the level of cooperation between players therein operating. In this regard, an
in-depth analysis on the public-private partnerships implemented
has to be considered as crucial in the process of elaborating the
reciprocal visibility and accountability of emerging spaces of
direct and indirect cooperation into concrete common projects of
sustainable development.

Renewable energy, as it is generated from resources which
are naturally replenished on a human timescale, represents a
medium of exchange that requires policy-makers to make reference to spatial and temporal categories which are essentially different from those that frame the production and distribution of
energy produced by fossil fuels. Designing policies aimed at
fostering sustainable solutions in countries where fossil fuels
represent the main source of energy is therefore particularly
critical since an original understanding of value circulation, business costs, benefits, and risks needs to be conceived and made
consistent with unexplored dynamics of accountability.

In Europe, during the 20th century and the beginning of 21st
century, the general form of urbanism was large scale, centrally
planned development; coherently, the electricity supply system
was highly monetized, external to users' homes and businesses,

administered in hierarchical and highly centralized ways. Only recently, energy markets have been liberalized. As a consequence of liberalization, electricity suppliers have been exposed to competition, and vertically integrated companies have been broken up into different players operating at the levels of electricity generation, transmission, distribution. Simultaneously the role of consumers has changed, as they have been asked to actively participate in the electricity markets and to determine from whom and under what conditions they would prefer to receive their electricity (Lambing, 2012 in Bollier & Helfrich, 2012).

Such a structural change was introduced on the expectation that competition would have somehow pushed the power supply industry to more cost-effective and demand-oriented structures, a higher degree of cost transparency, a reduction of excess capacity, reduced prices and more ecological innovations. In reality though, individual companies, at least at a preliminary stage of implementation, do not have any intrinsic motivation to promote anything else but maximum company profit. In spite of any sustainability policy, the necessity that utilities have to maximize profits incentivizes them to pursue market concentration and bypass directives to lower carbon dioxide emissions.

As it is, the process of construction of a sustainable liberalized market is facing contradictions and multiple structural failures: while major energy utilities force to keep a hierarchical and centralized business approach, decentralized energy systems close to the site of consumption are emerging as expression of a relatively new trend.

Policy makers particularly struggle to integrate into a comprehensive national planning small energy islands and stand-by-alone energy systems, which nevertheless produce an indirect impact on the electricity market overall. Reasons of such difficulty could be explained as follows.

- Small energy islands: there are many disadvantages that derive from small size, including a narrow range of resources, therefore undue specialization and risks of excessive external dependence; variable population density, which might, especially in some period of the year, increases the pressure on already limited resources; overuse of resources and premature depletion; relatively small watersheds and threatened supplies of fresh water; costly public administration and obsolete infrastructures, including transportation and communication; and limited institutional capacities and domestic markets and

limited export volumes, which are too small to achieve economies of scale.
• Stand-by-alone energy systems: micro-grids related to apparently self-sufficient small communities. The idea is that decentralization could empower local people to identify their own
environmental problems, allocate resources more efficiently,
reduce information costs and get alternative sense of ownership in decision; all the same, the risk of social atomization
and isolation of such systems needs to be considered in the
cross-border process of definition of a common policy of
sustainable development.

Generally, the development of efficient energy systems
requires the active involvement of the stakeholders in the decision
making process as well as in the process of implementation of
sustainability oriented programs, the availability of substantial
financial means and the integration of innovative technologies.

To develop efficient energy systems, it is first important to
define system-policies, that means policies capable to take inter-
dependencies between environmental, societal, economic and
institutional problems into account (Schmidt-Bleek, Wilenius, &
Lehmann, 2014 in Angrick, Burger, & Lehmann, 2014). The
State, the financing organizations and the development banks
could provide incentives for private investments through long
term and binding policy targets, economic and regulatory
measures (including carbon pricing, efficiency standards, technol-
ogy-specific support). However, the financing of infrastructure
investments and large scale projects, such as the extension of
energy transmission grids, would first need funding by states,
national and regional investment banks, and development banks,
because such projects frequently require high risks and large
sums of capital.

In a multilevel system, the governance of energy systems
would imply public side and private agents to be coordinated for
the sake of effectively dealing with market failures and implementing sustainable solutions. The liberalization of the energy
sector has led to a pronounced internationalization of the energy
market, all the same the impression is that the basis on which trying to integrate energy market players into a comprehensive network should be elaborated with reference to an original
interpretation of coordination between regional dimensions. In
this sense, China could be the pioneer in the process of construction of efficient energy systems.

References

Angrick, M., Burger, A., & Lehmann, H. (Eds.). (2014). *Factor X: Policy, strategies and instruments for a sustainable resource use*. Berlin: Springer.

Bollier, D., & Helfrich, S. (Eds.). (2012). *The wealth of the commons: A world beyond market and state*. Amherst, MA: Levellers Press.

Cheung, K. (2011). *Integration of renewables: Status and challenges in China*. Paris: International Energy Agency.

Ciwei, G., & Yang, L. (2010). Evolution of China's power dispatch principle and the new energy saving power dispatch policy. *Energy Policy, 38,* 7346–7357.

GWEC and Greenpeace International. (2012). *Global wind energy outlook*. Brussels: Global Wind Energy Council.

IEA International Energy Agency. (2011). *World energy outlook 2011*. Paris: IEA Publications.

Lambing, J. (2012). Electricity commons – Toward a new industrial society. In D. Bollier & S. Helfrich (Eds.), *The wealth of the commons: A world beyond market and state*. Amherst, MA: Levellers Press.

Li, J., Shi, P., & Gao, H. (2010). *China wind power outlook 2010*. Brussels: Global Wind Energy Council.

Pittman, R., & Zhang, V. Y. (2008). *Electricity restructuring in China: The elusive quest for competition*. Washington, DC: Economic Analysis Group.

Schmidt-Bleek, F., Wilenius, M., & Lehmann, H. (2014). The challenge of the whole: Creating system policies to tackle sustainability. In M. Angrick, A. Burger, & H. Lehmann (Eds.), *Factor X: Policy, strategies and instruments for a sustainable resource use*. Berlin: Springer.

Song, Y., & Zhang, X. P. (2007). The Chinese electricity market infrastructure and operation system: Current status and future development. Power Engineering Society General Meeting. IEEE.

Tawney, L., Bell, R. G., & Ziegler, M. (2011). *High wire act: Electricity transmission infrastructure and its impact on the renewable energy market*. Washington, DC: World Resources Institute.

11 Corporate Social Responsibility Standards in Green Energy Industry: A Comparison between European Union and China

Giuseppe A. Policaro and Paolo Rossi

ABSTRACT

Purpose – CSR is a relatively new concept which can be defined as the set of rules by which a company equips itself in order to ensure compliance to various regulations, as well as ethical and environmental standards, that have to be addressed in relation to the sector in which it operates. Despite this international definition, it is hard to deal with this notion in a legal perspective. The chapter investigates how the notion is operating in the European and Chinese Green Energy Industry.

Methodology/approach – The approach is functionalist in nature and is based on comparative law method.

Practical implications – The insights about the diverse notions of CSR in the energy industry can be useful for lawyers and compliance managers working in transnational contexts.

Social implications – CSR represents a way of marketing for consumers and society. Understanding the real functioning in the world of affairs beyond the policy declamations may increase the public accountability of the CSR processes.

Originality/value – The functionalist approach based on comparative law method has never been applied to the inter-twined issues about CSR in the energy industry.

Keywords: Corporate social responsibility; company law; international standards; soft law

Introduction

Neoclassical economy does not properly consider the value of environment and, in general, of Corporate Social Responsibility. CSR can be considered as a set of rules by which a company equips itself in order to ensure compliance with various regulations as well as ethical and environmental standards that must be adhered in relation to the sector in which it operates. In doing so, companies integrate social, environmental, and economic concerns into their values and operations in a transparent and accountable manner.

CSR allows an organization to take responsibility for the impact of its decisions and activities on society, the natural environment, and its own future profitability. Business models developed for such purposes tend to encourage the creation of long-term value, as well as increase confidence on stakeholders and shareholders (McWilliams & Siegel, 2000). CSR functions as a tool for corporations to monitor and ensure active compliance with the law, ethical standards, and international standards.

The United Nations has called this triad of concerns the triple bottom line: people, planet, and profit. Despite this international definition, it is hard to deal with this notion in a legal perspective. However, especially in the green economy the notion is even more adopted as policy motto. It is important to ascertain how this notion is operating as a legal principle. Some considerations in the European and Chinese contexts will be useful.

CSR Definition in the EU

The European Commission considers CSR as *"the integration, for a Business, of social and environmental issues in their business operations and in their relationship with stakeholders. Businesses have a socially responsible action if they decide to go beyond the minimum legal requirements and obligations defined through collective agreements to satisfy social needs."*

EC has also underlined the principle of subsidiarity in respect to the definition of CSR, that *"common practices inspired to the concept of CSR ... does not substitute public policies, but they can help to achieve a number of objectives pursued by them."*[1]

To support it, EC has also submitted in October 2011 a number of proposals aimed at encouraging the development of social entrepreneurship responsibility, in order to produce wide-ranging positive effects. This initiative was the result of a joint work carried out by the EC General Directorates Enterprise and Industry, Employment, Social Affairs and

---

[1]The European Commission has published a communication about a partnership for growth and jobs: making Europe a hub of excellence on corporate social responsibility, COM 136, which incorporates the concepts already expressed in the Green Paper on how to *"promoting an European framework for corporate social responsibility,"* COM 366 and reiterated in subsequent documents until the recent *Working document* on *Corporate Governance in Financial Institutions: Lesson to be drawn from the current financial crisis, best practices*, as reported in the Green Paper: Corporate governance in financial institutions and remuneration policies, COM 284 def in which it's stressed that between the duties of a board of a company there is a necessary arbitrage between "constituencies" suggesting, in order to ensure that managers will take care of stakeholders, the creation of specific fiduciary duties for these last.

Inclusion, Internal Market and Services, under the leadership of the latter one.[2]

Anyway, the vagueness of the definitions proposed by the EC is very high.

----

[2]The goals are many, including:

(1) to encourage responsible companies. In order to increase transparency in the payments made by the forestry industries and mining industries to the governments around the world, the Commission has proposed a system of reporting made Country by Country (CBCR). The goal is to report financial information for each of the (European) Countries in which a business operates: in particular, it will highlight taxes, royalties, and bonus that the holding pays to a host government, highlighting the financial impact on the Country's balances.

To achieve this, the Commission proposed a review of the Transparency Directive for the listed companies and accounting guidelines applicable to large non-listed companies

(2) to encourage new approaches to corporate social responsibility. The EC introduced a new definition of this goal, more relevant to principles and guidelines internationally recognized. To do it, in 2013, the EC set up a European Prize for corporate social responsibility.

(3) to support social entrepreneurship. Today the social economy represents 10% of all European businesses and it employs over 11 million employees.

The proposed actions aimed to support its development, by providing suggestions to improve access to social entrepreneurship grants (including EU funding through Structural Funds and the future creation of a financial instrument aimed to provide investment funds focused on social businesses and to financial intermediaries capital, debt, and risk-sharing instruments), instruments to improve their visibility and a simplified regulatory framework. Following this vision, the European Parliament adopted on November 20, 2012 a Resolution on the Initiative for Social Entrepreneurship. In this context, it also recalled the Adoption in April 2013 of a regulation on European funds for social entrepreneurship.

(4) Reduction of bureaucracy for SMEs. The EC intends to reduce the administrative tasks for small firms through specific accounting directives for SMEs.

Simplifying the rules for financial statements will also make easier a comparison, make them clearer and more understandable.

It will allow those who read a budget (shareholders, banks, and suppliers) to gain a better understanding of the results of its business and its financial situation. The potential saving costs for SMEs are estimated approximately 1.7 Billion Euro a year. Moreover, through the amendment of the Transparency Directive, the listed companies will no longer be obliged to print quarterly financial reports, helping them to reduce the costs and at the same time discouraging short-term capital markets.

It seems that CSR encompasses social issues, ethical concerns, suggestions inspired by the principle of subsidiarity in respect to public policies, up to reach extreme views in which business is considered more similar to a nonprofit organization than a profit enterprise (OECD, 2004).[3]

According to these definitions, it is difficult for a lawyer, for example, to extrapolate from these definitions of rules of governance for the European companies.

On the other hand, it is true that socially responsible behavior pursued by managers are not only those abiding certain standards but also (perhaps, most importantly) those set up independently from it, aimed to push the performance of business activities to respect some political, ethical, or social instances.

That idea reflects, however, the different theories that give to the administrators an arbitration role, concerning the different interests pursued by the big companies, without nevertheless recognizing a primacy of the interests of the shareholders.

These are the famous theories ranging from the old institutional conceptions "Unternehmen an sich" and the Anglo-Saxon type of company as "social institution" to the latest ideas that, based on contract ideas, says that in a public company there is public interest, nonconfrontational, and cooperation between shareholders and other stakeholders, in order to achieve the biggest satisfaction of mutual interests (Alchian & Demsetz, 1972; Blair & Stout, 1999).[4]

Outlining the excessive vagueness of definitions set up by EC concerning CSR, it will be important to look deep for more detailed rules in the various jurisdictions.

Among them, the Italian and the English definitions appear to be best suited to comply with these dictates.

1. In the Italian system there aren't rules that specify which kind of interests managers are required to pursue (those of the shareholders or, e.g.,, of other stakeholders). Some rules

---

[3]OECD documents on this issue are not so defined. In these documents it is stressed that the administrative function has to adhere to high ethical standards and to take into account the interests of *stakeholders*, whose role in the corporate governance is defined, with peculiar emphasis on its contribution to the competitiveness of the company. Furthermore, directives for multinational enterprises focused on the respect for human rights are listed within these documents.

[4]It is related to the Team Production Theory.

underline their responsibility in case of damages, in particular, to shareholders (such as Articles 2392, 2393, and 2393 bis of the Civil Code).

Anyway, there are some rules that contain reference to safeguards other than shareholders and, in most cases, they require the adoption of organizational models within the company that can be set up to prevent potential offenses that can damage the interests of third parties, or to "socially" justify some decisions of the board.

This is the case, for example, of the models provided by Legislative Decree no. 231/2001, of Anglo-Saxon inspiration (also inspired by the US Sarbanes-Oxley Act), aimed to prevent offenses committed by top managers and employees for the benefit of the company.

Or, in another case, the part of the Art. 103, paragraph 3-bis, says that, in case of tender offers or exchange, the board must make a report concerning all the useful information for the appreciation of the same offer with "an evaluation of the effects that the eventual success of the offer will be for the company, as well as on employment and location of production sites."

This is a case that reflects the implementation of the XIII EC Directive on the powers granted to the administrators and in case of protectable interests in the presence of a hostile takeover bid.

Apart from the above-mentioned rules, the managers have a much more important task than to create simple value for the company in the short term. While respecting their discretion and freedom of decision (according to the principles of the Business Judgment Rule), they should always consider the consequences of their decisions in the long term, pursuing the interest of sustainable growth value in respect of all stakeholders.

On the other hand, the sustainability of the creation of shareholder value is the principle that inspire the Recommendations of the EU and of the Financial Stability Board, as well as the regulatory requirements of supervisory authorities, in particular in the financial sector, related to the remuneration policy and the corresponding requirements of various regulatory codes, including that of the Italian Stock Exchange that, in arguing that the remuneration policies should set goals for the medium to long term, provide an interpretation of the way in which the managers are required to fulfill the duty to promote the welfare of shareholders.[5]

This means that the respect of CSR principles can only be possible in the long term.

2. At European level is the British system the one where we can find the largest number of references to the principles of CSR. The sec. 172 (1) of the Companies Act 2006 says that the administrators "must act in a way that he considers, in good faith, would be most likely to promote the success of the company for the benefit of its members as a whole."

It provides that, to do it, the following must be considered: (a) the consequences of any decision in the long term; (b) the interests of employees; (c) the relationships with suppliers, customers, and other subjects; (d) the impact of the company's operations on the community and the environment; (e) the opportunity that the company could maintain "a reputation for high standards of business conduct."

This rule has the fundamental goal of avoiding excessive discretion of the managers and their excessive involvement in an arbitrage between the different interests at the expense of economic growth and international competitiveness. It aims to

---

[5]The principle 7.P.2 of the Code of Conduct of the Italian Stock Exchange, as amended in March 2010, provides that "the remuneration of Executive directors and Top officials with strategic responsibilities is defined trying to align their personal interests with the priority objective of creating value for shareholders in the medium to long term."

The same is in Germany. In this country, the principle of aligning the remuneration policy of the Vorstand to a lasting increase in the value of the company in the long term, already contained in the Corporate Governance Kodex Deutsher of June 2008, has been incorporated in the amendment to the text of § 87 AktG introduced by July 31, 2009 Law on the adequacy of the remuneration of the Board of Management (Gesetz zur Angemessenheit der Vorstandsvergütung) that, for listed companies, expressly provides that the structure of the remuneration should be related to sustainable development of the firm. The principle on remuneration incorporates, therefore, an implicit recognition of the duty of the managers to pursue the interest of a sustainable growth of the value of the company in long term, but in an institutionalist perspective, exceeding the theory of value creation for shareholders that is clearly spelled out in principle 4.1.1. the new version of the Corporate Governance Kodex in June 2009 according to which "the Vorstand must manage the company aiming to create value, on its own responsibility and in the interest of the firm: this means to consider the interests of shareholders, its workers and stakeholders."

pursue the growth and value creation for the company in the long term, from a point of view that we could assimilate to the CSR principles (Grantham, 1998; MunozSlaughter, 1997; Worthington, 2001).

In any case, it's a provision requiring to the managers to take care of the interests of stakeholders, in a perspective anchored to the promotion of the success of the company, for the benefit of its shareholders, that in any case does not undermine their power (Bainbridge, 2013).

CSR Definition in the People's Republic of China

Nowadays, the Chinese government puts greater emphasis on safeguarding the legal rights and interests of citizens and has established a well-founded and complete legal system, in which, many laws and regulations, such as "Cleaner Production Promotion Law of the People's Republic of China," "Provisions on Special Protection for Juvenile Workers," "Production Safety Law of the People's Republic of China," "Labour Law of the People's Republic of China," "Regulations on Enterprise Minimum Wage," "Law of the People's Republic of China on the Protection of Rights and Interests of Women," "Trade Union Law of the People's Republic of China," and "Code of Occupational Disease Prevention of the People's Republic of China" contain CSR elements and requirements.

Over the past decade, the development of CSR in China has gone through three stages:

The first stage was from the mid-1990s to the early 21st century.

During this time, driven by the consumer market, CSR requirements were mainly applied to the international supply chain and international retailers and brand owners began to pay attention to the CSR issue, establish and implement CSR codes of conduct, standards, or systems. At the same time, some Chinese enterprises, which had joined the global supply chain, began to accept factory auditing by multinational corporations. The management of these export-oriented enterprises was the first social group contacting CSR concept.

The second stage was from the early 21st century to 2003.

At that time, Chinese academic institutions, nongovernment organizations, and international organization in China began to systematically introduce this concept and carry out extensive study and discussions. CSR concept was introduced to the society, drawing wide attention and debate and under the background of global economic integration and fast growing foreign trade, trade authorities called on all interest parties to pay attention to CSR, so as to avoid the negative impact it may bring to trade.

At the same time, government departments began to show concerns to the development of CSR among enterprises. The Ministry of Labour, the Ministry of Commerce, and the Chinese Enterprise Confederation (CEC) all created CSR investigation committees to study the development of CSR in China.

The third stage began from 2004. It is a stage of active actions.

This was the time when Chinese government departments, industries, and enterprises all have realized that developing CSR is an effective means to build a harmonious society, carry out the scientific approach to development, and realize sustainable development. Accordingly, they have taken a series of positive measures to promote the maturity of CSR movement. The most important measure has been adopted by the State Owned Asset Supervision and Administration Commission (SASAC) initiative under the State Council activities.

In 2008, SASAC, the majority shareholder and ultimate owner of many China's largest business groups, issued the Notification on Issuance of the Guidelines on Fulfilling Social Responsibility by Central Enterprises, which required State Owned Enterprises to comply with SASAC 2008. The State Council publicly demonstrated its support for CSR by enacting and disseminating the 2008 SASAC law. The notification is a strong indication that CSR is being widely and politically authorized and that companies should implement their own such measures (Ip, 2009; Kolk, Hong, & van Dolen, 2010).

However, China is still in the initial stage of developing a standardized, systematic, and widely participated CSR social movement.

CSR in the Green Energy Industry: EU and Chinese Approaches

CSR is largely adopted in the debate about the green economy. If we have a look to the Green Energy Industry, we can observe a different approach in the EU and China. The European way to CSR is strictly linked to environmental issues, while the Chinese one to quality standards.

The EU has provided a number of certifications for the companies in terms of CSR principles and environmental protection. One of the most important is the brand "Ecolabel" set up by the Regulation of the European Parliament and of the Council 1980/ 2000 on July 17, 2000, for products with low environmental impact. This mark can be used by those companies that can provide consumers an accurate, non-deceptive, and scientifically based information report on the environmental impact of their products. The system is based, on one hand, on providing to entrepreneurs a marketing tool to advertise the quality of their product, and, on the other hand, it gives clear information and educative notes to the consumers.[6]

Companies that wish to be certified must ensure that their products follow environmental compatibility criteria in all its production, marketing, and disposal phases. This is guaranteed by specifically appointed inspection bodies, and the licensing of the use of the mark is subject to a specific contract, governed by Decision 2000/729 of the EC, signed between the applicant and the national body which carried out the audit work.

Due to the voluntary nature of the request for this kind of certification, the EC decided that in case of failed compliance with the criteria, no sanctions will be considered, but only the loss of the right to use the trademark.

However, the Regulation on the ecolabel does not exclude the coexistence of other national eco-brands. In any case, the EC and the Member States must work to coordinate the European system and the national systems.

Another environment certification is the EMAS certification, introduced by Regulation 1836/93/CEE, amended in 2009, always on a voluntary basis, that involves a complex systematic

---

[6]The criteria for awarding the label are defined and regularly updated by a Regulatory Committee, made by a Consultative Forum of stakeholders, which represents all stakeholders (service providers, trade unions, NGOs, environmental associations, representatives of industries) and from bodies designated by national authorities, which decide to whom the brand is given. The criteria for eco quality are so identified subject to the approval of the EC.

and periodic evaluation of all the environmental management system of the requesting parties.[7]

In China, there is a clear assumption that the market-based regime relies a competitive advantage among market competitors and CSR is part of it. The consumers that drive market-based regimes now include sophisticated investors interested in sustainable business, a concept that encompasses attention to human rights. Consumers may also directly affect a business by refusing to purchase products produced by companies that do not comply with human rights standards. The effects of the market-based regime on CSR compliance is limited to many Chinese enterprises, especially State owned, due to long-standing (albeit declining) insulation from relevant market forces.

In China, publicly traded companies are subject to a Code of Corporate Governance that requires such companies to consider stakeholder interests including those of the community as well as to pursue sustainable development.

The 2006 Company Law requires in Art. 5 that "when undertaking business operations, a company shall comply with the laws and administrative regulations, social morality and business morality. It shall act in good faith, accept the supervision of the government and the general public, and bear social responsibilities." The extent to which this imposes an enforceable obligation is contested, however "some scholars understand it as an exhortatory rather than mandatory provision, and in practice this is currently its effect, due to a lack of access to legal remedies" (Lin, 2010).

The SA8000 protocol is a private initiative that uses international human rights norms and labor laws to create an auditable international standard for companies. The protocol is widely adopted in the official documents of Green Energy Enterprises in China. The standard SA8000 was created by Social Accountability International, a nongovernmental organization advised by a broad range of stakeholders from trade unions, other nongovernmental organizations, government representatives, and business members.

---

[7]See Regulation n. 1221/2009 of the European Parliament and of the Council of November 25, 2009, on the voluntary participation of the organizations to a common eco-management and audit scheme (EMAS), in the OJEU L 342 of December 22, 2009.

Certification in accordance with SA8000 is a distinguishing characteristic that allows consumers and others to easily identify human rights compliance by a subject company. Participation in SA8000 is voluntary and can take the form of certification via independent auditing against the protocol, or participation in the Corporate Program, which is intended to assist companies with implementation of SA8000 principles in company operations. The Corporate Program gives member companies access to resources that can enable it to better understand and more effectively integrate SA8000 into corporate policies. In addition, Social Accountability International offers relevant training programs to support CSR programs in compliance with SA8000.

There are also VPs that are a CSR standard specific to the extractive and energy sector and largely diffused in China. Created by a consortium of governments, extractive/energy sector corporations, and nongovernmental organizations, the VPs are intended to address human rights specifically and CSR generally, and provide guidelines for discussing, promoting, and protecting human rights interests through the activities of a range of stakeholders.

The VPs acknowledge the varying roles and responsibilities of government and corporate stakeholders with respect to human rights, as well as the potential impact of nongovernmental organizations and other less formal interest groups.

Corporate adherents of the VPs are expected to work in conjunction with host governments to ensure law and order, as well as security for government, corporations, and private citizens.

Primary responsibility belongs to governments, which are responsible under the VPs to maintain rule of law in accordance with international human rights standards.

However, companies that adopt the VPs are expected to support local authorities in complying with the standards and to work to mitigate potential human rights abuses. As an example, adopting companies are meant to promote three principles in their use of private security: (a) not employing individuals credibly implicated in human rights abuses to provide security services; (b) using force only when strictly necessary and to an extent proportional to the threat; and (c) not violating the rights of individuals while exercising the right to exercise freedom of association and peaceful assembly, to engage in collective bargaining, or other related rights of company employees as recognized by the Universal Declaration of Human Rights and the ILO Declaration on Fundamental Principles and Rights at Work.

In addition to encouraging policies that are further compliant with relevant international norms, the VPs also require companies to actively monitor and report human rights abuses to government authorities, to proactively prevent future human rights abuses by pressuring local government to investigate and take action when violations do occur, and to ensure that company-provided equipment is not used in the violation of human rights. Equipment in this context refers to the tools provided to security forces, including lethal and nonlethal weapons. Companies providing equipment are required under the VPs to comply with relevant law with respect to the equipment and to mitigate any potential human rights abuses that may occur if the equipment is misappropriated or diverted in transport.

The VPs are especially important because they reflect a broad consensus of industrialized countries, influential nongovernmental organizations, and leading multinational corporations participating in the extractive and energy sectors.

The two-pronged approach of the VPs, addressing both the needs of private industry in protecting their operations and the human rights and fundamental freedoms of local communities, speaks of commercial and individual interests. For a company to be recognized as a participant, it must implement the VPs in a transparent manner and engage in dialogue to further the goals of the VPs with other governmental, nongovernmental, and corporate participants.

When a host country is unable to satisfactorily protect human rights, the VPs call on companies to engage private security forces to act as local police, subject to the same principles that apply to official government forces. Therefore, a participant of the VPs not only maintains the ability to protect its interests in a host country but it can do so within an internationally recognized framework and community dedicated to furthering both security concerns and human rights within the context of the energy sector.

Beyond generally private international initiatives like SA8000 and the VPs, the UN has spearheaded the Global Compact, which collects universally accepted principles for the sustainable conduct of business in an increasingly globalized world. The principles speak to support human rights, compliance with labor standards, environmental responsibility, and anti-corruption efforts. The human rights principles, like SA8000 and the VPs described earlier, draw from the Universal Declaration of Human Rights to guarantee individual rights to equality, life, and security, as well as personal, economic, social, and cultural freedom.

The environmental responsibility standards are intended to promote public-private cooperation through the types of partnerships encouraged by the UN Environment Programme's existing environmental law initiatives, and in compliance with the goals set forth in the multiple existing treaties for environmental protection. Finally, the anti-corruption principle speaks to the rule of law issues that can undermine sustainable development, with a focus on why controlling corruption is beneficial from both an ethical and a business stance.

The labor standards follow the ILO Declaration of Fundamental Principles and Rights at Work, which addresses worker rights to unionize, as well as the elimination of forced labor, child labor, and discriminatory employment practices. Corporate participation in the Global Compact is voluntary. It requires only a written letter of commitment from a company Chief Executive Officer and an annual financial contribution in support of Global Compact initiatives, with a suggested amount based on the company's annual sales/revenues. Participating companies are expected to incorporate the guiding principles of the Global Compact into all levels of their regular business processes, provide aid toward fulfilment of development goals including the Millennium Development Goals, and publicize and advocate compliance with the Global Compact. In return, the company receives the benefit of an established, recognized CSR framework, the ability to participate in a community of like-minded stakeholders engaged in pursuing similar objectives, and access to resources to support sustainable development efforts.

Acknowledgments

The paper reports some findings of an extensive research developed during the POREEN project and also thanks to the support of the Italian Foundation CARIPLO under the Project Grant "Going East."

References

Alchian, A. A., & Demsetz, H. (1972). Production, information costs and economic organisation. *American Economic Review*, 62, 777.

Bainbridge, S. (2013). *Preserving director primacy by managing shareholder interventions*. UCLA School of Law, Law-Econ. Research Paper No. 13-09. Retrieved from http://ssrn.com/abstract=2298415

Blair, M. M., & Stout, L. (1999). A team production theory of corporate law. *Virginia Law Review*, *85*, 247.

Grantham, R. (1998). The doctrinal basis of the rights of company shareholders. *Cambridge Law Journal*, *57*(3), 554.

Ip, P. K. (2009). The challenge of developing a business ethics in China. *Journal of Business Ethics*, *88*, 211–224.

Kolk, A., Hong, P., & van Dolen, W. (2010). Corporate social responsibility in China: An analysis of domestic and foreign retailers' sustainability dimensions. *Business Strategy and the Environment*, *19*, 289–303.

Lin, L.-W. (2010). Corporate social responsibility in China: Window dressing or structural change? *Berkeley Journal of International Law*, *28*(1), 64–100.

McWilliams, A., & Siegel, D. (2000). Corporate social responsibility and financial performance: Correlation or misspecification? *Strategic Management Journal*, *21*(5), 603–609.

MunozSlaughter, C. (1997). Corporate social responsibility: A new perspective. *Company Lawyer*, *18*(10), 313.

OECD. (2004). Principles of corporate governance.

Worthington, S. (2001). Shares and shareholders: Property, power and entitlement: Part II. *The Company Lawyer*, *22*(10), 307–314.

12 Energy Investments in China and the Role of Environmental Regulation: The Legal Perspective

Changmian Zhang and Piercarlo Rossi

ABSTRACT

Purpose – A balance between environmental protection and sustainable development of the energy industry is fostered in the majority of nations. China's economic growth has been rapid in the past few decades, with the unfortunate side effect of environmental pollution and ecological deterioration in the country. In this chapter, we provide a study of Chinese legal rules about civil liability for environmental damages in the light of objectives of sustainable development of the energy industry.

Methodology/approach – The research approach is based on the Regulatory Impact Assessment.

Practical implications – International funds and private investors, especially those working in FDI, have to cope with the legal framework more or less favorable to investment and innovation deriving from experimentation and development of new energy products and processes. In each jurisdiction, the mechanism of civil liability is crucial in determining such a legal framework.

Social implications – The real functioning of civil liability as applied by the doctrinal and judicial interpretation has to be taken into account for minimizing the mass damages for the environment and individuals.

Originality/value – Different from other assumptions based on administrative rules or policy issues, the balance between environmental protection and sustainable development is considered in this chapter under a view that emphasizes the role of legal rules from a civil law perspective.

Keywords: Civil law; tort law; mass damages liability; environmental protection; sustainable development

Introduction

A balance between environmental protection and sustainable development of the energy industry is fostered in the majority of nations. Today, energy companies may be subjected to two types of liability with regard to environmental disasters. The first is related to the adoption of any measures, including fines, approved by national authorities or determined by administrative law. The second is related to the payment of damages under civil law for damages caused to third parties in consideration of their actions or omissions.

However, there are many differences in the national legislations about these liability regimes. The extension of liability conditions may vary, from a complete restoration of the damaged habitat in some countries to only compensation measures in others. Liability can import criminal charges in some countries. Liability is based on a negligence rule in some jurisdictions, while strict liability is the model in many others, where an energy company may be held responsible without any occurred fault. Even the concept of environmental damage changes according to the diverse national legal definitions; it may encompass all or some of elements such as adverse and measurable loss, natural resources, biological resources, and environmental services.

The balance between environmental protection and sustainable development of the energy industry is differently articulated not only as a direct consequence of national policy decisions but also as an indirect result caused by the liability regimes.

China's economic growth has been rapid in the past few decades, with the unfortunate side effect of environmental pollution and ecological deterioration in the country. In fact, some observers have rightly demonstrated the fact that the spectacular economic growth in China has come at high environmental costs (Faure & Liujing, 2014). As China has overtaken the United States in energy consumption and become the world's biggest energy consumer (Swartz & Oster, 2010), the China's impact on the environment becomes an international concern at least in terms of climate problem.

Within the country, the escalated environmental or ecological damages have been becoming a crucial and striking problem, since it is directly related with the sustainability of the nation's development. Thus, the Chinese government is paying more and more attention to the environmental pollution. From a legal perspective, the government has made some progress in order to improve the legal system of environmental law. The civil liability, together with the administrative/criminal liability, constitutes one of the significant mechanisms to protect the environment.

Materials and Methods

Several laws and regulations have been enacted with regard to the civil liability for environmental damage, since the promulgation of Tort Liability Law of the People's Republic of China (hereinafter, "TLL") in 2009. In particular, the Environmental Protection Law (hereinafter, "EPL") revised in 2014 is of paramount importance. As to case law, there are two decisions that are fundamental to ascertain the issues about the role of civil liability for environmental damage: the Interpretation of the Supreme People's Court on several Issues concerning the Application of Law in the Trial of Liability for Environmental Tort (hereinafter, "IIALTLET") issued on Third July 2015[1] and the Interpretation of the Supreme People's Court on Several Issues concerning the Application of Law in the Conduct of

---

[1]Available at http://www.chinacourt.org/law/detail/2015/06/id/148253.shtml

Environmental Civil Public Interest Litigations (hereinafter, "IECPIL") issued on January 7, 2015. The review proposed in this study is developed from a perspective of Regulatory Impact Assessment in order to demonstrate that the statutory design of legal rules on civil liability could be more or less efficient in obtaining a balance between environmental protection and sustainable development of the energy industry. Even if RIA is not deliberately employed in China as a process for continuous regulatory reform, the cost and benefit of the enactment of laws can be analyzed under a theoretical perspective (Glachant, 1998). Civil liability can be considered as an element of an environmental protection system that encompasses ex ante remedies and ex post remedies (Friehe, 2009; Schwartz, 1997).

Results

Despite its reference to civil law tradition, Chinese civil liability for environmental damages is different from those of other jurisdictions. In particular, five elements are to be noticed.

THE REQUIREMENT OF UNLAWFULNESS

As in other civil law tradition country, the Chinese scholars are consent on the constitutive elements of civil torts, namely (1) damages; (2) conduct of tortfeasor; (3) causation between the damage and conduct; and (4) fault. Despite this consent, nevertheless there has been a debate on the issue of unlawfulness. That is to say, to be qualified as a Tort, the conduct should violate a regulation or not? Some scholars, partly on the basis of pandectists tradition, the German tradition in particular, insist this element. On the other hand, some scholars disagree, arguing that the fault itself already infers something unlawful. As far as the environmental liability is concerned, the debate became much more articulate, when the positive rules are not always clear and inconsistent.

Theoretically, the General Principles of Civil Law of 1986 (hereinafter "GPCL") has provided the environmental liability in article 124:

> Any person who pollutes the environment and causes damages to others in violation of State provisions for

environmental protection and the prevention of pollution shall bear civil liability in accordance with the law.[2]

As one can readily find, a violation of a regulation is regarded as condition for liability. Additionally, it appears to be a supportive argument to this position the recent enactment in the Real Right Law (2007), which formulates in article 90 that

> No holder of realty may discard solid wastes or discharge such harmful substances as atmospheric pollutants, water pollutants, noise, light and magnetic radiation with violation of the related provisions of the state.[3]

The special statutes, however, do not require this condition for liability. For example, the revised Water Pollution Prevention and Control Law (2008) (hereinafter, "WPPCL") in the Section 1 article 85 that

> The party whose rights and interests are damaged by a water pollution accident is entitled to ask the party discharging pollutants to eliminate the damage and make compensation for their losses.[4]

Hence, the law seems to introduce the possibility of liability without violating any regulation. Similar regulations, furthermore, one can trace in Prevention and Control of Atmospheric Pollution Law (2000 Revision) (hereinafter, "PCAPL"),[5] in Prevention and Control of Pollution from Environmental Noise Law of 1996[6] (hereinafter, "PCPENL"), and so on.

To clarify the regulatory contradiction, the Chinese legal scholarship tended to be in favor of the non-requirement of the unlawfulness – on the basis not only of the legal-technical ground, among others, the priority of special statutes respect to the general law, the reinterpretation of the expression in GPCL

---

[2]GPCL, article 124.
[3]Real Right Law, article 90.
[4]WPPCL, article 85, section 1
[5]PCAPL, article 63: *Any unit that has caused an atmospheric pollution hazard shall have the responsibility of removing the hazard and of making compensations to the units or individuals that have suffered direct losses.*
[6]PCPENL, article 61: *"Any unit or individual suffering from the hazards of environmental noise pollution shall have the right to demand the polluter to eliminate the hazards; if a loss has been caused, it shall be compensated according to law."*

"State provisions for environmental protection and the prevention of pollution" but also of the economical ground (Chen & Li,
2008; Wu, 2009) – until the enactment of TLL in 2009. The
latter seems to end up the debate in favor of unnecessary unlawfulness. In the general definition of tort in article 2,[7] one can trace
nothing about the condition of unlawfulness. Furthermore,
according to an authoritative opinion (Wang, 2012), the adaptation of the conception "civil right and interest" in TLL (article 2)
and the absorption of unlawfulness in fault (section 1 of article 6[8])
are sufficient to prove that the Chinese tort law exclude the unlawfulness as a constitutive requirement of tort. The crucially important fact is that the provision of liability for environmental
pollution has no mention of this requirement.[9] In fact the interpretation issued by the Supreme Court in July 2015 (IIALTLET)
confirms this assertion, stating that the polluter's exception based
on the fact that the discharge of pollutants meets the statutory or
local requirements, shall not be supported by court.[10]

THE NOTION OF ECOLOGICAL DAMAGE

Ecological damage is distinguished from traditional damage
(such as personal injury and property) partly due to the fact that
ecological damage not only causes eventually the individual
economic loss but also, much more important, brings about
the social loss, and in many cases, the social loss is not readily
seen or even discernable, because it may not be diagnosed until
several years after exposure.[11] This distinction may constitute

---

[7]TLL, article 2: "*Those who infringe upon civil rights and interests shall
be subject to the tort liability according to this Law.*"
[8]TLL, article 6: *One who is at fault for infringement upon a civil right
or interest of another person shall be subject to the tort liability.*
[9]TLL, article 65: "*Where any harm is caused by environmental pollution, the polluter shall assume the tort liability.*"
[10]IIALTLET, article 1. In practice, a guiding case (issued by the super
court) in which the defendant's argument of meeting the standard has
been rejected by court is accordance with the interpretation. The case is
available at http://www.chinacourt.org/article/detail/2014/07/id/1329676.
shtml
[11]One may take Songhua River pollution for example to illustrate this
point. The Songhua River pollution caused by PetroChina Cooperation
on November 13, 2005, led to a temporary stop in water supply for
Harbin city, and resulted in direct economic losses of up to 1.5 billion
RMB in that city alone.

a challenge in pursuit of compensation by the traditional tort law, since the latter covers only the compensation of individual loss.

At this point, it's opportune to overview the coverage of the Tort Law taken in effectiveness into force on July 1, 2010. The article 1,[12] which clarifies its scope partly as the protection of individual rights and interests, seems to exclude the ecological damages. However, the model that determines the scope leaves a slim chance to direct interpretation to the contrary.

In civil law tradition, there are mainly two models to define the scope of protection. One, denominated as a "list model," is represented by the BGB, which enumerates specific rights that must be protected in §823 I.[13] The other, named as general provision model, may be represented by the France Model (Code Civil) and by Italy (Code Civil). According to article 1382[14] of French Civil Code, for instance, any act which causes damage to another obliges the one by whose fault it occurred, to compensate it. Article 1383[15] further provides that everyone is liable for the damage he causes not only by his intentional act but also by his negligent conduct or by his imprudence. So the almost same provision is offered by Italian code in article 2043.[16]

---

[12]TLL, article 1: "*In order to protect the legitimate rights and interests of parties in civil law relationships, clarify the tort liability, prevent and punish tortious conduct, and promote the social harmony and stability, this Law is formulated.*"

[13]BGB., §823 I: "=*"Wer einen anderen zu einer Verrichtung bestellt, ist zum Ersatz des Schadens verpflichtet, den der andere in Ausführung der Verrichtung einem Dritten widerrechtlich zufügt. Die Ersatzpflicht tritt nicht ein, wenn der Geschäftsherr bei der Auswahl der bestellten Person und, sofern er Vorrichtungen oder Gerätschaften zu beschaffen oder die Ausführung der Verrichtung zu leiten hat, bei der Beschaffung oder der Leitung die im Verkehr erforderliche Sorgfalt beobachtet oder wenn der Schaden auch bei Anwendung dieser Sorgfalt entstanden sein würde.*"

[14]Code Civil, article 1382: "*Tout fait quelconque de l'homme, qui cause à autrui un dommage, oblige celui par la faute duquel il est arrivé à le réparer.*"

[15]Code Civil, article 1383: "*Chacun est responsable du dommage qu'il a causé non seulement par son fait, mais encore par sa négligence ou par son imprudence.*"

[16]Codice Civile, article 2043: "*Qualunque fatto doloso o colposo, che cagiona ad altri un danno ingiusto, obbliga colui che ha commesso il fatto a risarcire il danno*".

The Chinese Tort Law seemed to have followed the eclectic model. On one hand, the article 6[17] stipulates the general provision of civil liability for Torts (Zhang, 2012); on the other hand, the article 2[18] gives a protection list including as many as 18 civil rights and interests. However, a widely accepted opinion (L. Wang, 2010; S. Wang, 2010) is that the list is anything but exhaustive. In particular, the concept "Civil rights and interests" is an open conception, tending to comprehend the newly developed civil right, as time passed. Especially during the occasion of amendment of EPL in 2013, scholars have discussed whether it should be added as an article related to right to environment. The statement of this article is suggested as *"All the unit and individual have the right to enjoy a cleaning and healthy environment"* (Cai, 2013). Thus, the right to Environment, identified with an individual right, could be estimated as one of civil rights protectable in TLL so that it could be fully protected. However, unfortunately, the revised EPL has not adopted the suggestion.

Other authoritative scholars, rather to reinterpret the article 2 of TLL, tend to interpret directly the article 65 which regulates the environmental liability, arguing that the term "environment" appeared in the article has a boarder meaning than that in the GPCL of 1986, including both living environment and the ecological environment (Yang, 2010). This assertion is confirmed by the revised EPL, which, in article 64,[19] leads the TLL to govern

---

[17]TTL, article 6:

"*One who is at fault for infringement upon a civil right or interest of another person shall be subject to the tort liability.*"

"*One who is at fault as construed according to legal provisions and cannot prove otherwise shall be subject to the tort liability.*"

[18]Article 2: *Those who infringe upon civil rights and interests shall be subject to the tort liability according to this Law.*

"*Civil rights and interests" used in this Law shall include the right to life, the right to health, the right to name, the right to reputation, the right to honor, right to self image, right of privacy, marital autonomy, guardianship, ownership, usufruct, security interest, copyright, patent right, exclusive right to use a trademark, right to discovery, equities, right of succession, and other personal and property rights and interests.*

[19]EPL, article 64: "*Where any damage is caused by environmental pollution or ecological disruption, the tortfeasor shall assume tort liability in accordance with the relevant provisions of the Tort Law of the People's Republic of China.*"

this type of damages, though the article 2,[20] which gives a definition of the term, according to some scholars, has nothing to do with the ecological environment or sustainable development (Mo, 2011). In this direction, there is no doubt that if the ecological disruption turns out to infringe the individual right and interests, the tortfeasor shall assume the civil liability under the TLL. It arises, however, the doubt when the ecological disruption doesn't result to damage of individual right and interests, since in the article 65 of TLL appears the term "harm." To be specific, whether it shall be applied the concrete rules provided in TLL in terms of environmental pollution: among others, the principle of non-fault liability, the reversed burden of prove. In fact, after the enactment of TLL, some scholars viewed the absence of ecological damage protection in TLL as a heavy "negligence" (Dai, 2011; Dong, 2012).

Seeing the different terms used in article 2 (civil right and interest), 67 ("harm") of TLL, one environmental law scholar asserts that one can infer from the difference that the "harm" includes the "ecological harm" (Huang, 2010). However, the recent judicial interpretation IIALTLET[21] limited this applicable scope within civil cases concerning about environmental pollution and ecological disruption. That is to say, only ecological disruption resulted in civil/individual damages can fall in scope of this interpretation. Thus, the rules specified in IIALTLET, as we will examine later, such as causation and third-party conduct, cannot be applied in the circumstance in which the ecological disruption does not infringe directly the civil right. Therefore, IIALTLET has no intention to clarify such a doubt. In any case, it's rather worthy to illustrate two institutes related to the ecological damages. One is the action of public interest, the other is kind of political, the *Measures for the Accountability for the Leaders of the Party and Government in ambit of Ecological*

---

[20]EPL, article 2: "*For the purposes of this Law, 'environment' means the entirety of all natural elements and artificially transformed natural elements that affect the survival and development of human beings, including but not limited to air, water, seas, land, minerals, forests, grasslands, wetland, wildlife, natural and cultural relics, nature reserves, scenic spots, historical sites, and urban and rural areas.*"
[21]IIALTLET, article 18, section 1: "*The present interpretation shall be applied to trail of the civil cases concerning environmental pollution and ecological disruption ...*"

Damages[22] (hereinafter, MAED) issued in August 2015. Let's begin with the recent one. Generally speaking, the MAED has the intention to impose a rather strict responsibility on the Leader of the Party and Government in regards with the ecological damages. Articles 5–8 provide different cases in which the Leaders in charge should burden a responsibility. Though the article 17 requires the local government to make specific measures to rend effective MAED, one can hardly predict its practical effects in future. However, it shows the endeavor of the Party to improve the ecological environment, and thus, one could expect that in future the individual could raise action for the ecological environment. Nevertheless, the action of public introduced in EPL demonstrates a prudent attitude of the government. The revised Civil Procedure Law (2012) (Hereinafter, "CPL") provides, in general, the action of public interest in article 55.[23] Following the CPL, the revised EPL (2014) specifies the action in ambit of environmental damages on which it's worthy to take a detailed examination. First of all, different from the CPL which regulates only the environmental pollution conducts, the EPL rends included also the ecological damages.[24] The IECPIL coming into force on January 7, 2015, determines or broadens

---

[22]Available at http://news.xinhuanet.com/2015-08/17/c_1116282540.htm

[23]CPL, article 55: "*For conduct that pollutes environment, infringes upon the lawful rights and interests of vast consumers or otherwise damages the public interest, an authority or relevant organization as prescribed by law may institute an action in a people's court.*"

[24]EPL, article 58: "*For an act polluting environment or causing ecological damage in violation of public interest, a social organization which satisfies the following conditions may institute an action in a people's court:*

(1) *It has been legally registered with the civil affairs department of the people's government at or above the level of a districted city.*
(2) *It has specially engaged in environmental protection for the public good for five consecutive years or more without any recorded violation of law.*

A people's court shall, according to the law, accept an action instituted by a social organization that satisfies the provision of the preceding paragraph.

A social organization may not seek any economic benefit from an action instituted by it."

the scope of regulation, including not only the conduct that has damaged the public interest but also the ones having the major risk of it.[25] However, its rigid qualification as plaintiff may construe an obstacle to be taken in practice. As the EPL holds in section 2 of article 58, only the social organization is qualified to institute an action on behalf of public interest. Though the IECPIL intends to extend the plaintiff, holding in article 2[26] that, apart from the social organization in narrow sense, the private non-enterprise entity and foundation, if registered in the civil affairs administrative department at or above the level of a districted city, could be determined as a social organization in board sense, the individual nevertheless is excluded by this category of action. Furthermore, the conditions to be satisfied seem pretty demanding. The condition that the organization should be legally registered with the civil affairs department at or above the level of a districted city (although the IECPIL extends it to the prefecture-level city not divided into districts[27]) may make less functional the social organization below the district which has a direct connection with the environmental conducts. The second condition provided in EPL as "specially engaged in environmental protection for the public good" is further delineated in article

---

[25]IECPIL, article 1: "*Where an authority or relevant organization as prescribed by law files a lawsuit against any conduct that pollutes the environment and damages the ecology, which has damaged the public interest or has the major risk of damaging the public interest, in accordance with the provisions of Article 55 of the Civil Procedure Law, Article 58 of the Environmental Protection Law, and other laws, if the provisions of item (2), (3) or (4) of Article 119 of the Civil Procedure Law are complied with, the people's court shall accept the lawsuit.*"

[26]IECPIL, article 2: "*A social organization, private non-enterprise entity, or foundation, among others, registered in the civil affairs administrative department of the people's government at or above the level of a districted city in accordance with laws and regulations may be determined as a social organization prescribed in Article 58 of the Environmental Protection Law.*"

[27]IECPIL, article 3: "*The civil affairs administrative department of the people's government at or above the level of a districted city, autonomous prefecture, league or region, prefecture-level city not divided into districts or a district of municipality directly under the Central Government may be determined as the "civil affairs administrative department of the people's government at or above the level of a districted city" prescribed in Article 58 of the Environmental Protection Law.*"

4 of IECPIL,[28] according to which, organization's tenets and main business scope are requested to maintain the public interest and it engages in public environmental protection activities. It indeed demands a lot. The thing goes worse, when the second section of article 4 of IECPIL provides that the public interest involved in the lawsuit filed by a social organization shall be related to its tenets and business scope. The third condition, expressed as "without any recorded violation of law" in EPL, is specified, or better to say, limited within its business activities by IECPIL.[29] Compared to the other legal systems, the EPL and its judicial interpretation provide some so strict limitation that it excludes the possibility of participation from the private individual. However, in relation to the scope of compensation, the IECPL holds in the article 21 that the tortfeasor assumes the loss of service functions caused by the ecological damage.[30] It's evident that the compensation for such loss shall be utilized to restore the damaged ecological environment.[31] The performed examination allows us to reach a primary conclusion. Despite the recent endeavor in particular represented by the environmental scholars in occasion of amendment of EPL, it's fair to affirm that in the current legal system the ecological damage, if not resulted

---

[28]IECPIL, article 4: "*Where a social organization's tenets and main business scope specified in its articles of association are to maintain the public interest and it engages in public environmental protection activities, it may be determined as "specially engages in public environmental protection activities" prescribed in Article 58 of the Environmental Protection Law.*

The public interest involved in the lawsuit filed by a social organization shall be related to its tenets and business scope."
[29]IECPIL, article 5: "*Where no administrative or criminal punishment is imposed on a social organization due to any violation of law or regulation in its business activities within five years before filing a lawsuit, it may be determined as "has no record of violations of laws" prescribed in Article 58 of the Environmental Protection Law.*"
[30]IECPIL, article 21: "*Where the plaintiff requests the defendant to pay expenses for the loss of service functions from the period when the ecological environment is damaged to the restoration thereof, the people's court may support such a request in accordance with law.*"
[31]IECPIL, article 24: "*The expenses for restoring the ecological environment, the loss of service functions from the period when the ecological environment is damaged to the restoration thereof and other expenses that shall be assumed by the defendant according to the judgment rendered by the people's court shall be used to restore the damaged ecological environment.*"

to infringe the individual civil right, can doubtfully be covered by Tort Law. One shall use the legal mechanism of action of public interest to protect the ecological environment. This affirmation appears to be consolidated by the provision in article 29 of IECPIL,[32] which seems to confirm the twofold system: the infringement of individual right by environment-damaging conduct, the infringement of public interest by the same conduct. Nevertheless, such legal mechanism, introduced by CPL in 2012, is redefined in the EPL and its explanation, which prescribe some strict limitation for the qualification of plaintiff in this action.

LIABILITY WITHOUT FAULT

TLL provides the principle liability without fault in article 7 which states:

> one who shall assume the tort liability for infringing upon a civil right or interest of another person, whether at fault or not, as provided for by law, shall be subject to such legal provisions.[33]

The environmental liability, given, in particular, its technical complexity and economical unbalance between tortfeasor and victim, together with other categories,[34] falls in the scope of liability without fault. Pursuant to the article 65 of TTL, pollution that causes damage, standing alone, will suffice to hold the polluter for tort liability. To some extent, the TTL reiterates some provisions in other existent statutory law. For example, the Water Pollution Prevention and Control Law of the People's Republic of China (1984, now substituted by the revised law in 2008) holds in article 41 that "the unit which has caused a water

---

[32]IECPIL, article 29: "*The filing of an environmental civil public interest litigation by any authority or social organization prescribed by law shall not affect the filing of an action by any citizen, legal person or any other organization that suffers from personal injury or property damage due to the same conduct that pollutes the environment and damages the ecology in accordance with the provisions of Article 119 of the Civil Procedure Law.*"
[33]TLL, article 7.
[34]Product liability (TTL, article 41–47), Liability for Motor Vehicle Traffic Accident (article 48–53) Medical malpractice liability (article 54–64), Liability for Ultrahazardous Activity (article 70–77), Liability for Harm Caused by Domestic Animal (article 78–84) some categories of Liability for Harm Caused by Object (articles 86, 88, 89), etc.

pollution hazard has the responsibility to eliminate it and make compensation to the unit or individual that suffers direct losses." Following the TLL, some statutory laws, in occasion of their revision, adopted expressly and clearly the principle of non-fault liability. The *Marine Environment Protection Law of the People's Republic of China* (2013 Amendment) (hereinafter, MEPL), which in article 90[35] introduces the principle.

In terms of non-fault liability in environmental liability, one shall keep in mind two issues: (1) the subjectivity of the principle to the ecological damages liability; (2) the exemption rules.

As far as the first issue is concerned, some scholars (Chen, 2008; Zhao, 2012) insisted that, given the non-fault liability principle, it shall be applied only if provided by law, the ecological damage liability, because of the absence of special provision, shall fall in general principle of liability, namely the fault liability.[36] However, as we discussed above, the issue is still under shadow, and need to be clarified by legislation or by judicial interpretation.

Now we discuss the second issue. Pursuant to the article 66 of TLL,[37] the polluter could waive the liability by proving certain circumstances as provided for by law. In other words, there exist the exemption rules. The TLL provides some general circumstances for waive liability in the third chapter, namely the Intentional Conduct of Plaintiff (article 27),[38] force majeure (article 29),[39] self-defense (article 30),[40] and necessity (article 31).[41]

---

[35]MEPL, article 90: "*Any party that is directly responsible for a pollution damage to the marine environment shall relieve the damage and compensate for the losses;......*"

[36]TLL, article 6.

[37]TLL, article 66: "*Where any dispute arises over an environmental pollution, the polluter shall assume the burden to prove that it should not be liable or its liability could be mitigated under certain circumstances as provided for by law or to prove that there is no causation between its conduct and the harm.*"

[38]TLL, article 27: "*The actor shall not be liable for any harm that is caused intentionally by the victim.*"

[39]TLL, article 29: "*Where any harm to another person is caused by a force majeure, the tortfeasor shall not be liable, except as otherwise provided for by law ....*"

[40]TLL, article 30: "*Where any harm is caused by self-defense, the person exercising self-defense shall not be liable ....*"

[41]TLL, article 31: "*Where any harm is caused by any conduct of necessity, the person causing the occurrence of danger shall be liable ....*"

It appears that the self-defense can hardly be utilized in environmental tort. Thus, the circumstances of exemption of liability shall be (1) Intentional Conduct of Plaintiff; (2) force majeure; (3) necessity.

However, the special laws provide in a different way. For instance, The *Water Pollution Prevention and Control Law of the People's Republic of China* (2008 Revision) (hereinafter, "WPPCL") gives two circumstances: the Intentional Conduct of Plaintiff and Force majeure.[42] Differently, the PCAPL (2000 Revision) stipulates only one circumstance with some qualification.[43] Moreover, the *Marine Environment Protection Law of the People's Republic of China* (2013 Amendment) (hereinafter, "MEPL") on one hand excludes the intentional conduct of plaintiff; on the other hand, specifies the circumstances in article 92:

> Where damage to the marine environment caused by a pollution cannot be avoided despite prompt and reasonable adoption of measures, and where the pollution is entirely attributable to any of the following circumstances, the parties concerned held responsible shall be exempt from liability:
>
> (1) War;
> (2) irresistible natural calamities; or
> (3) negligence or other wrongful acts in the performance of a department responsible for the maintenance of beacons or other navigation aids.[44]

One may easily find that this norm, on one side, defines, and, in the same time, limits the general conception of Force majeure; on the other side, extends the circumstances provided in TLL, by adding the negligence.

---

[42]WPPCL, article 85: "...

If the damage is caused by force majeure, the party discharging pollutants bears no liability for compensation, unless it is otherwise prescribed by law.

If the damage is caused by the victim on purpose, the party discharging pollutants bears no liability for compensation ..."

[43]PCAPL, article 63: "*If atmospheric pollution losses result directly from uncontrollable natural disasters which cannot be averted even after reasonable measures have been promptly taken, the party concerned shall be exempted from any liability.*"

[44]MEPL, article 92.

In this situation, there arises the question: which law has the priority? The IIALTLET in section 2 article 1 prefers the special laws.

It may be opportune to notice the third-party action. Under article 68 of the TLL,[45] if the harm is caused by environmental pollution as the result of the fault of a third party, the victim may require compensation from either the polluter or the third party. After paying compensation, the polluter is entitled to reimbursement from the third party. Thus it's clear that to hold the third party liable, in addition to his conduct attributive to the pollution, the third party must be at fault. It has been emphasized by the Interpretation in section 3 of article 5. Furthermore, the section 1 of the same article allows the victim to raise independently an action toward the third party. However, from the norm, it seems difficult to infer the solution about the issue whether the third party can be utilized by the polluter as a circumstance to mitigate, even waive the liability. The earlier "WPPCL" stipulates not in a dissimilar way:

> If the damage is caused by a third party, the party discharging pollutants has the right to, after making compensation according to law, recover the compensation from the third party.[46]

Nor the "MEPL"[47] offers a solution. In Chinese scholarship, the issue has been discussed rather articulately. Some scholars respond affirmatively, arguing that if the third party's action "disrupts" the causal connection between the damages and the conduct of polluter, the polluter doesn't have to assume any liability or his liability shall be mitigated (Cai, 1995; Li, 1997; Wang, 2004). Other scholars, on the basis that the principle of non-fault liability intends to protect the victim in a strict way, hold that the third-party conduct shall not be estimated as an exemption of liability (Zhang, 2007). This is not the opportunity to discuss that

---

[45]TLL, article 68: "*Where any harm is caused by environmental pollution for the fault of a third party, the victim may require a compensation from either the polluter or the third party. After making compensation, the polluter shall be entitled to be reimbursed by the third party.*"
[46]WPPCL section 4 of article 85.
[47]MEPL, article 90: "*... in case the pollution damage to the marine environment is entirely caused by an intentional act or a fault of a third party, that third party shall relieve the damage and be liable for the compensation.*"

the argument presented by the affirmative response, in its essence, leads to prove no causation between the conduct and damages in order to free from liability.[48] The IIALTLET seems to close the discussion, by the statement in section 3 of article 5:

> The polluter's claim to waive or mitigate the liability on basis of the third party's fault shall not be supported by court.

CAUSATION AND THE REVERSED BURDEN OF PROOF

One of the most crucial respects of tort liability for environmental tort could be proving the causal connection between the damages and the pollution. In many cases, the damage is not easily seen or even discernible, for it may not be diagnosed until several years after exposure. To prove the causation, whatever the causality theory is adopted,[49] often requires sophisticated devices and technology. Therefore, it would be too burdensome and unfair for the plaintiff to prove causation. Thus, early in the 2001, the Supreme Court's interpretation introduced the presumption of causation by providing that the polluter ought to prove that there is no causal relationship between the act and harmful consequence.[50] Following this interpretation, both the revised Law of the People's Republic of China on the Prevention and Control of Environmental Pollution by Solid Wastes (2004)

---

[48]See TLL, article 66: "*Where any dispute arises over an environmental pollution, the polluter shall assume the burden to prove that it should not be liable or its liability could be mitigated under certain circumstances as provided for by law or to prove that there is no causation between its conduct and the harm.*"

[49]The various causality theories, see Zhao Hu, *supra* note 53, p. 59–62.

[50]Some Provisions of the Supreme People's Court on Evidence in Civil Procedures, article 4 section 3:

"*The burden of proof in the tort actions shall be assumed according to the following rules:*

(3) In a compensation lawsuit for damages caused by environmental pollution, the infringing party shall be responsible for producing evidence to prove the existence of exemptions of liabilities as provided in laws or that there is no causal relationship between the his act and the harmful consequences."

(hereinafter, "LPCEPSW")[51] and the revised WPCL[52] adopted the reversed burden of proof on the causation.[53] Given this, the TLL's introduction in article 66[54] couldn't be estimated as an innovation. According to article 6 of IIALTLET, the no causal connection could be confirmed in following typical circumstances:

(1) There is no possibility that the discharged pollutants could cause such damage
(2) The discharged pollutants which could cause such damage have not arrived the place where the damages occurred
(3) The damages occurred before the discharge of pollutants.[55]

Different from the traditional view, pursuant to which, the plaintiff in environmental tort shall prove only the conduct and damage, the IIALTLET adds in article 6 another fact to be proved by plaintiff: "the connection between the discharged pollutants or the sub-pollutants and the damages." However what such connection exactly refers to is anything but univocal, though the officer of Supreme Court explains that the standard of proving the connection is pretty much lower than that of proving the causation.[56]

---

[51]LPCEPSW, article 86: "*For a damage suit arising from the environmental pollution by solid wastes, the inflicter shall assume the burden of proof for the statutory causes for exemption and the nonexistence of causation between its act and harmful consequences.*"
    The "LPCEPSW" is revised once more in 2013, but this rule remains intact in article 86.
[52]WPCL (2008), article 87: "*For an action of damage due to a water pollution accident, the party discharging pollutants shall assume the burden of proof for legally prescribed exemptions and the nonexistence of relation of cause and effect between its act and the harmful consequences thereof.*"
[53]Even if the presumed causation has been fixed early in China, the judicial practice didn't always comply with this rule. See Hu Xuejun's recent case study: *Comments on the causation and its prove in Environmental Tort*, in *China Law Science*, 05/2013, pp. 163–170.
[54]TLL, article 66: "*Where any dispute arises over an environmental pollution, the polluter shall assume the burden to prove that it should not be liable or its liability could be mitigated under certain circumstances as provided for by law or to prove that there is no causation between its conduct and the harm.*"
[55]The chapter establishes a so-called Miscellaneous Provisions: "*other circumstances in which could be valued non-existing causation.*"
[56]Available at http://www.legaldaily.com.cn/xwzx/content/2015-06/01/content_6107283.htm?node=53628

References

Cai, S. (1995). *Environmental law textbook*. Beijing: Law Press.

Cai, S. (2013). From environmental rights to environmental protection obligations of the state and environmental public interest litigation. *Modern Law Science*, *11*, 3−4.

Chen, C., & Li, A. (2008). The illegality of acts is not the constituting element of environmental tort liability. *Public Administration and Law*, *4*, 108−110.

Chen, K. (2008). Studies on categorization of environmental torts. *Public Administration and Law*, *5*, 66−69.

Dai, M. (2011). On the necessity of further improving the legislation on civil liability for environmental tort: Comment on environmental pollution responsibility terms in the tort liability law. *Hebei Law Science*, *1*, 156−164.

Dong, S. (2012). On improving of environmental liability institute. *Legal System and Society*, *12*, 52−53.

Faure, M. G., & Liujing (2014). Compensation for environmental damage in China: Theory and practice. *Pace Environmental Law Review*, *31*, 226−230.

Friehe, T. (2009). Precaution v. avoidance: A comparison of liability rules. *Economics Letters*, *105*, 214–216.

Glachant, M. (1998). The use of regulatory mechanism design in environmental policy: A theoretical critique. In S. Faucheux (Ed.), *Sustainability and firms: Technological change and the changing regulatory environment* (pp. 179–188). Cheltenham: Edward Elgar.

Huang, P. (2010). Further discussion on constitutive elements of environmental pollution liability: A long with the relevant provision of "Tort Liability Law". *Public Administration and Law*, *12*, 77–80.

Li, Y. (1997). *Compensation for environmental damages*. Beijing: Economic Press.

Mo, Z. (2011). Tort liabilities and torts law: The new frontier of Chinese legal horizon. Richmond Journal of Global Law and Business, *10*, 487.

Schwartz, G. T. (1997). Mixed theories of tort law: Affirming both deterrence and corrective justice. *Texas Law Review*, *75*, 1801.

Swartz, S., & Oster, S. (2010). China Tops U.S. in Energy Use. *Wall Street. Journal.* Retrieved from http://online.wsj.com/article/SB10001424052748703720504575376712353150310.html. Accessed on July 18, 2010.

Wang, L. (2004). *Studies on the principle of imputation for tort liability*. Beijing: CUPL Press.

Wang, L. (2010). On characteristics of the scope of protection Chinese tort liability law provided. *Journal of Renmin University of China*, *4*, 1−8.

Wang, L. (2012). Our tort law has adopted the unlawfulness? *Peking University Law Journal*, *1*, 5−23.

Wang, S. (2010). *Explanations to the tort liability law of the People Republic of China*. Beijing: China Law Press.

Wu, P. (2009). The illegality of acts is not the constituting element of environmental tort liability. *Legal System and Society*, *12*, 58−59.

Yang, Y. (2010). *Detailed explanation to the tort liability law of the People's Republic of China*. Beijing: Intellectual Property Press.

Zhang, X. (2012). The interpretation and application of the general provision in tort law. *Journal of Law Application, 10*, 28–29.

Zhang, Z. (2007). Analysis on the obstacles about solution mechanisms of environmental disputes. In Id (Ed.), *Studies on advanced problems about solution mechanisms of the environmental dispute*. Beijing: Tsinghua University Press.

Zhao, H. (2012). *Research on civil liability of environmental tort*. PhD thesis, Wuhan University.

Part III
Alternative Fuels and Low Carbon Buildings: Research Trends in Europe and China

13 The Feasibility of Liquefied Methane as an Alternative Fuel in Europe and China

Marco Spitoni, Fabio Polonara and
Alessia Arteconi

ABSTRACT

Purpose – This chapter outlines the potential market of methane (especially LNG) as vehicle fuel in Europe and China.

Methodology/approach – A comprehensive report on the existing framework in terms of market capacity, regulations, and incentives is presented. Moreover, the feasibility of using biogas as environmental friendly source gas is considered.

Findings – The transport sector represents a major element in the global balance of greenhouse gas (GHG) emissions. Natural gas is considered the alternative fuel that, in the short-medium term, can best substitute conventional fuels in order to reduce their environmental impact, because it is readily available at a competitive price, using technologies that are already in widespread use. It can be used as compressed gas (CNG) or in the liquid phase (LNG). The former is more suitable for light vehicles, while the latter for heavy-duty vehicles. Some barriers need to be overcome for the diffusion of this alternative fuel, especially concerning the supply problem. The incentive policy has been shown to cover a major influence in the feasibility evaluation.

Originality/value – This work shows the state of the art of natural gas as fuel, especially from biogas source, in Europe and China and assesses the incentive scheme necessary to make liquefied biomethane feasible on the basis of the existing scenario in Italy.

Keywords: Alternative fuels; LNG; CNG; LBG; GHG emissions

Introduction

Nowadays, there is a growing interest in renewable energy sources and more sensitivity toward environmental issues. Over the past century, the carbon dioxide (CO_2) concentrations in the atmosphere have been increasing significantly. During 2012, electricity and heat generation sectors and transport sector accounted for 42% and 23% of the total emissions, respectively (IEA, 2014). Thus, the transport sector represents a major item on the global balance of greenhouse gas (GHG) emissions. It is forecasted that energy use and GHG emissions in this sector will increase by 50% by 2030 and more than 80% by 2050. The emission level and growth in transportation sector in 2012 was mainly driven by the road sector, which increased by 64% since 1990 (IEA, 2014). The Intergovernmental Panel on Climate Change (IPCC) advices that global GHG emissions must be reduced by at least 50% by 2050 (IEA, 2009). In order to reduce the environmental impact and GHG emissions, some measures must be applied. Regarding transport sector the key point is to lower the carbon emissions during combustion. This could be achieved by introducing more efficient engines or other kinds of new cars (such as electrical or hybrid vehicles) or introducing new fuels, to make the combustion cleaner. In this context, natural gas and biomethane could play a significant role in reducing GHG emissions in the short-medium period.

GHG Emission Reduction in Transport Sector

THE EUROPEAN SITUATION

In Europe, the GHG emission reduction is achieved by means of mandatory targets, set depending on the vehicle size. Up to now, these targets have been set for passenger vehicles and vans. The final goal is to reduce CO_2 emissions from transport sector by roughly 60% by 2050, compared to 1990 levels, as reported in the European Commission website (EC, 2015a).

Passenger cars are responsible for about 12% of total CO_2 emissions in Europe. Law imposes that the new car emissions do not exceed more than 130 g CO_2/km by 2015 (average limit). This emission level must be further reduced up to 95 g CO_2/km by 2021 (average limit), corresponding to 4.1 l/100 km of petrol or 3.6 l/100 km of diesel consumption, respectively (EC, 2015b). Compared with the average emission level in 2007 (158.7 g/km), these levels represent a reduction of about 18% and 40%, respectively, for the 2015 and 2021 targets. Since 2010, the emission levels have decreased by 17 g CO_2/km (an average of 12%) and in 2014, the average emission level for a new car was 123.4 g CO_2/km, well below the 2015 target, as reported in the monitoring of CO_2 emissions provisional data (EEA, 2009).

These emission targets have been set according with a limit value curve that imposes the maximum allowable level of emissions for every year from 2012. Penalties are foreseen for those manufacturers having a fleet with an average emission level higher than such annual level. The penalty depends on the value of exceeding emissions: 5€ for the first g/km of exceedance, 15€ for the second, 25€ for the third, and 95 for each subsequent g/km. From 2019, the penalty will be 95€ from the first gram exceeding the limit.

Some incentives are granted under certain circumstances: if the manufacturer equips his vehicles with innovative technologies, he can gain credits up to a maximum of 7 g/km per year for his fleet. Moreover, incentives are foreseen for those manufacturers able to produce vehicles with a very low emission level (lower than 50 g/km). The incentive will be proportional to the number of low emitting vehicles that, depending on the year, will be enumerated as reported in Table 1.

Table 1: Incentive for Those Manufacturers Able to Produce Passenger Vehicles or Light Trucks with an Emission Level Lower than 50 g/km (EEA, 2009).

Passenger Vehicles (First Stage)	Passenger Vehicles (Second Stage)	Light Trucks
3.5 vehicles in 2012 and 2013	2 vehicles in 2020	3.5 in 2014 and 2015
2.5 in 2014	1.67 in 2021	2.5 in 2016
1.5 in 2015	1.33 in 2022	1.5 in 2017
1 from 2016 to 2019	1 from 2023	1 from 2018 onwards

Smaller manufacturers have different targets:

- Manufacturers with a sales volume between 10,000 and 300,000 cars per year can decide to lower their average emission level of 25% from 2012 to 2019, compared with that of 2007, and of 45% starting from 2020, compared with that of 2007.
- Manufacturers with a sales volume between 1,000 and 10,000 cars per year can decide to set their own targets that must be approved by the commission.
- Manufacturers with a sales volume lower than 1,000 new cars per year or cars manufactured for a special purpose have no mandatory target to respect.

Regarding vans (light commercial vehicles), they represent about 12% of the European light-duty vehicles market and a similar regulation has been set in order to reduce the GHG emissions related with them. The targets are mandatory for those vehicles used to carry goods, weighing up to 3.5 tons and less than 2.61 tons when empty. Law imposes that the new van emissions do not exceed more than 175 g CO_2/km by 2017 (average limit). This emission level must be further reduced down to 147 g CO_2/km by 2020 (average limit), corresponding to 5.5 l/100 km of diesel (EC, 2015c).

As for passenger vehicles, penalties are foreseen if the average CO_2 emissions of a manufacturer's fleet exceed its limit value in any year from 2014. The penalty is the same of that for the light-duty vehicles.

Also for vans, credits up to a maximum of 7 g/km per year for the fleet will be granted for those manufacturers that equip their vans with innovative technologies. Moreover, if the produced vans have a very low emission level (less than 50 g/km, the same as for passenger cars), each one will be considered as reported in Table 1. This incentive is recognized for a maximum of 25,000 vans from 2014 to 2017.

Also in this case, smaller manufacturers have different targets:

- Manufacturers with a sales volume between 1,000 and 22,000 cars per year can decide to set their own targets that must be approved by the commission.
- Manufacturers with a sales volume lower than 1,000 have no mandatory target to respect.

Moreover, manufacturers can join together to meet these targets.

Regarding heavy-duty vehicles (HDVs), they represent roughly a quarter of road transport emission and about 5% of total GHG emissions in Europe with a growth of about 36% from 1990 to 2010. To meet the targets for 2050, some actions are necessary. However, up to now, accurate measures and reports from this sector are missing so it is actually not possible to define any goal. Some studies have shown that the current technology level could permit to reduce GHG emissions by at least 30% and this reduction is cost-effective (EC, 2015d). At present, the commission has developed a simulating tool able to measure CO_2 emissions from new HDVs.

THE CHINESE SITUATION

Since the beginning of the century, especially in the last decades, the vehicle annual sales in China has been growing by an unexpected rate. More than 23 million vehicles were sold in China in 2014, making the Chinese auto-market the largest in the world (United Nations Environment Programme, 2015). Consequently, Chinese GHG emissions in transport sector have become the highest in the world, accounting for about 6% of global CO_2 emissions. These emissions are expected to increase more than 50% by 2020 from 2010 levels. Chinese government have set targets for 2020 in order to reduce and control air pollution and, to meet those targets, the emissions growth must be approximately halved.

In 2004, fuel economy standards were introduced by means of fuel consumption standards definition and dividing the vehicle market into 16 classes based on the vehicle mass. Several steps or phases were defined, also differentiating manual transmission (MT) and automated transmission (AT). At present, for the smallest weight class (MT), the consumption target for 2015 was set to be equal to 5.2 l/100 km. From Figure 1, it can be seen in detail the phase targets for each weight class. After the second phase (end of 2011), the third phase began and mandatory average targets based on weight classes were set. These targets foreseen an average fuel consumption equal to 6.9 l/100 km. By implementing the first two phases, a reduction of about 11.5% in fuel consumption was achieved. In 2009, during the second phase, started in 2008, the fuel consumption level was equal to 7.78 l/100 km (180.5 g/km). However, by 2010, this level had risen by 0.6% (7.83 l/100 km), most likely because larger engine

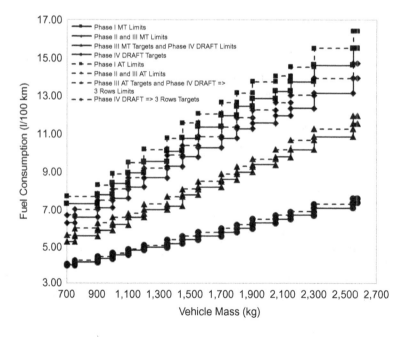

Figure 1: China Weight-Based Passenger Vehicle Fuel Consumption Limits (Phases I, II, and III) for Automatic Transmission (AT) and Manual Transmission (MT) Vehicles (iCET, 2014).

and high fuel consuming cars increased their market share (United Nations Environment Programme, 2015). In order to facilitate the achievement of this mandatory emissions level, a fourth phase has been recently released, providing useful guidelines (Figure 1).

Moreover, in 2009 gasoline and diesel excise tax was increased, from 0.2 Yuan to 1 Yuan and from 0.1 Yuan to 0.8 Yuan per liter, respectively. Due to the decreasing fuel price during 2013 and 2014, the central government increased the gasoline excise tax up to 1.52 Yuan per liter (United Nations Environment Programme, 2015). In addition, incentive and subsidies are given to consumers in order to encourage the purchase of new-energy vehicles or small engine vehicles. This subsidy is not directly given to consumers but to the manufacturers, who lowers the vehicles price. An additional subsidy is also given to those consumers who purchase a passenger vehicle (any type) with an engine capacity under 1.6 l, consuming at least 20% less than the government standards (United Nations Environment Programme, 2015).

The Chinese law scheme includes also penalties in the form of excise taxes for manufacturers and consumers in order to promote the purchase of vehicles with smaller engines. In Table 2, updated excise taxes rate is reported. It can be seen that taxation for vehicles with small engines was reduced while for vehicles with bigger engines it was increased. For engines in the category 1.5–2 l, it remained the same.

Table 2: Tax Rate over the Years Depending on the Engine Displacement (United Nations Environment Programme, 2015).

Category by Engine Displacement (l)	Tax Rate Prior to 1 April, 2006 (%)	Tax Rate April 4, 2006–31 August, 2008 (%)	Tax Rate Beginning 1, September, 2008 (%)
< 1.0	3	3	1
1.0–1.5	5	3	3
1.5–2.0	5	5	5
2.0–2.5	5	9	9
2.5–3.0	8	12	12
3.0–3.5	8	15	25
4.0 and larger	8	20	40

Natural Gas Vehicles Diffusion at Present

One possibility to reduce environmental impact and lower air pollution and GHG emissions in the short-medium term is to substitute conventional vehicle fuels with natural gas (NG). The advantages of natural gas are:

- environmental benefits;
- availability;
- competitive price;
- reduction of dependency on imported oil.

In the transport sector, the natural gas could be used in its compressed (CNG) or liquefied (LNG) form. This depends on the vehicle weight: CNG is more appropriate for small vehicle while LNG, for its high energy density, is required for HDVs, such as trucks, buses, and so on. For these reasons, LNG can be considered as a substitute for diesel.

From the CO_2 production point of view, the well-to-wheel life cycle analysis indicates that, compared to diesel, CNG and LNG reduce GHG emissions by 14% and by 3–10% (on the basis of the supply option), respectively (Arteconi, Brandoni, Evangelista, & Polonara, 2010). Refueling, storing, as well as burning LNG are already available technologies. At present, the development of a wide infrastructure is an important issue for the diffusion of this alternative fuel: the distance between refueling stations and time necessary for refueling a car are important aspects for the public acceptance. Some studies confirm that to solve this problem, natural gas refueling stations should be in a number equal to 10–20% of conventional gasoline and diesel stations (Yeh, 2007). Another important issue to be overcome, that is the most important in order to increase the market penetration of natural gas as vehicle fuel, particularly in its liquid form (LNG), is the problem of supply (Arteconi & Polonara, 2012). Actually, the simplest way to supply LNG is to buy it at LNG terminals or, as alternative, liquefy natural gas from pipeline. The use of this alternative fuel in the transport sector has grown considerably lately. Up to now, more than 20 million NG vehicles are existing worldwide, including also LNG buses and trucks.

EUROPEAN NGVS SITUATION AND POLICIES

One of the target for the 2020 in Europe is about renewable sources share. By 2020, each EU member state should guarantee that in the transport sector this share would be at least 10% of the total energy used for transportation. The final target is to reduce GHG emissions from this sector by 10%, to be achieved as follows (EC, 2015e):

- 6% by means of biofuels;
- 2% by means eco-innovations;
- 2% by means of CMD credits for flaring reduction not directly linked to EU oil consumption.

As part of these targets, natural gas as vehicle fuel is supported in order to reduce GHG emissions. Biomethane is also considered as a valuable renewable source for air pollution reduction. At present, the current situation about NGV and refueling stations in Europe is reported in Tables 3 and 4 for the main countries.

As it can be seen, the share of NGVs in some cases is negligible and a lot of efforts are necessary in order to encourage NGV diffusion. For this reason, several policies have been adopted in Europe to promote natural gas as vehicle fuel. Efforts for NGVs in Europe can be divided into measures concerning the fuel, measures concerning the vehicles, and measures concerning the infrastructure.

For the fuel, a reduced taxation was applied for both natural gas and biomethane in order to support their diffusion. In Germany, a reduced tax was set for CNG from 2006 until 2018 (from 31.8€/MWh to 13.9€/MWh). This causes a cost saving for NGVs of about 50% and 30%, compared with petrol and diesel. Moreover, to encourage the biomethane production, feed in tariff programs have been introduced in countries like France and Sweden (NGVA, 2014b).

Measures about vehicles produce mainly benefits for consumers. In fact, consumers can gain subsidies to purchase a new NGV or to substitute a conventional car with an NGV. In Italy, for example, this incentive is up to 1,500€ for buying a new NGV or 500€ for converting a traditional car. Several countries adopted this kind of measures with considerable results, like Austria where the incentive is given to those consumers that purchase or convert a traditional car (up to 1,000€) and also to taxies and school buses (up to 3,000€). Other incentives related

Table 3: NGVs Situation in the Main European Countries (NGVA, 2014a).

Country	Total NGVs	Light-Duty Vehicles	Buses	Trucks	Other	% in the Country	% in the Area
Italy	885,300	880,000	2,300	3,000	0	2.16	77.04
Ukraine	388,000	19,400	232,788	135,793	19	5.13	33.77
Armenia	244,000	192,000	17,300	34,700	0	55.45	21.23
Germany	98,172	95,708	1,735	176	553	0.20	8.54
Russia	90,050	65,000	10,000	15,000	50	0.25	7.84
Bulgaria	61,320	61,000	280	40	0	1.83	5.34
Sweden	46,715	43,795	755	2,163	2	0.92	4.07
France	13,550	10,050	2,400	1,100	0	0.04	1.18
Switzerland	11,640	11,278	173	129	60	0.25	1.01
Austria	8,323	8,100	167	54	2	0.16	0.72
Total (other 32 countries)	1,899,602	1,427,467	275,716	195,037	1,382	0.55	100.00

Table 4: Natural Gas Stations Situation in the Main European Countries (NGVA, 2014a).

Country	All Stations	CNG Stations	% in the Area	L-CNG Stations	LNG Stations
Italy	1,049	1,040	31.70	8	1
Germany	920	920	28.00	0	0
Armenia	345	345	10.50	0	0
Ukraine	324	324	9.90	0	0
France	310	310	9.50	0	0
Russia	253	252	7.70	1	0
Sweden	213	205	6.30	4	4
Austria	180	180	5.50	0	0
Switzerland	141	139	4.20	1	1
Bulgaria	110	110	3.40	0	0
Total (other 32 countries)	4,581	4,501	100.00	43	37

to the vehicle are about taxation schemes in terms of road taxes, parking fees, and so on (NGVA, 2014b).

Regarding the infrastructure, as already mentioned, it is of paramount importance to develop an appropriate refueling station network. This aspect encourages both consumers' demand and manufacturers' new NGVs models offer. At present, two projects are ongoing in this direction:

- The GasHighWay project;
- The LNG Blue Corridors project.

The aim of the GasHighWay project is to increase the use of natural gas as vehicle fuel and promote the upgrading of biogas in order to obtain biomethane to be used in the same way. Moreover, the project wants to create a network of refueling stations for both natural gas and biomethane distributed on the European territory from the northern regions (Finland) to the southern ones (Italy). The project aims also at spreading the best technologies available for natural gas vehicles and refueling stations as well as promoting knowledge transfer and support for those companies and organization interested in this field (GasHighWay, 2009).

On the other hand, the LNG Blue Corridors project regards LNG infrastructure and diffusion. The aim of this project is to create an appropriate infrastructure in terms of "blue corridors" of LNG refueling stations for HDVs running with liquefied natural gas. Core of the project is the construction of 14 LNG or L-CNG refueling stations, located in critical points (corresponding to four "blue corridors") and the realization of a fleet of about 100 HDV, running along those corridors (Blue Corridors, 2013).

CHINESE NGVS SITUATION AND POLICIES

In the transportation sector, Chinese government needs to improve energy efficiency and to optimize the energy mix by means of electric vehicles and developing the biofuel sector. Regarding natural gas, although its consumptions share represents a small fraction of the total energy consumption, in 2014 its demand has risen up to 180 billion cubic meters per annum. This quantity is about four times the quantity of 2005 and makes China the largest natural gas consumer, before the United States and Russia. In 2012, transportation sector represented roughly 9% of the natural gas consumption and the market continues to grow as a result of Chinese policies to reduce air pollution (Rory, 2015). Moreover, the government wants to reduce the coal and oil consumption in order to increase the alternative fuels share, in particular natural gas (NGVA, 2015).

Natural gas as vehicle fuel has been promoted by means of several pilot projects, aimed at building and developing the infrastructure and the NGV industry. Also private investments in this way were encouraged, as mentioned in the "12th Five-Year Plan." The main efforts of Chinese government consisted in reducing its dependence on natural gas importations. In 2010, this dependence was more than 15%, foreseen to be more than 35% by 2015 (China's National People's Congress, 2011). For this reason in 2012, as part of the "12th Five-Year Plan," the National Development and Reform Commission, the Ministry of Finance, the Ministry and the National Energy Board issued the "shale gas development plan (2011–2015)." This plan aims at creating the foundation for the "13th Five-Year Plan," in which a large-scale development of shale gas will take place.

In addition, the 12th Five-Year Plan has set other targets for 2015 about improving infrastructure capacity (gas pipeline length and extensiveness) and gas storage facility for supply reasons. It is foreseen that by 2015 it will be possible to supply roughly 18% of the total population, corresponding to about 250 million people. The implementation mechanism is structured as follows:

- Strengthen coordination and management planning to create favorable conditions for the planning and implementation. Local governments at all levels and relevant enterprises must refine the implementation of the main objectives and priorities defined in the plan.
- Require continuous adjustment in order to meet the goal of domestic natural gas production practice and international natural gas market. The focus is to protect the security and stability of supply and promote the healthy and the sustainable development of the natural gas industry.
- Formulate the annual implementation plan to guide the various regions and relevant enterprises to work in accordance with national strategic intention and policy and establish the evaluation and reward system to ensure the smooth implementation of planning goals and tasks.

Therefore, the plan has the effect to boost natural gas development in every sector, included NGVs, with particular attention for HDVs. From 2009 to 2015, buses production tripled, up to 50,000 units, while truck production grew by 50% in just two years. The ENN, one of the largest companies for NGVs in China, said that by the end of 2015 the number of HDVs will rise up to 300,000 units. Also LNG refueling stations have been built intensively in recent years. Up to now some companies are planning to build up more than 1,000 LNG refueling stations in the next 5 years (NGVA, 2015).

Another aspect of Chinese natural gas policies is the pricing reform. This was partially addressed in the "2007 Gas Policy" and specified more in detail in the "2012 Gas Policy." Important aspects of both documents are reported later (Blumental, Yong, Deemer, & Zhang, 2013):

- 2007 Gas Policy: "deepen the pricing reform of natural gas and improve the pricing mechanism, gradually rationalize the ratio between natural gas prices and alternative fuel prices and fully utilize the role of natural gas price in adjusting supply and the demand."

- 2012 Gas Policy: "expedite the establishment of price linkage between natural gas price and the prices of alternative fuels, establish and improve the price linkage from upstream to downstream, encourage the study and implementation of differential pricing policies including seasonal price and interruptible price in regions with large fluctuation in gas demand, provide guidance on the reasonable consumption of natural gas, increase the utilization of natural gas and support an innovative trading system in connection with natural gas."

As it can be seen, the "2012 Gas Policy" explains more in detail how natural gas pricing should be reformed.

Finally, reforms in the natural gas sector in China had the consequence to boost the development of natural gas vehicles and refueling stations. Tables 5–7 describe the current NGV vehicles and refueling stations in China and the growth trend in this sector since 2010.

As it can be seen, although the Chinese policies are not specifically oriented to natural gas vehicles production and diffusion in terms of infrastructure development, China's growth rate in this field was impressive, making China the first Country in terms of both NGVs and refueling stations.

Table 5:   Natural Gas Vehicles Market Comparison between Different Countries (Li, 2015).

Ranking	Country	NGVs (10,000)	Refueling Stations
1	China	441.4	4,455
2	Iran	400	2,220
3	Pakistan	370	2,997
4	Argentina	248.7	1,939
5	India	180	936
6	Brazil	178	1,805
7	Italy	88.5	1,049
8	Colombia	50	692
9	Thailand	45.7	497
10	Uzbekistan	45	213
Total	Other 83 countries	2274.6	26,523

Table 6: CNG Vehicles and Refueling Stations in China over the Years (Li, 2015).

Year	CNG Vehicles (10,000)	Annual Growth (%)	CNG Stations	Annual Growth (%)
2010	110	22.2	1,800	28.6
2011	148.5	35	2,300	27.8
2012	208.5	40.4	3,014	31
2013	323.5	55.2	3,732	23.8
2014	441.1	36.6	4,455	19.4

Table 7: LNG Vehicles and Refueling Stations in China over the Years (Li, 2015).

Year	LNG Vehicles (10,000)	Annual Growth (%)	LNG Stations	Annual Growth (%)
2010	1	–	About 100	–
2011	3.8	280	About 200	100
2012	7.5	97.4	More than 600	200
2013	13	73.3	1,844	207
2014	18.4	33.5	2,500	35.6

Biomethane as Gas Source

As already said, one of the main issues to overcome in order to make natural gas market competitive is the problem of supply. One option is to use biomethane as renewable source of feedstock gas. Biomethane is produced from biogas of landfills or from anaerobic digesters. In the anaerobic digestion, biogas is obtained by means of microorganisms that digest biomass as crops, industrial wastes, sewage sludge, and so on. Raw biogas is composed mainly of methane (50–70% v/v), carbon dioxide (25–45% v/v), and other minor components, namely nitrogen (1–5% vol), water vapor (1–2% vol), and hydrogen sulfide (0.1–0.5% vol) (Aebion European Biomass Association, 2009). For this reason, raw biogas cannot be directly used as vehicle fuel so a purifying process, called upgrading, is required in order to remove the carbon dioxide (other minor compounds are removed by means of a pretreatment). At present, several upgrading technologies are available such as pressure water scrubbing (PWS), chemical scrubbing, and membrane separation (Xu, Huang, Wu, Zhang, & Zhang, 2015). In addition, it could be possible to recover CO_2 during the upgrading phase and sell it as by-product (Yang, Ge, Wan, Yu, & Li, 2014). Moreover, a cryogenic upgrading process can also be performed in order to both remove and recover CO_2 and liquefy biomethane in order to obtain liquefied biogas (LBG) (this process is still in a development phase). By comparison with other alternative fuels, biomethane presents several advantages:

- It is the alternative fuel with the highest energy density due to its high methane content;
- CO_2 emission from its combustion are the same of that captured during the biomass growth;
- It is less dependent on natural gas importations;
- It could be injected into the national gas grid.

For these reasons, biomethane represents an interesting combustion fuel to be used as vehicle fuel, whose technology is already available and mature. In addition, it can be used in a liquid form as well as common natural gas and, at this moment, several LBG plants exist, especially in the United States and Sweden.

EUROPEAN SITUATION

As one of the European targets, by 2020 at least 20% of the total energy consumption must be from renewable sources. At present, biomass represents the renewable energy source mostly used in Europe and biogas has an important role. In 2014, more than 15,000 biogas plants were in operation with an equivalent installed power of about 8,000 MW (Stambasky, 2015). In Figure 2, the European biogas plants distribution is reported for 2013. Moreover, more than 300 biomethane plants exist, accounting for about 1 billion cubic meters of biomethane produced (Stambasky, 2015). Some studies indicate that the biogas potential in Europe is still largely unexploited and this sector is expected to grow more and more in next years. Table 8 shows the biomethane technical potential for each biomass resource.

In future, the use of biogas is expected to grow considerably and is foreseen that by 2030 the 30% of the technical potential will be reached (15% within 2020). Moreover, biomethane share

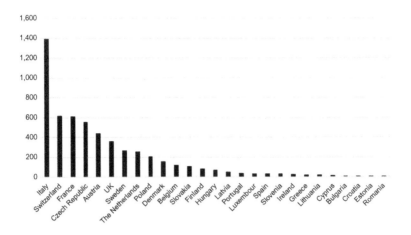

Figure 2: European Biogas Plants Distribution by Country. Germany has 9,000 Plants, Not Represented. *Source:* Adapted from Stambasky (2015).

Table 8: Biomass Feedstock and Biomethane Potential in Europe (Stambasky, 2015).

Biomass Resource	Potential (Per Year)	Percentage
Woody biomass	66 billion cubic meters	43.7
Herbaceous biomass	11 billion cubic meters	7.3
Wet biomass residues	26 billion cubic meters	17.2
Energy crops	48–143 billion cubic meters	31.8
Total	**151–246 billion cubic meters**	100

on biogas production is expected to pass from 2% in 2010 to 26% by 2020 and up to 37.5% within 2030. Consequently, the biomethane share on total natural gas will grow from 3% in 2010 to 5% by 2020 and up to 8% within 2030 (Stambasky, 2015).

CHINESE SITUATION

In China, as well as in Europe, biogas production represents an important sector and here the first biogas plant in the world was built at the end of the 19th century (Deublein & Steinhauser, 2008). Biogas produced from anaerobic digestion is very important and it comes also from domestic production with more than

Table 9:   Biomass Feedstock and Biogas Potential in China
(Bischoff, 2014).

Biomass	Quantity	Biogas Achievable (Per Year)
Agricultural straw	700 million tons (50% can be used)	100 billion cubic meters
Animal waste and wastewater	3 billion tons	108 billion cubic meters
Industrial waste and wastewater	2.7 billion tons	11 billion cubic meters
Organic municipal solid waste	77 million tons	9 billion cubic meters
Municipal sewage sludge	2.11 million tons	2 billion cubic meters

30 million household digesters (Jyothilakshmi & Prakash, 2015). As part of the 12th Five-Year Plan (2011), the Chinese government is increasing its investments in this sector and biogas infrastructure is growing rapidly. One reason for that is the fact that biogas potential in China is very high. In Table 9, biomass feedstock and biogas production achievable are reported (Bischoff, 2014).

As it can be seen, biogas potential from waste material is about 230 billion cubic meters per year corresponding to a biomethane potential of about 150 billion cubic meters per year. Therefore, biomethane in China can play a significant role in both energy production and vehicle fuel market.

THE FEASIBILITY OF LBG: AN ITALIAN CASE STUDY

In Italy, as in other European countries, incentives for biomethane production are provided. Table 10 reports the complete incentive scheme for biomethane as transportation fuel.

At present, the value of CIC is unknown due to the ongoing establishment of the relative market, thus some studies were made in order to evaluate the minimum incentive necessary to make biomethane feasible. In particular, the feasibility of LBG was analyzed (Arteconi, Spitoni, & Polonara, 2015). By varying the CIC value, the LBG production cost was evaluated, depending on the considered scenario (Arteconi, Spitoni, Polonara, & Spigarelli, 2015). Thus, considering a retail price for LBG equal to $1 \unicode{x20AC} \cdot kg^{-1}$ (Arteconi & Polonara, 2013), the minimum CIC value

Table 10: Summary of the Italian Incentives Scheme for Biomethane Fuel from Digesters by Varying the Feedstock Composition and Plant Features. Base Incentive is Named CIC (DM, 2013).

Feedstock Composition	Number of CIC			
	New plant		Existing plant	
	Sold to others refueling station	Own refueling station	Sold to others refueling station	Own refueling station
By-products < 70%	1	1×1.5 (1−10 years)	1×0.7	$1 \times 0.7 \times 1.5$ (1−10 years)
		1 (11−20 years)		1×0.7 (11−20 years)
By-products ≥ 70%	1.7	1.7×1.5 (1−10 years)	1.7×0.7	$1.7 \times 0.7 \times 1.5$ (1−10 years)
		1.7 (11−20 years)		1.7×0.7 (11−20 years)
By-products = 100%	2	2×1.5 (1−10 years)	2×0.7	$2 \times 0.7 \times 1.5$ (1−10 years)
		2 (11−20 years)		2×0.7 (11−20 years)

CIC: base incentive (€/10 Gcal biofuel).

to make LBG feasible was assessed. As shown in Figure 3, this value is about $0.11€/Nm^3$, $0.13€/Nm^3$, and $0.24€/Nm^3$ for a by-product percentage equal to 100%, 75%, and 50%, respectively. This scenario considers a new biogas plant using PWS upgrading technology, in which the biomethane produced is liquefied, stored, and refueled on site (the refueling station belongs to the biogas owner).

Conclusions

The transport sector accounts for about 23% of global CO_2 emissions and it will continue to grow in the future. For this reason, it is of paramount importance to intervene with policies intended to lower and control GHG emissions.

Both Europe and China had adopted similar actions by setting limits for cars emissions, introducing tax schemes, and promoting alternative fuels usage. As a consequence, some

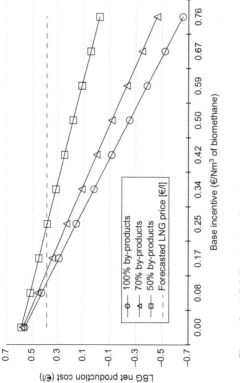

Figure 3: LBG Production Cost Depending on the Base Incentive.

targets have already been achieved, but a lot of work is still required. In Europe, these policies refer to passenger cars and light trucks and set maximum emissions, penalties, and incentives for manufacturers. HDVs have not been considered yet due to lack of information about their emission level. In China, limits in the CO_2 emissions were set as well. Moreover other measures like tax instruments and penalties are used.

Similar considerations could be made regarding biofuels policy concerning agricultural policy, blending mandates, subsidies, and tax instrument referring especially to ethanol and bio-diesel fuels. Several plans were also made for natural gas as alternative fuel in transport sector but NGVs share in both Europe and China is still too low. However, despite information about China's policy were not available in detail, natural gas vehicles industry has known an impressive growth of about 300% in NGVs, more than 1,700% in LNG vehicles and about 150% in refueling stations. In addition, big efforts were put inside the gas development plan as part of the "12th Five-Year Plan."

An important role could be played by biomethane as vehicle fuel. With this purpose, in Europe, incentive policy exists with several examples in different countries, promoting green energy and NGVs diffusions. In Italy, for example, an interesting incentive scheme for biomethane has been introduced and it is an opportunity to make the LBG production feasible. On the other hand in China, it can be seen that there is a huge and growing market for biogas and at present there are several biogas plants producing biomethane as vehicle fuel. The 12th Five-Year Plan for Biomass Energy Development claims ambitious targets but up to now an incentive scheme for biomethane is missing. However, Chinese government is increasing its investments in biogas infrastructure.

References

Aebion European Biomass Association. (2009). *A biomass road map for Europe.* Retrieved from http://www.seai.ie/Renewables/AD_In_Ireland_22nd_October/A_Biogas_Roadmap_for_Europe.pdf

Arteconi, A., Brandoni, C., Evangelista, D., & Polonara, F. (2010). Life-cycle greenhouse gas analysis of LNG as a vehicle fuel in Europe. *Applied Energy, 87,* 2005–2013.

Arteconi, A., & Polonara, F. (2012). LNG as vehicle fuel in Italy. *Proceedings of the 12th Cryogenics IIR conference,* Paper 041, September 11–14, Dresden, Germany.

Arteconi, A., & Polonara, F. (2013). LNG as vehicle fuel and the problem of supply: The Italian case study. *Energy Policy*, *62*, 503−512.

Arteconi, A., Spitoni, M., & Polonara, F. (2015). The feasibility of Liquid Biomethane (LBG) in Italy. *Proceedings of the 24th IIR International Congress of Refrigeration ICR2015*, Paper 504, August 16−22, Yokohama.

Arteconi, A., Spitoni, M., Polonara, F., & Spigarelli, F. (2015). The feasibility of liquid biomethane as alternative fuel: European and Chinese markets comparison. *International Journal of Ambient Energy*, in press, doi:10.1080/01430750.2016.1191040

Bischoff, M. (2014). Biogas and bio-methane in China from a German perspective. In The Deutsches Biomasseforschungszentrum (DBFZ), Biogasrat e.V. and Renewable Energy Association (Coordinators), *BioGasWorld*. Berlin: International Exhibition Grounds.

Blumental, D., Yong, X., Deemer, P., & Zhang, S. (2013). *United States: China issues new natural gas utilization policy*. Retrieved from http://www.mondaq.com/unitedstates/x/217828/Oil+Gas+Electricity/China+Issues+New+Natural+Gas+Utilization+Policy

China's National People's Congress. (2011). *12th Five-Year Plan*.

Decreto ministeriale. (2013, dicembre 5). Modalità di incentivazione del biometano immesso nella rete del gas naturale (in Italian).

Deublein, D., & Steinhauser, A. (2008). *Biogas: From waste and renewable resources (An Introduction)*. Weinheim: Wiley-VCH Verlag GmbH & Co. KGaA.

European Commission. (2015a). *Climate action, reducing emissions from transport*. Retrieved from http://ec.europa.eu/clima/policies/transport/index_en.htm

European Commission. (2015b). *Climate action, reducing CO_2 emissions from passenger cars*. Retrieved from http://ec.europa.eu/clima/policies/transport/vehicles/cars/index_en.htm

European Commission. (2015c). *Climate action, reducing CO_2 emissions from vans*. Retrieved from http://ec.europa.eu/clima/policies/transport/vehicles/vans/index_en.htm

European Commission. (2015d). *Climate action, reducing CO_2 emissions from heavy duty vehicles*. Retrieved from http://ec.europa.eu/clima/policies/transport/vehicles/heavy/index_en.htm

European Commission. (2015e). *Climate action, fuel quality*. Retrieved from http://ec.europa.eu/clima/policies/transport/fuel/index_en.htm

European Environment Agency. (2009). *Monitoring of CO_2 emissions from passenger cars − Regulation 443/2009*. Retrieved from http://www.eea.europa.eu/data-and-maps/data/co2-cars-emission-8

GasHighWay. (2009). Retrieved from http://www.ngvaeurope.eu/the-gashighway

Innovation Center for Energy and Transportation. (2014). *Performance of the Chinese new vehicle fleet compared to global fuel economy and fuel consumption standards (clean transportation program)* (pp. 25−28). Retrieved from http://icet.org.cn/english/reports.asp?fid=20&mid=21

International Energy Agency. (2009). *Transport, energy and CO_2* (pp. 43–49). Retrieved from https://www.iea.org/publications/freepublications/publication/transport2009.pdf

International Energy Agency. (2014). CO$_2$ emissions from fuel combustion highlights (2014 ed.) (pp. 10–11). Retrieved from https://www.iea.org/publications/freepublications/publication/CO2EmissionsFromFuelCombustionHighlights2015.pdf

Jyothilakshmi, R., & Prakash, S. V. (2015). Production of biogas using small-scale plug flow reactor and sizing calculation for biodegradable solid waste. *Renewables, Wind, Water and Solar, 2*(6), 1–4. doi:10.1186/s40807-015-0006-0

Li, Y. (2015). *China's natural gas car ownership rose to first in the world.* China Energy Network. Retrieved from http://www.china5e.com/news/news-905755-0.html

LNG Blue Corridors. (2013). Retrieved from http://lngbc.eu/

Natural & Bio Gas Vehicle Association Europe. (2014a). *European NGV statistics.* Retrieved from http://www.ngvaeurope.eu/european-ngv-statistics

Natural & Bio Gas Vehicle Association Europe. (2014b). *Catalogue of incentives and best practices in Europe for NGVs.* Retrieved from https://ec.europa.eu/energy/intelligent/projects/sites/iee-projects/files/projects/documents/gashighway_catalogue_of_incentives_and_best_practices_in_eu_en.pdf

Natural & Bio Gas Vehicle Association Europe. (2015). *Air pollution policies spark NGV market in China.* Retrieved from http://www.ngvaeurope.eu/air-pollution-policies-spark-ngv-market-in-china

Rory, J. (2015). *Energy briefing (China).* Global Economics.

Stambasky, J. (2015). Biogas & biomethane in Europe. In *Agriculture and renewable energy: The biogas/biomethane value chain* (promoted by the Municipality of Reggio Emilia). Italy: Loris Malaguzzi International Centre.

United Nations Environment Programme. (2015). *The Chinese automotive fuel economy policy* (pp. 1–16). Retrieved from http://www.unep.org/transport/gfei/autotool/case_studies/apacific/china/CHINA%20CASE%20STUDY.pdf

Xu, Y., Huang, Y., Wu, B., Zhang, X., & Zhang, S. (2015). Biogas upgrading technologies: Energetic analysis and environmental impact assessment. *Chinese Journal of Chemical Engineering, 23,* 247–254.

Yang, L., Ge, X., Wan, C., Yu, F., & Li, Y. (2014). Progress and perspectives in converting biogas to transportation fuels. *Renewable and Sustainable Energy Review, 40,* 1133–1152.

Yeh, S. (2007). An empirical analysis on the adoption of alternative fuel vehicles: The case of natural gas vehicles. *Energy Policy, 35,* 5865–5875.

14 Vapor Compression Heat Pumps and District Thermal Energy Networks for Efficient Building Heating and Cooling

Neil Hewitt, Ye Huang, Mingjun Huang and Caterina Brandoni

ABSTRACT

Purpose – Currently heating and cooling in buildings is responsible for over 30% of the primary energy consumption in the United Kingdom with a similar amount in China. We analyze heat pumps and district thermal energy network for efficient buildings. Their advantages are examined (i.e., flexibility in choosing heat sources, reduction of fuel consumption and increased environmental quality, enhanced community energy management, reduced costs for end users) together with their drawbacks, when they are intended as means for efficient building heating and cooling.

Methodology/approach – A literature review observed a range of operating conditions and challenges associated with the efficient operation of district heating and cooling networks, comparing primarily the UK's and China's experiences, but also acknowledging the areas of expertise of European, the United States, and Japan. It was noted that the efficiency of cooling networks is still in its infancy but heating networks could benefit from lower distribution temperatures to reduce thermal losses. Such temperatures are suitable for space heating methods provided by, for example, underfloor heating, enhanced area hydronic radiators, or fan-assisted hydronic radiators. However, to use existing higher temperature hydronic radiator systems (typically at a temperatures of $>70°C$) a modified heat pump was proposed, tested, and evaluated in an administrative building. The results appears to be very successful.

Findings – District heating is a proven energy-efficient mechanism for delivering space heating. They can also be adaptable for space cooling applications with either parallel heating and cooling circuits or in regions of well-defined seasons, on flow and return circuit with a defined change-over period from heating to cooling. Renewable energy sources can provide either heating or cooling through, for example, biomass boilers, photovoltaics, solar thermal, etc. However, for lower loss district heating systems, lower distribution temperatures are required. Advanced heat pumps can efficiently bridge the gap between lower temperature distribution systems and buildings with higher temperature hydronic heating systems

Originality/value – This chapter presents a case for district heating (and cooling). It demonstrates the benefits of reduced temperatures in district heating networks to reduce losses but also illustrates the need for temperature upgrading where building heating systems require higher temperatures. Thus, a novel heat pump was developed and successfully tested.

Keywords: High temperature heat pumps; district heating

Introduction

At the present time in the United Kingdom, heating (and cooling) requirements in buildings, (space heating/cooling and hot water provision) are met predominantly by relatively small systems designed to either serve an individual building, or sometimes, in cases of buildings with multiple occupancy, individual apartments or flats.

By contrast in China in urban areas, district heating fueled predominantly by coal is well established with 2,810,220 TJ of heat supplied in 2011. District heating systems are however generally at a scale for which carbon capture and storage (CCS) is not considered to be a viable option, that is, the UK Government's CCS Cost Reduction Task Force estimated CCS costs in 2012 to be in the region of £161/MWh compared to a pulverized coal plant (£90/MWh) and onshore wind energy (£85/MWh). Thus, efficiency, utilization, and flexibility improvements appear more appropriate.

Heating systems in both countries are predominantly fossil fuel based (gas in the United Kingdom, coal in China) with emissions generated at the point of end use, which for some fuels can lead to poor local air quality. There is to date in the United Kingdom only limited use of district heating (and cooling) systems designed to serve multiple buildings or city districts (2% of heat in the United Kingdom, over 72% of networks serve an average of 35 dwellings with a further 17% serving an average of 190 dwellings), the majority of networks were constricted before 1990. In other parts of Europe including Germany, Sweden, and Denmark district heating is well developed; in 2010, 13% of heat supply to the residential and service sector in the EU27 was by district heating with over 6,000 different systems installed.

Currently, heating and cooling in buildings is responsible for over 30% of the primary energy consumption in the United Kingdom with a similar amount in China. Increasing wealth leads to concomitant expectations of improved control of indoor temperatures required to provide occupant comfort; it is thus probable that energy consumption associated with both space heating and cooling of buildings will increase. The ambitious targets for greenhouse gas reduction in the United Kingdom and the aim of initially stabilizing and then reducing emissions in China embodied in the Chinese carbon plan will make the decarbonization of heating and cooling in buildings essential in both countries. District heating and cooling is an approach that in towns and cities has been shown to offer excellent prospects for both saving energy and reducing pollution and will be an important component in the transition from a carbon intensive heat supply system to a low-carbon heat supply system. Based on the levels of deployment in mainland Europe, considerable scope to increase district heating deployment in the United Kingdom exists with, major barriers currently appearing to be commercial and planning issues. However, improvements in technology are required to enable low/zero carbon district heating to be realized and these, will lead to stronger commercial cases and increased numbers of suitable sites for application.

The Building Challenge

The heat load of many buildings in temperate climates is strongly dependent on the seasons with a significant space heating load in the winter months with minimal or zero space heating load in the summer. Cooling loads for most buildings except those with large casual or solar gains are opposite to this. The requirement for hot water at present is generally much smaller than that for space heating, but it is, however, more constant throughout the year. A district heating system that can provide both heating and cooling, therefore, will prove much more attractive and cost-effective than a system designed to provide only heat or coolth, particularly in climates with cold winters and hot summers.

Most district heating system consists of three main components:

- Heat sources
- Transmission and distribution networks
- Building interface.

Heat sources that provide heat to the network can be a single system in a single location or multiple systems distributed throughout the district heat network. Heat sources that have been used include gas, coal and biomass boilers, CHP systems, solar thermal systems, geothermal heat, large-scale heat pumps, or industrial waste heat. Due to large seasonal variations in heat required for space heating when multiple heat sources are available, an order of priority of heat source dispatch is required to ensure that greater operational time is allocated to the lowest cost/CO_2 intensive heat source.

In a heating network, the transmission (from a remote heat source to the region of demand) and distribution networks (in the region of demand) composed of flow and return pipes that are used to convey hot water from the heat sources to and from loads, substations, or building interface units. The typical operational temperatures for direct systems in which the district heat network directly supplies radiators and other hydronic heating systems are in the range (temperature flow/temperature return), T_f/T_r 85/65°C to T_f/T_r 68/34°C. Indirect systems operate at higher temperatures with temperatures up to T_f/T_r of 140/75°C being typically used. The pipe network can be installed either above or below ground; in both cases it is essential that it is well insulated to minimize heat loss. Variable speed drive circulating pumps provide the required flow rate to meet the heat loads in the most energy-efficient way. Pressures used can typically be up to 16 bar in indirect distribution networks and 25 bar in transmission mains, while direct systems are operated at lower pressures. Local distribution systems within buildings can lead to significant parasitic heat loads with unoccupied spaces being heated to high temperatures caused by, for example, inadequate levels of insulation or insulation being removed and not replaced during maintenance.

The building interface is where the DH system enters the building. In direct systems, the water from the DH network is circulated through the building's heating system which imposes restrictions on both the pressure and temperatures that can be used. In indirect systems a heat exchanger is used between the DH network and the buildings heating system. For provision of domestic hot water in both systems, a heat exchanger is required; this can be used to charge a local thermal store or provide instantaneous hot water.

Thermal storage systems provide increased operational flexibility and can be used to maximize utilization of heat generated from heat sources with high priority or low CO_2 emissions that have variable output that does not occur concurrently with demand. Storage capacity and duration can be large to enable shifting of, for example, solar heat from summer to winter or smaller (of shorter duration) to allow peak loads to be met without recourse to low-utilization gas boilers.

The development of new towns and cities allows a planned approach to heating and cooling to be adopted. New buildings built to current building regulations should not require interventions to improve envelope performance allowing future heating/cooling loads to be accurately predicted. If suitable appropriately sized district heat distribution networks are installed from the outset when other services are being installed, costs can be minimized. Since improving building fabric performance increases cost (and embodied energy) and reduces heat loads, a system optimization is required against the delivery cost achieved by different configurations and capacities of district heating systems. Direct systems operating at lower temperatures and pressures are considered to be more suitable in such applications because lower temperature heat sources can be used, heat loss from pipe networks will be smaller and the heat loads to be met are lower, engendering continuous use even through periods of building performance improvement, thereby reducing investment risk. In pursuing this flexible, low-energy, long-lived option, the development of low-cost/short payback upgrade technologies becomes paramount.

Existing cities present major challenges and opportunities for district heating deployment. Key challenges include

- A strong/compelling reason to change from existing heat supply systems will be required to guarantee a high level of adoption and commercial viability.
- Retrofit of building fabric to improve envelop performance and reduce heat losses will reduce heat loads and impact financial viability.
- Building density and use varies significantly within cities and towns leading to irregular spatial distribution of heat loads.
- Deploying the required pipe network infrastructure will be disruptive and significantly more complicated and expensive than on a virgin site.
- Changes in building use and activities may mean that waste heat sources cease to be available.
- Fossil fuel-based CHP, although attractive, at present is only a transition to a low-carbon supply system and unless fuel is decarbonized or CO_2 is sequestered, it may require early substitution impacting on commercial viability.
- To reduce costs and allow use of existing heat distribution systems in buildings, an indirect DH system will in many cases be required leading to higher distribution temperatures and network losses.

Key opportunities include

- Heat loads of existing buildings are likely to be larger than for new buildings due to poorer thermal performance of their envelopes leading to higher heat loads and greater revenue for the DH operator.

- Existing unutilized heat sources can if at appropriate temperature be incorporated in the DH network possibly at little cost.
- Large base heat loads, for example, hospitals, shopping centers, universities if present provide a nexus around which to build a DH network and improve financial viability.
- The enabling technologies proposed in this chapter facilitate the expansion of these opportunities through allowing a wider use of heat sources and delivering to the broader needs of more varied customers (Heat Upgrade), facilitation of heat use at different times (Storage), and all-year round viable economic usage (the addition of heat driven Cooling).

Current District Heating Technologies

In China, the majority of district heating systems were initially based on waste heat from nuclear electricity generation systems. However, a more recent focus has been on the recovery of waste heat from tradition power stations, for example, coal. As major cities expanded, the power stations were engulfed by residential and business districts and provided the cooling needs of the power station could be maintained, new developments had a readymade source of heat for those parts of China requiring space heating. Recent applications have seen the incorporation of renewable energy (e.g., solar and biomass) and geothermal heating systems (Gong & Werner, 2015). However, coal is the dominant district heating source (Figure 1).

It has been generally considered that district heating was for northern China only (Guo, Huang, & Wei, 2015). However, Guo et al. (2015) goes on to state that "In 2012, a proposal that the District Heating Systems in North China should be extended to South China was put forward to The Fifth Session of the 11th CPPCC National Committee." This is in recognition of the fact that southern regions of China do require space heating, and this is often achieved through more inefficient individual or distributed heating systems. Thus, there is an opportunity to increase the efficiency of district heating systems in these potentially new areas of expansion as well as in existing systems.

In the United Kingdom, district heating only makes up to 2% of UK heat demand and is represented by almost 300 projects in operation or under development. This is radically different from other European countries where, for example, Finland supplies

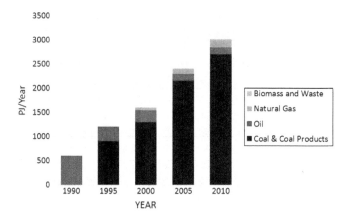

Figure 1: Expansion of China District Heating. *Source*: Adapted from Gong and Werner (2015).

49% of its total heat via district heating and Denmark provides almost 60% of its total heat by district heating. In the United Kingdom, a cost review was carried out by Davies and Woods (2009) with the costs illustrated in Figure 2. It can be seen that some of the renewable energy approaches are commercially less mature as are the "energy from waste" approaches. Combined heat and power (CHP otherwise known as Cogeneration) typically encounter economic barriers to deployment.

So the British government is trying to increase the number of households connected to district heating networks. The Department for Environment and Climate Change (DECC) would like to see the number of connected properties increased from the 2% (just under 200,000 nationwide) to 20% by 2030 and 40% by 2050. To facilitate this, DECC has made £7 million available to councils to carry out feasibility of studies for district heating systems. More than 50 UK local authorities have taken the government up on its offer. Between them they have been awarded £4 million and there is £3 million remaining in the pot.

For example, Heat Networks Delivery Unit (HNDU) funding round offers grant funding and guidance to local authorities in England and Wales for the feasibility studies of heat network projects. HNDU support is not currently available in Scotland or Northern Ireland. HNDU can only support heat network projects. HNDU cannot provide support for any other activity including activity that looks at heat sources only where supplying a heat network is not the primary function of a plant.

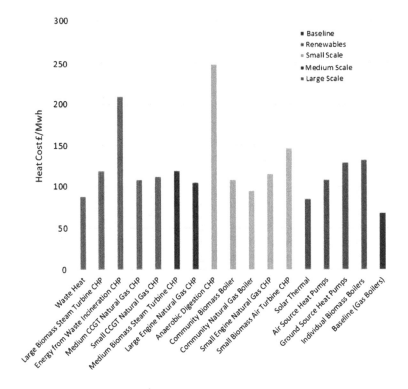

Figure 2: Cost of Heat Provision in the United Kingdom. *Source*: Adapted from Davies and Woods (2009).

For example, feasibility for an energy from waste plant (EfW) as a whole would not be eligible for support, whereas a feasibility study to investigate the potential for a specific EfW plant to supply a heat network would be eligible.

HNDU grant funding will meet up to 67% of the estimated eligible external costs of feasibility studies (which means the money paid by the local authority to third parties to deliver the heat network development stages). The local authority will have to secure at least 33% in match funding. It is up to the local authority to ensure the match funding (e.g., third-party funding) is not breaching any state aid or any other funding restriction rules in its use of other funding streams. DECC is not placing any additional constraints on whether the 33% match funding is sourced from the local authority's own reserves or from a third-party funder. However, subsidies cannot be the basis of any successful industry and therefore more efficient systems will be required.

Opportunities for Greater Efficiency in District Heating

One of the major challenges of district heating networks is utilization of the waste heat. In China with the potential increase of district heating networks into thermally marginal areas, over capacity will lead to inefficiency coupled with the potential of overheating and thermal comfort challenges if controls are inadequate. Furthermore, there is the perception that district heating (especially that delivered from waste heat recovery) is a low-cost option and therefore reduces the incentive for deploying building energy efficiency measures, for example, building fabric upgrades (Berger et al., 2016). As the major source of waste heat is electricity generation plants, their adaptation to recover waste heat is of paramount importance. A simplified diagram of a power station process is outlined in Figure 3.

For heat recovery, the main area of interest is "Q_{81}," that is, the heat from the steam cycle to allow condensation is provided by a low pressure liquid water for pumping ("W_{12}"). But what is the optimum temperature? Given the ranges of temperatures of T_f/T_r district heating, that is, 85/65°C to T_f/T_r 68/34°C and with indirect systems operating at higher temperatures with temperatures of up to T_f/T_r of 140/75°C, the loss in electrical efficiency performance is compensated by an increase in the overall

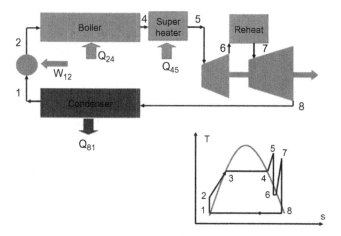

Figure 3:   Power Station Schematic and Temperature Entropy Diagram.

performance through heat recovery and the displacement of fossil fuels for district heating.

Lund and Mohammadi (2016) demonstrated the value of improved insulation in district heating networks with the highest standards being appropriate if energy costs are higher. This study illustrated that the investment in state-of-the-art district heating pipework represents a 20% uplift in installation costs.

Heat losses can be reduced by reducing the flow temperatures (Baldvinsson & Nakata, 2016). Low-temperature district heating system design at T_f/T_r of 60°C/30°C results in marginally larger pipe sizes and improved efficiency but given the marginal improvements, the cost penalty of larger pipes for more hot water to meet heating demands will demand a detailed cost-benefit analysis for each application. Such fourth-generation systems (Köfinger et al., 2016) might also involve heat pumps and lower temperature heat delivery systems, especially those associated with space heating, for example, underfloor heating and fan-assisted or extended area hydronic radiators.

District Cooling Challenges

When comparing the United Kingdom and China, the United Kingdom is only a marginal market for district cooling applications. This of course may evolve if future climate predictions of up to an average of 4°C rise in temperature for in particular the south of the United Kingdom come to fruition. However, an emerging area not only in the United Kingdom but also globally are data centers. Davies and Woods (2009) noted that data centers already consume some 1.5% of UK electricity and it is projected to grow to over 20% by 2020. Thus, heat rejected from such systems could be utilized in heating networks.

It is acknowledged that district cooling began in Denver, Colorado, the United States in 1889. By the 1990s, 20 cities in the United States had district cooling systems (Seeley, 1996). While Europe has examples in France, Germany, Italy, Sweden, and Finland, for example, Japan has over 150 district cooling systems.

Roppongi Hills is an 11.6-hectare site near the center of Tokyo. It is a mixed used site housed in 11 buildings, the center-piece being the 54-storey Mori Tower. The 11 buildings equate to more than 750,000 m^2 of floor space. The surrounding complex includes major hotel chains, shops, entertainment, commercial activities such as television companies and a limited and expensive, residential area. The distributed nature of the site however did not discourage the developers in supplying electricity, heating, and cooling from their own energy supply center.

Despite the fact that there are 11 blocks of housing either a single business entity or containing a mixture of business and residential activities, the developers made the conscious decision to provide electricity through their own 6-kV distribution network and hot and cold water through a piped system. The electricity distribution network is paralleled for security of supply and also grid-connected to provide backup.

The electricity is supplied via a cogeneration system based on 6 × 6,360 kW Rolls Royce gas turbines of the RR 501 KH5 type. The gas turbines provide the motive power for the generators as well as high-grade waste heat for the 8 × 8,350 kW Ebara absorption chillers that provide the cold water for the air-conditioning circuits in the floors of each building.

Both the electricity generation and heating/cooling provision is supported by eight steam boilers with steam capacities ranging from 40 to 70 tons per hour. These provide both electrical backup and support via a 500 kW back pressure steam turbine and additional heating/cooling capacity through both re-firing and co-firing in association with the waste heat from the gas turbines.

The strategy for sizing and operating this equipment is somewhat different from that encountered in the United Kingdom. The objective is to meet all electricity demands via the gas turbines. Thus, there must be considerable periods of time when the turbine output is excessive, and therefore heavy reliance is made of the relatively quick response to variable loads that is the forte of gas turbines. The additional boilers and the back pressure steam turbine also give a degree of flexibility to match the electricity, heating, and cooling demands.

The strategy outlined above leads to a range of efficiencies encountered in this first year of operation. When utilizing a maximum steam output from the gas turbines, an overall efficiency (heating, cooling, and electricity) of 74.6% is achieved. This is broken down into 45.9% for the steam for absorption coolers and 28.7% associated with electricity production.

For a maximum electricity output from the gas turbines, an overall efficiency of 47.3% was achieved. This can be broken down to 11.9% for the steam for absorption chillers and 35.4% for electricity production. The peak load to base load ratio = 2:1 and the overall goal is a yearly efficiency of 60%.

The energy center is found 35 m below the Mori Tower. It houses the energy service company (ESCO) that controls and distributes the energy from gas turbines, boilers, and absorption chillers found in the adjacent basement. To appreciate the scale of the plant room, it occupies over 100 m^2 of space and houses equipment weighing over 5,000 tons!

However, it is the processes that are carried on here that are of interest. First of all there is the double-effect absorption cooling. The Japanese climate in the greater Tokyo area requires significant air-conditioning during the spring-summer-autumn months. Waste heat from the gas turbine systems at temperature of a maximum of 500°C is very well suited to the needs of double-effect absorption cooling.

Double-effect absorption cooling has a coefficient of performance for cooling (COPc) in excess of 1.0, that is, for every kW of waste heat, a kW of cooling can be provided. This is compared with the UK practice of using single-effect absorption systems. Such systems are further down-rated when used in conjunction with the waste heat from engine-based cogeneration systems. The low-grade waste heat available (typically less than 100°C) only allows a COPc of 0.5–0.7. Therefore, to summarize, the use of gas turbines, while having a lower electricity generation capacity when compared with state-of-the-art engine-based systems, offer greater efficiencies elsewhere.

The delivery of cooling is achieved through water/brine loops around the site as it would be impossible to utilize directly the water/lithium bromide of the double-effect absorption chiller. Its circulation to any particular point is, however, limited by the building energy management system which utilizes ambient air before calling on the services of the chilled water. This variable-air-volume (VAV) approach has also found favor in the United Kingdom but for slightly different reasons.

Flexible air-conditioning can be achieved as above by varying the amount of chilled air or by varying the amount of refrigerant flowing in the air-conditioning circuit (variable refrigerant volume – VRV). If the traditional UK vapor compression air-conditioning systems utilize hydrofluorocarbons (HFCs), for example, it tends to favor VAV systems to reduce the amount of refrigerant that is used in the building.

Further flexibility in the facilities provided at Roppongi Hills is achieved by a number of fixed rate water/brine circulation pumps supported by a number of variable speed pumps for hot/cold water delivery. This allows each floor on each building to be kept at the desired temperature and humidity desired by the occupiers.

However, the overall goal for the Roppongi Hills cogeneration system is an annual efficiency of 60%. This may be considered as modest in UK terms but it is based on the sizing strategy selected. The strategy is that of meeting 100% of the electricity load internally and thus there must be spare capacity. While gas turbines are capable of meeting variable loads, this is at an efficiency penalty under part load conditions.

The driver behind this scenario is the competition being created by the deregulation of the energy market within this case, natural gas championing over grid-based electricity as the lower cost energy provider for Roppongi Hills. Energy demand reduction measures in the buildings consist of double glazing to reduce heat loss and heat gains. One innovative approach is the fact that the blinds close at midnight to reduce morning solar gain. However, these are subsequently controlled by tenants and thus the ESCO must typically meet the cooling needs from then on.

Lighting is a considerable part of the energy load in the buildings and new low-energy light bulbs have reduced the lighting load from 22 W/m^2 to 16 W/m^2. The staircases, normally used for emergency exists have been installed with motion sensors so that when they are only illuminated when in use. The operation of the Roppongi Hills complex reveals a peak heat load 93 W/m^2 and a peak electricity load 40 W/m^2, that is, a total energy load of 133 W/m^2. The plant is designed to typically deliver 1.3 times peak loads and thus it has the potential to operate inefficiently.

Therefore, it would appear that Roppongi Hills is somewhat inefficient by UK standards. The Roppongi Hills ESCO recognizes that in order to influence their tenants and improve the overall efficiency, they must first understand in detail what each building is using. Thus, they are implementing a monitoring and targeting program that will utilize (when completed in the near future) 160,000 sensors, one for each 30 m^2 of floor area. The aim is for their energy consumption to be 35% below the national standard.

China's experience with district cooling is outlined by, for example, Gang, Wang, Xiao, and Gao (2016) who discuss the design challenges encountered by district cooling systems in the different climate zones of China. Typically, water circulation is at

3–12°C and driven by absorption chillers. As in the Japan example, flexibility in cooling load was achieved through turbine operation when in combined heat and power mode. This type of operation requires an element of redundancy in that additional gas boilers are provided for either additional cooling (heat for the absorption chillers) or additional heating in winter.

Integration of Low-Temperature District Heating Networks and Vapor Compression Heat Pumps

It has been established that lower temperature district heating systems have reduced losses but require underfloor heating or other increased surface area or fan-assisted hydronic systems. Thus, a building with a higher temperature hydronic system (T_f = 70°C or greater) would need an alternative heat pump. Ulster has developed such a unit and its performance is reported here.

The development of a heat pump to address the issue of integration with a lower temperature district heating network as a heat source to meet a building's heating needs was initially considered in the modification of a cascade heat pump. In a cascade heat pump, a lower temperature stage utilizing R410a, for example, would heat an upper temperature stage utilizing R134a, for example. A test program was devised around a Daikin Altherma HT heat pump paying specific attention to the temperature of the heat exchange between the R410a low-temperature circuit and the R134a high temperature circuit. Initially, it was thought that the modification of this cycle would serve as a complete heat pump/STES system, allowing the air-source R410a lower temperature unit to be operated when heat from the STES was exhausted. Figure 4 illustrates the concept, the system under tests and results focusing on the intermediate heat exchanger temperatures. Results indicated that under maximum conditions, that is, warmest air in the test chamber (12°C) and warmest hot water supply temperature (75°C), the R134a higher temperature stage reached a maximum temperature of approximately 49°C in its "evaporator." Thus, it was concluded that the use of R134a with conventional equipment was more than likely not appropriate for this situation.

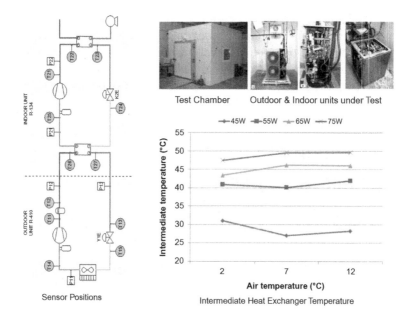

Figure 4:   Cascade Heat Pump Evaluation Summary.

While maintaining the belief that off-the-shelf equipment was appropriate for this task, a number of working fluids were examined whose properties were such that pressures at temperatures of 75°C and below were in keeping with traditional pressure ranges of, for example, R134a compressors, that is, −25°C to 15°C or 1 barA to 5 barA. R245fa emerged as a likely candidate with temperatures of 14.8°C and 62.7°C for 1 barA and 5 barA, respectively. The challenges are then compressor lubrication (oil viscosity, miscibility, etc.) and electric motor temperature when operating at elevated evaporator temperatures. Heat transfer proved to be marginally challenging as major brazed/welded compact plate manufacturers incorporated R245fa properties in their design portfolios. However, expansion valve manufacturers required new algorithms to address superheated properties of R245fa. These solutions, where appropriate, were incorporated into a small-scale water to water heat pump facility at Ulster utilizing a scroll compressor, compact plate heat exchangers, and an electronic expansion valve to test the theory of R134a equipment suitability.

The water to water heat pump was initially tested with R134a at EN14511 standards to establish correct operation and a baseline performance. The performance map was extended to higher temperatures to allow meaningful R245fa tests. Figure 5 illustrates comparative performance between the two fluids. Thus, there was a confidence in moving the tests forwards to a full-sized demonstrator capable of heating a larger building.

A series of models were devised to illustrate the likely performance of R245fa for a range of equipment. The compressor was initially of variable speed (30–70 Hz speed control) but it was decided to suspend its installation and make use of an available 1 m^3 hot water buffer tank. In general, the results show an improvement in the performance of R245fa over R134a (Figure 6).

However Figure 7 illustrates that under certain conditions, the heat pump cannot displace the entire boiler requirement and would suggest a larger heat pump. However, there was an electrical constraint placed on the heat pump that limited its electrical supply. Thus, this is the largest compressor that can be safely deployed.

The heat pump utilizes possible off-the-shelf components. R134a compressors were utilized in the model after a discussion with manufacturers. Such discussions confirmed that the existing

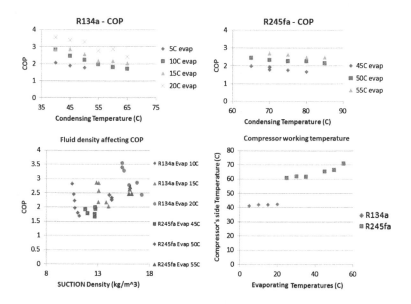

Figure 5: R134a/R245fa Comparisons.

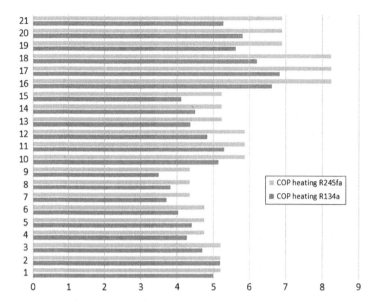

Figure 6: R245fa/R134a Performance Comparison for a Range of Relevant Conditions.

compressor oil was deemed to be suitable for operation with R245fa, part load operation at low-temperature lifts may require additional compressor cooling and the use of the buffer tank ensured that satisfactory run times would be obtained under all conditions. Heat exchangers were selected with R245fa and water in mind but the larger expansion valve proved difficult to obtain R245fa operating values. It was operated with the compromise setting of R123 which was deemed closest to the pressure/temperature levels of R245fa.

The system layout and construction are noted in Figure 8. A simple layout was proposed due to the constraints of space in the building plant room. The main components are as follows: Compressor – Emerson 6MU-40X-AWM/D-D, Heat Exchangers – SWEP B120T × 90 and SWEP V200T × 50, expansion device – Alco ETS6 and its controller EC3-X33, coupled with a Carly 15-l receiver to manage capacity changes. Just a charge of 13 kg of R245fa was utilized.

The heat pump was installed in the administration building and initially operated from a low-temperature network with a temperature of approximately 40°C. After installation and commissioning with cross checks to the extensive control system,

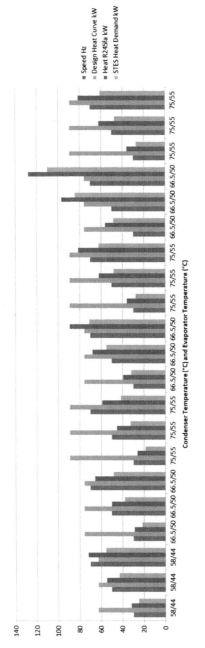

Figure 7: Modeled R245fa Heat Pump Performance.

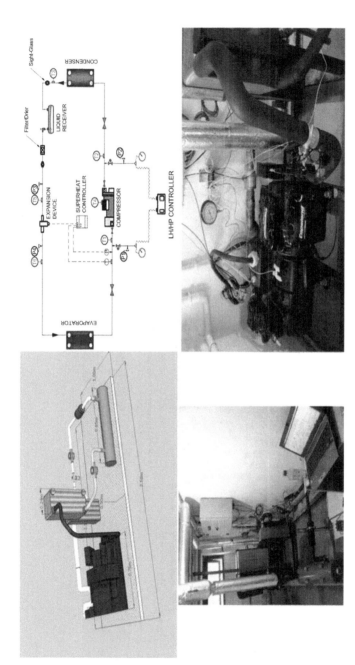

Figure 8: Schematic, Sensor Positions, and Images of the Heat Pump On-Site.

36 hours of operation were carried out at the time of writing. The results are as follows with a typical start and run illustrated in Figure 9.

The role of a heat pump utilizing off-the-shelf equipment and an alternative working fluid has been proven in the case of upgrading heat from a seasonal thermal energy store to meet the demands of a building that in this case utilized space heating via higher temperature hydronic radiators. A number of challenges exist that are partially related to design optimization criteria as well as availability of dedicated components. However, as an overall initial assessment, the heat pump appears to be successful in this field of upgrading lower temperature heat to that required by the building (Table 1).

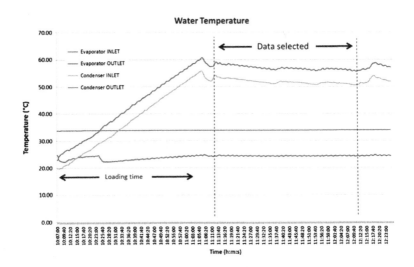

Figure 9: Start and Run Cycle.

Table 1: Heat Pump Performance.

Date	Heating Capacity kW	Power IN kW	COP kW/kW	η isen %	Cr
December 1	40.36	7.82	5.16	75.48	3.63
January 9	28.33	6.12	4.63	51.64	4.13
February 18	38.63	6.97	5.54	70.15	3.31
February 19	37.84	6.76	5.59	66.67	3.34

The electrical supply limitation of the building is not an uncommon problem. Should space allow, temperature upgrading of the heat to smaller compact thermal store for daily cycling, for example, based on phase change materials or thermochemical materials may facilitate a form of demand side response to maximize electricity usage at off-peak times. This can potentially reduce running costs through lower off-peak electricity tariffs and to reduce the stress on the existing electricity supply infrastructure.

Upgrading waste heat is a major market opportunity. Globally, the value of waste heat is in the region of €500 billion. It is estimated that the EU is wasting €55 billion per year (800 TWh) in recoverable waste heat. Vast quantities of surplus heat from industry sector activities exist; however, it is mainly allowed to dissipate unused into the atmosphere, often requiring additional energy usage to achieve this. The end result is that only 6.9 TWh of industrial excess heat is recycled in the whole EU27 (Connolly et al., 2012). Since energy costs can represent up to 40% of total production costs of heat-intensive industries, measures to improve heat recovery and site energy efficiency, will reduce operating costs and improve competitiveness. Recovery of surplus heat implies a significant potential for reducing fuel demand, thereby increasing energy security, reducing costs, and CO_2 emissions, each key aims of the EU2020 program. The Energy Roadmap 2050, published by the European Commission, acknowledges that renewable heating and cooling is vital to decarbonization, hence the capture of industry waste heat should be designed into any future energy efficiency implementation plans.

However, by its nature, waste heat is a waste product. Why is it a waste product? It is because it is deemed to have no value. Lower grade waste heat typically between 40−60°C can be utilized for underfloor space heating systems, swimming pools, etc. End users of waste heat need to be adjacent to waste heat suppliers to minimize heat transport costs, although the use of thermochemical storage systems integrated into containerized transport may challenge this in the future. Alternatively, district heating is not a globally accepted approach but in regions where it is a common place, temperature upgrading to or from such systems may benefit from the deployment of this heat pump.

Finally, what are the limitations of R245fa? A simple REFPROP model indicates that a COP of <2 is possible at 150° C, which is primarily the impact of operation near the critical point for this refrigerant. Thus, very high vapor compression heat pumps with refrigerants fulfilling the criteria of zero ozone depletion, near zero global warming potential (R245fa > 950) may require radical thinking in that a ratio of 3:1 must typically be observed when comparing electricity price to gas price. Products from Honeywell may well address this.

So what might the options be? An alternative with potential may be the 3M Novec series of fluids. Little is known about this Organic Rankine Cycle fluid but its vapor pressure appears to be about 30 BarA at 200°C. If its thermodynamic properties are acceptable, an acceptable COP may be achieved at 150°C and therefore industrial heat recovery and upgrading becomes a reality for advanced heat pumps.

Conclusions

District heating is a proven energy-efficient mechanism for delivering space heating. They can also be adaptable for space cooling applications with either parallel heating and cooling circuits or in regions of well-defined seasons, on flow and return circuit with a defined change-over period from heating to cooling. Renewable energy sources can provide either heating or cooling through, for example, biomass boilers, photovoltaics, solar thermal, etc. However, for lower loss district heating systems, lower distribution temperatures are required. Advanced heat pumps can efficiently bridge the gap between lower temperature distribution systems and buildings with higher temperature hydronic heating systems.

References

Baldvinsson, I., & Nakata, T. (2016). A feasibility and performance assessment of a low temperature district heating system – A North Japanese case study. *Energy, 95*(15), 155–174.

Berger, T., Amann, C., Formayer, H., Korjenic, A., Pospichal, B., Neururer, C., & Smutny, R. (2016). Impacts of external insulation and reduced internal heat loads upon energy demand of offices in the context of climate change in Vienna. *Austria Journal of Building Engineering, 5*, 86–95.

Connolly, D., Mathiesen, B. V., Østergaard, P. A., Möller, B., Nielsen, S., Lund, H., ... Werner, S. (2012). Heat roadmap Europe 2050: First pre-study for the EU27. Aalborg University, Halmstad University, PlanEnergi.

Davies, G., & Woods, P. (2009). *The potential and costs of district heating networks - a report to the Department of Energy and Climate Change*. Oxford: Pöyry Energy (Oxford) Ltd.

Gang, W., Wang, S., Xiao, F., & Gao, D. (2016). District cooling systems: Technology integration, system optimization, challenges and opportunities for applications. *Renewable and Sustainable Energy Reviews, 53*, 253−264.

Gong, M., & Werner, S. (2015). An assessment of district heating research in China. *Renewable Energy, 84*, 97−105.

Guo, J., Huang, Y., & Wei, C. (2015). North−South debate on district heating: Evidence from a household survey. *Energy Policy, 86*, 295−302.

Köfinger, M., Basciotti, D., Schmidt, R. R., Meissner, E., Doczekal, C., & Giovannini, A. (2016). Low temperature district heating in Austria: Energetic, ecologic and economic comparison of four case studies. *Energy*, in press, doi:10.1016/j.energy.2015.12.103

Lund, R., & Mohammadi, S. (2016). Choice of insulation standard for pipe networks in 4th generation district heating systems. *Applied Thermal Engineering, 98*, 256−264.

Seeley, R. S. (1996). District cooling gets hot. *Mechanical Engineering, 118*(7), 82.

15 Research on Biomass Energy Utilization in Chinese Rural Area

Xu Zhang, Mingling Zhai, Yanyan Wang, Yulei Gao, Haoliang Zhao, Xiang Zhou and Jun Gao

ABSTRACT

Purpose – In order to verify the feasibility of different techniques, this chapter further studies the adaptability of two massive straw biomass applications in rural areas in China.

Methodology/approach – The methods of assessing biomass power generation project with Life Cycle Assessment (LCA), survey and field test of one biogas station, and game-theoretic analysis are adopted.

Findings – The following conclusions can be drawn: The air pollution costs account for more than 60% of the total environmental cost, followed by depreciation expense and maintenance fee of 18%, compared to that of biomass power generation at 0.01711 CNY/kWh. The adopted greenhouse sunlight technology of Solar Biogas Plant in Xuzhou, China, raises the inside average temperature by 11.0 °C higher than outside and keeps the pool temperature above 16 °C in winter, ensuring a gas productivity of biogas project in winter up to $0.5-0.7$ m^3/m^3 by volume. This chapter also analyzes the information cost incurred by asymmetric information in biomass power generation via game theory method and illustrates the information structure with game results. It provides not only a foundation for the policy research in promoting straw power generation but also theoretical framework to solve the problem of straw collection.

Social implications — These studies will propose solutions to relevant problems arisen in the running process.

Originality/value — These studies are all based on real cases, field research, and appropriate theoretical analyses, so, they can reduce the relevant costs and promote the application of relevant technologies.

Keywords: Biomass power generation; LCA; sola biogas plant; centralized gas-supply; game theoretical analysis with asymmetric information

Agricultural biomass comprises a wide variety of resources such as straw and the livestock manure. In China, crop residues account for 38.9% of the total biomass resources available for energy production. These sources are considered to be carbon-neutral and an ideal alternative to fossil fuels. They are considered to be helpful to alleviate environmental pollution and reduce China's dependence on imported fuels. According to a report from World Bioenergy Association [WBA] (2010), the reasonable and sustainable utilization of global biomass energy could meet global energy demand.

China has a rich stock of crop residues. According to one study, the annual production of net available crop residues is about 505.5 million tons per year, and total bioenergy potential is about 253.7 million tons of standard coal per year. In 2010, the theoretical amount of crop residues was 729 million tons, among which only 147–334 million tons were of energy consumption. Unfortunately, open field burning of agricultural residues after harvest causes severe air pollution in China. Due to the practice of open burning of crop residues, black carbon emissions increased from 14.05 Gg in 1990 to 67.87 Gg in 2005, while organic carbon emissions increased from 57.37 Gg to 267

Gg over the same period. In Chengdu, China, the peak $PM_{2.5}$ emissions from intensive biomass burning surpassed 500 μg from May 18 to 21 in 2012. Besides, open burning of straw biomass can also cause other hazards (see Figure 1), such as diminishing visibility detrimental to air traffic safety and fire hazard.

Cost Optimization of Biomass Power Generation in China

Since biomass power generation is a highly efficient way to utilize biomass energy, recent years has witnessed the establishment of a patch of straw biomass power plants in China, whereas the majority ran into operational difficulties or even production halts in the practice. Therefore, it is of great significance to precisely analyze the cost composition of the biomass power plants to improve the operation.

Figure 1: Open Burning of Straw Causes Other Hazards, Such as Diminishing Visibility Detrimental to Air Traffic Safety, Fire Hazard, etc.

Research on the cost optimization of biomass power generation can help to solve the supply and demand dilemma of straw resources, reduce the power generation cost, raise its market competitiveness, and make indirect contributions to the national planning of biomass utilization and the cause of energy saving and emission reduction.

Typical Chinese way of biomass power generation is biomass combustion power generation fueled by crop straw, mainly including wheat, corn, rice, cotton, and tuber crops. According to the statistic from National Statistics Bureau in 2013, the primary crop straw in China consists of wheat, corn, rice, cotton, and tuber crops, with a total yield of 590 million tons, among which the three major crops (corn, rice, and wheat) account for over 80% in total, with 38.8%, 25.3%, and 22.1% for corn, rice, and wheat respectively, followed by 5.1% cotton, 4.8% tuber crops, and 3.9% beans as the yield of rest crop straw. Figure 2 illustrates the principle of biomass power generation.

DYNAMIC COST ANALYSIS OF A TYPICAL BIOMASS POWER PLANT IN CHINA

Dynamic cost analysis is to analyze generation cost with economic methods, monitor, calculate, and study the changing status of cost, characterized by dynamism and instantaneity. The former indicates fuel consumption and generation cost under

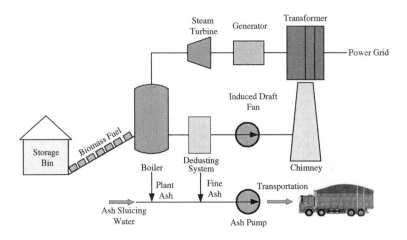

Figure 2: Diagram of the Principle of Biomass Power Generation.

various operating conditions and generating loads, rather than annual average generation cost, while the latter refers to monthly, daily, or even hourly cost in view of an annual financial calculation. Dynamic cost analysis of a typical biomass power plant can provide decision-making information on production and operation management for the plants, produce substantial references for generation cost so as to improve the market competitiveness of biomass power generation technology.

Cost Composition Analysis of Biomass Power Generation Technology

Biomass power generation costs are composed of fixed costs, namely depreciation fees, repair costs, material expenses, complements and benefits and other fixed costs, included in power generation costs through distribution, as well as variable costs, including fuel costs, water and electricity bills of the plant, which are directly taken into account in power generation costs. Though settled annually, the depreciation fees in the analysis can be amortized monthly or daily. In this chapter, the depreciation fees are amortized monthly, as different types of biomass fuel are used each month. In addition, water and electricity bills in variable costs remain relatively stable, while fuel costs vary greatly with the type of fuel used.

Dynamic Cost Analysis

So far, the majority of domestic biomass power plants encounter difficulties in operation due to confusion about cost composition analysis of biomass power generation technology. The adoption of dynamic cost analysis can provide a clearer view of the plants' cost composition.

A typical biomass power generation plant with an initial cost of 300 million RMB yuan and 40 years of longevity is taken as an example. After studying the setting, we can draw a conclusion that the minimum and maximum generation costs are 0.61 yuan/(kWh) and 0.69 yuan/(kWh) respectively, when straw price is at 200 yuan/ton; 0.68 yuan/(kWh) and 0.77 yuan/(kWh) for straw price at 250 yuan/ton; 0.75 yuan/(kWh) and 0.85 yuan/(kWh) for straw price at 300 yuan/ton, as shown in Table 1.

By break-even analysis, we can conclude that the plant will remain profitable all-yearlong except certain months when the electric price is 0.75 yuan/(kWh); by sensitivity analysis we can conclude that variation of fuel prices exerts major influence on the generation cost, accounting for 50% of the cost, followed by depreciation fees and electricity bill. Therefore, decreasing

Table 1: The Generation Cost vs. Each Fuel Price.

Straw Price (yuan/ton)	Minimum Generation Cost yuan/(kWh)	Maximum Generation Cost yuan/(kWh)
200	0.61	0.69
250	0.68	0.77
300	0.75	0.85

the fuel price and initial cost and extending the power generation duration can lead to significant cost reduction. Hereinto, a drop of 10% and 20% of the fuel price under the set context will, respectively, lead to 5.09% and 10.17% cost reduction of power generation.

ENVIRONMENTAL COST ANALYSIS OF TYPICAL BIOMASS POWER PLANT IN CHINA

In respect of biomass power generation plants, environmental costs can be generalized as quantitatively calculated expenses resulted from the process of alleviating environmental burden or environmental protection measures in compliance with relevant government policies.

A large quantity of pollution will be produced in the construction and production process of the plant, for example, the converting procedure of material procurement consumes energy and releases pollution since a mass of human and material resources are demanded to collect, store, and transport the biomass fuel due to its diversification and broad distribution.

Conventional thermal power generation emits 2.23 kg SO_2, 277.78 kg CO_2, and 1.39 kg NO_X to the atmosphere for every 1 GJ energy it generates, while the numbers turn to 0.2030 kg SO_2, 228.0704 kg CO_2, and 0.7287 kg NO_X for every 1 GJ energy biomass power generation plant produces based on Life Cycle Assessment, indicating the pollution emission of the biomass power generation is way less than its thermal counterpart. Thence biomass power generation becomes an effective way to reduce greenhouse gas emission in power sector.

Biomass direct combustion generation system has a greater impact on solid waste, dust, and fume than on acidification, eutrophication, and global warming, namely there is greater impact on locality than on regions and the globe in the biomass power generation project.

At present, a biomass power plant with installed capacity at 25 MW requires an input of environment protection equipment at 5 million yuan or so. By calculating the environmental cost of biomass power generation project, we can discover that the environmental cost of biomass direct power generation, at only 0.01711 yuan/(kWh), is less than that of its coal-burning counterpart. In addition, we can draw a conclusion by Activity Cost Analysis that air pollution costs most environmentally, accounting for over 50% of the total environmental cost and equipment expense for 18%. Therefore, reduction of air pollution emission plays a key role in cutting down the environmental cost.

COST OPTIMIZATION OF BIOMASS SUPPLY CHAIN FOR POWER PLANT

The leading problem among those popping up in the industrialization of biomass power generation technology is the collection, storage, and transportation of the fuel, particularly difficult in China given the piecemeal farming lands per family as a result of a traditional pattern of household-based production unit in China, plus small vehicles as major transportation means in rural areas that insinuates an increase of delivery frequency and cost. Meanwhile, the roads in the rural areas are not able to support large trucks. If the collection radius is extended, so will the cost. Therefore, it casts a major challenge not only to the collecting organization but also to the cost management. In addition, biomass power generation technology involves a much more complex process of collection, package, transportation, grinding, and burning compared to a traditional thermal generation system. Precisely speaking, the process involves delivering the reaped and dried biomass straw to the agent who packages and transfers it to the power plant where the straw is comminuted and conveyed to furnace by belts after its moisture is measured. The cost composition of the whole process is sophisticated, including fuel cost of straw, etc. and substantial cost of transportation, processing, storage, fuel loss, and environment. In consequence, the choice of fuel and optimization of generation cost is attached with growing significance now.

In view of the complexity of manufacturing and delivering process of biomass straw fuel, the model is assumed as follows for analysis: (1) The crop type is not taken into consideration. It is assumed that the crop is of uniform distribution in the collecting area, of a single breed and the same yield per unit. (2) The supplying fuel of the biomass power plants within the model spectrum is straw only due to its large planting areas, and can totally suffice the demand of generation. (3) The regional and seasonal characters of the crops are not considered here. (4) The collecting and transporting capacity is assumed full regardless of the impact of other factors (traffic, weather, etc.) on the crop collection. (5) In the worst scenario, the uncovered areas are directly procured by the biomass power plants.

As the collection radius and the straw quantity vary in the process, the transportation costs cannot be simply calculated as straw delivery expense by multiplying straw quantity by distance. Since the collection cost is related to the distance, with straw quantity constant, the station may prefer the nearby straw. Accordingly, the collection area can be viewed as a circular, and the collection cost will be calculated with definite integration in the Advanced Mathematics.

Assuming the radius of collection station is R_1, the transportation model is shown in Figure 3, and straw in uncovered areas is directly procured by the plant.

The above simplified model can be applied when the collecting area of the biomass power plant approximates a circular; when the coverage approximates a square, it can be solved by analogizing it to a circular and apply the aforementioned method. Straw from uncovered areas will be delivered to the plant by agents. The method is shown in Figure 4.

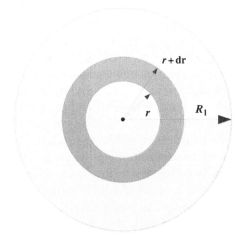

Figure 3: Transportation Model of Straw Collection of Biomass Power Plants.

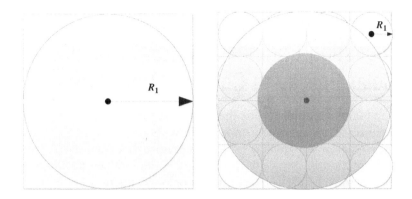

Figure 4:   Simplified Model of Collecting Area.

$$Y_1 = \int_0^{R_1} f\rho r t_1 \cdot 2\pi r \mathrm{d}r = \int_0^{R_1} 2\pi f \rho t_1 \cdot r^2 \mathrm{d}r = \frac{2}{3}\pi f \rho t_1 R_1^3$$

where f — coefficient of available straw; ρ — yield per unit cultivated area; r — radius; R_1 — radius of collection; t_1 — transportation cost.

By optimizing the fuel collecting area and the whole generation system, we can discover that the transportation cost is proportional to the third power of the radius, indicating an optimization of radius probably leads to reduction of transportation cost. By solving the collection model built on actual conditions, we can conclude that the optimal layout of the first circle of straw collection stations around the biomass power plant is to set nine stations with each of the collection radius at $0.25R$. This will save $0.22\pi f t_1 R^3$ compared to zero station; while 16 stations on the outermost circle and 10 on the following circle are needed when establishing the second circle of stations with an optimized collection radius at $0.16R$, which will save $0.27\pi f t_1 R^3$. Such a model can also be applied in solving the optimal layout of multiple circles of stations around the plant. Taking example of a biomass power station that consumes 20 tons rice straw annually, we can find out the optimal radius is 49.10 km.

Application of Crop Straw Anaerobic Digestion Engineering Combined with Solar Energy in Chinese Rural Area

The major prerequisite for the production of methane is the sustenance of the digester temperature within narrow limits. Tests show that when the digester temperature is below 10 °C, the fermentation bacteria are in a dormant state. When the digester temperature is above 20 °C, the biogas production rate can be 0.4 $m^3/(m^3 \cdot d)$−0.5 $m^3/(m^3 \cdot d)$ (Zhang, 2005). Therefore, it becomes difficult for most of the straw biogas plants in northern China to operate in winter when the natural digester temperature is below 10° C. The digester needs additional heating mainly with electricity, gas, oil, etc. However, application of these sources of energy will lead to excessive heating costs that are not economical (Zhao & Tan, 2009). Biogas production from crop straw combined with economical passive solar energy can solve these problems.

INTRODUCTION OF BIOGAS TECHNOLOGY WITH PASSIVE SOLAR ENERGY

Passive solar energy heating technology refers to the technology using solar greenhouse for collecting solar energy to heat the digester. The construction of solar greenhouse is simpler and costs less. The following is an example for application of the passive solar heating biogas technology. This project is located in central and eastern regions of China. The solar greenhouse is 200 m^2 large and the digester is 300 m^3. The process and system are shown in Figures 5 and 6. Crop straw is chopped by a machine, and mixed with water, ammonium bicarbonate, livestock, and poultry manure. Then the mixture is pumped into the fermentation tank. The methane produced will then be sent into the biogas tank to supply 100 households as cooking energy through the pipe network from the biogas tank.

To test and verify the warming effect of the solar greenhouse in winter, we had field tests for nearly two weeks in the winter of 2014. The main test parameters were temperature inside and outside the sunlight greenhouse. Variation of hourly air temperature inside and outside the greenhouse on a sunny winter day is shown in Figure 7. The temperature inside the greenhouse is

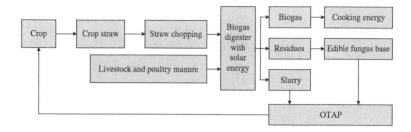

Figure 5:   Process Flow Diagram.

Figure 6:   Biogas Digester System with Solar Energy.

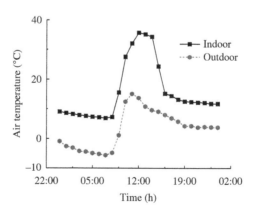

Figure 7:   Variation Regulation of Temperature Inside and Outside the Greenhouse on a Sunny Winter Day.

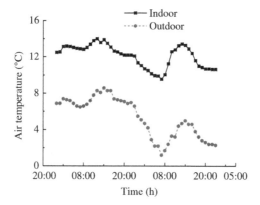

Figure 8: Variation Regulation of Temperature Inside and Outside the Greenhouse on Rainy and Cloudy Winter Day.

averagely 12.56 °C higher than that of outside. Figure 8 shows indoor and outdoor hourly temperature variation in two days. The first day is rainy and the second day is cloudy. The temperature variation is not significant. The average temperature is 12.9 °C inside the greenhouse and 7.3 °C outdoor on the rainy day. On the cloudy day, the average temperature is 11,3 °C inside greenhouse and 3.3 °C outdoor.

The heating effect of the sunlight greenhouse is remarkable. The average temperature is 15.2 °C inside the greenhouse in winter days, the lowest temperature is 6.6 °C, and the manure temperature is above 16 °C during the time which guarantees the biogas production. The biogas producing rate can reach $0.5-0.7 \text{ m}^3/(\text{m}^3 \cdot \text{d})$.

DEMAND OF BIOGAS ENERGY FOR RURAL RESIDENTS

The annual domestic gas consumption is calculated by the following formula (1). The rate of gasification refers to the ratio of the number of residents who use gas to the total population:

$$Q_a = \frac{Nkq}{H_l} \tag{1}$$

where Q_a – annual domestic gas consumption (Nm^3/a); N – population; k – rate of gasification (%); q – domestic gas

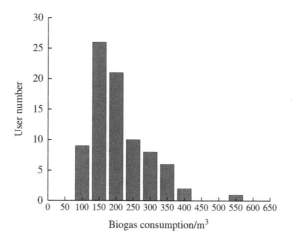

Figure 9: Distribution Map of Annual Biogas Consumption.

consumption quota per person (kJ/a); H_l — low-calorific value (kJ/Nm^3).

Through household survey of 100 household users, we got the basic information and consumption law of the biogas of each family. We analyzed the biogas consumption records from the biogas station by the rule of Grubbs test and selected out normal annual consumption data of 83 users from 100 users. According to the filtered biogas data, we draw the histogram whose class interval is 50 m^3 as shown in Figure 9. Biogas consumption of 69% households is between 92−229 m^3/a.

The arithmetic mean annual biogas consumption per person is 1422.4 MJ, lower than that of residents living in urban areas. Indicators of gas for domestic use in urban areas of east and central south China is 2,093−2,303 MJ/person·a that contains cooking and hot water. In this village, 83% of the residents use electricity and 28% use crop straw besides biogas, some even use liquefied petroleum gas or coal as live energy for various reasons. Almost every family has the solar water heater that contributes to the less use of the biogas energy.

The temperature decreases while the biogas consumption increases. In conclusion, we set the domestic gas consumption quota of 2,100 MJ/(person·a) as the design basis for further development. The biogas demand of a village with 100 families in this area will be 840,000 MJ/a, equal to 40,000 m^3 biogas.

RESOURCE POTENTIAL OF BIOGAS IN CHINESE RURAL AREAS

The crop residue amount that can realize energy regeneration is calculated by the equation:

$$CR_{Ei} = Q_{ci} \cdot r_i \cdot f_i \cdot e_i \qquad (2)$$

where CR_{Ei} – crop residue amount (kg); Q_{ci} – crop production (kg); r_i – residue to product ratio (RPR); f_i – collecting coefficient; e_i – coefficient of crop residue energy regeneration.

Theoretical straw biogas quantity is calculated by the equation:

$$B = \sum_{i=1}^{n} CR_{Ei} \cdot F_{ai} \qquad (3)$$

where F_{ai} – gas production factor under the condition of 35 °C (m^3/kg), B – biogas quantity (m^3).

Fermentation raw material mainly comes from the local user's wheat and maize straw. For the calculation of the crop straw amount, we assume there are four people each family of the 100 families in the village and 0.06 hectare farmland per capita. Then the whole village has a sum of 24 hectare arable land. Figure 10 shows shares of different use of crop residues in Jiangsu province (Cai, Qiu, & Zhi gang, 2011).

According to the above formula, the calculation process is shown in Table 2 as follows. The annual biogas production is

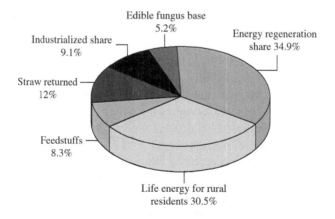

Figure 10:   Shares of Different Use of Crop Residues in Jiangsu.

Table 2: Theoretical Biogas Production.

	Wheat	Corn
Grain output per μ/kg·hectare^{-1}	5,250	9,000
RPR	1.28	1.25
Collecting coefficient	0.74	0.95
Coefficient of energy regeneration	0.654	0.654
Total solid/%	82	80
Factor (35 °C)/m^3·kg^{-1}	0.425	0.442
Biogas production/m^3	27201.49	59316.75

86518.25 m^3. The theoretical straw biogas quantity in Table 2 is calculated under 35 °C fermentation temperature. When the temperature drops to 20 °C, the gas production rate is about 60% of that under 35 °C.

The village is abundant in straw resources, whereas a significant portion of the resources is left unused. At present, many families use the solar water heater as a living hot water source and have no heating in the winter. Developing biogas water heater can be a way of further utilization of straw resources.

CONCLUSION

In this chapter, a biogas station combined with passive solar greenhouse in a village of Xuzhou is introduced. The greenhouse is economical and can be used to absorb and store solar energy to make full use of solar energy resources. The average temperature in greenhouse could be 11.0 °C higher than outside in winter. Temperature in greenhouse can enjoy an increase of 12–15 °C on sunny winter days or 5–8 °C on rainy days on average, which ensure the biogas engineering operates normally in winter. We analyzed the straw resource of the village and calculated the theoretical biogas production. Biogas consumption has obvious seasonal variation and daily variation which is similar to its urban counterparts. Results show that there are rich straw resources which can meet the cooking energy demand of residents. The use of straw biogas can not only realize the recycling of agricultural waste, reduce the straw burning and harmful gas emissions, but can also reduce the users' cost of living.

Game-Theoretic Analysis of Some Fundamental Problem of Rural Biomass Energy Utilization

GAME-THEORETIC ANALYSIS OF A BASIC PROBLEM OF BIOMASS SUPPLY FOR THE BIOMASS POWER GENERATION

As for the supply of crop residues for power plants in China, price fluctuation of biomass and input costs will affect Chinese farmers to a greater extent, who may not benefit from the biomass trade. There will be significant uncertainty as to whether the farmer will supply his/her biomass to biomass power plant (BPP). The farmer's decisions will affect the development of BPP, and the existence and development of BPP will in return affect the farmer's decisions.

We propose the basic problems that whether the farmer supplies the biomass and whether BPP purchases the biomass are determined independently to maximize their individual interests. For the farmer, the main problem is the distribution of his own labor, which is a central idea. Second, when there exists asymmetric information, how do the parties make decisions? If there are many farmers in a certain area, BPP will face uncertainty considering whether it can purchase the biomass from a farmer at a certain price to maximize income. Third, what are the effects of the different factors of the models on the game equilibriums? This is known as a two-party decision-making problem, and we adopt a game-theoretic approach to analyze it in detail.

These problems mentioned above should be analyzed with game theory from the perspective of multiple participants: farmer, biomass power plant, and government. Game theory is a very useful tool to analyze these problems from the perspective of multiple participants. Game-theoretic approaches have been widely applied in electronic market analysis (Hu et al., 2008; Wang, Zhou, & Botterud, 2011) in addition to studies of biomass energy generation technology.

The Game Model

We consider a game involving two players: BPP and the farmer. Other parts of biomass supply chain involved, such as brokers, are considered to be parts of BPP. BPP just purchases the biomass from one farmer at once. We consider the trade between the individual farmer and BPP as a game. The game is played statically in Figure 11, and they make decisions at the same time.

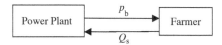

Figure 11: The Game between the Power Plant and the Farmer.

Basic assumptions are as follows:

1. The farmer and BPP are rational economic entities.
2. The farmer's strategy set is {collecting biomass and selling it at a certain price; discarding the biomass and saving labor to make money}. BPP's strategy set is {purchasing biomass from the farmer at a certain price; using other kinds of fuel instead of biomass}.
3. If the farmer gathers biomass, the purpose is for sale only.
4. The asymmetric information is p_l. There are different values of p_l for different farmers. The farmer knows the exact value of his p_l, $f(p_l)$, and all the information of BPP; BPP only knows the $f(p_l)$ and other information about the farmer that is the common knowledge. The probability distribution of p_l, $f(p_l)$ is as follows:

$$f(p_l) = \begin{cases} 0 & p_l < 0 \\ 1/p_l^u & 0 \le p_l \le p_l^u \\ 0 & p_l > p_l^u \end{cases} \tag{4}$$

$$F(p_l) = \begin{cases} 0 & p_l < 0 \\ p_l/p_l^u & 0 \le p_l \le p_l^u \\ 1 & p_l > p_l^u \end{cases} \tag{5}$$

5. The farmer and BPP are intelligent and risk neutral.
6. There is no competition between BPP and other enterprises.

The payoffs of the farmer's strategies are as follows:
The payoff of the strategy of collecting biomass and selling it at a certain price is

$$\pi_{11} = p_s Q - c_f = p_s Q - \beta Q^{3/2} \tag{6}$$

The payoff of the strategy of discarding the biomass and saving labor to make money is

$$\pi_{12} = p_l \Delta t = p_l Q/\alpha = p_l \kappa q A/\alpha \tag{7}$$

The farmer's profit-optimization problem is given by

$$\text{Max}\{\pi_{11}, \pi_{12}\}$$
$$\text{subjected to: } Q_s \geq 0, \ p_s \geq 0, \ p_l \geq 0 \tag{8}$$

The payoffs of BBP's strategies are as follows:

The payoff of the strategy of purchasing biomass from the farmer at a certain price is

$$E\pi_{21(p_b^*)} = P\left[p_e \gamma Q - \varepsilon Q - p_b^* Q - \left(c_{tf} + Lc_{tr}Q\right)\right] - (1 - P)c_{tf}$$
$$= PQ\left(p_e \gamma - \varepsilon - p_b^* - Lc_{tr}\right) - c_{tf} \tag{9}$$

The payoff of the strategy of using other kinds of fuel instead of biomass is

$$\pi_{22} = 0 \tag{10}$$

BPP's profit-optimization problem is given by

$$\text{Max}\{\pi_{21}, \pi_{22}\}$$
$$\text{subject to: } Q_b \geq 0, \ p_b \geq 0, \ p_e \geq 0 \tag{11}$$

Equilibrium of the Game Model

The two players must speculate about each other's decisions. The farmer speculates about the price p_b^* and BPP also chooses the appropriate p_b^* to maximize its own benefit. We describe the equilibrium in the form of the p_b^* equations as follows:

$$p_b^* = \begin{cases} \text{any value} & p_b^* < \beta Q^{1/2} \\ 0.5\left(p_e \gamma - \varepsilon - Lc_{tr} + \beta Q^{1/2}\right) & \beta Q^{1/2} \leq p_b^* \leq p_l^u/\alpha + \beta Q^{1/2} \\ & \text{and } Q p_l^{*2}/\left(\alpha p_l^u\right) \geq c_{tf} \\ \text{any value} & p_b^* > p_l^u/\alpha + \beta Q^{1/2} \\ & \text{when } Q_d = 0 \end{cases}$$

$$\tag{12}$$

When $Qp_l^{*2}/(\alpha p_l^u)<c_{tf}$, there is no value of p_b^*, where $p_l^* = \alpha(p_b^* - \beta Q^{1/2}) = 0.5\alpha(p_e\gamma - \varepsilon - Lc_{tr} + \beta Q^{1/2})$.

$$EQ_d = \begin{cases} 0 & p_b^*<\beta Q^{1/2} \\ 0.5\alpha Q(p_e\gamma - \varepsilon - Lc_{tr} - \beta Q^{1/2})/p_l^u & \begin{matrix}\beta Q^{1/2} \leq p_b \leq p_l^u/\alpha + \beta Q^{1/2} \\ \text{and } Qp_l^{*2}/(\alpha p_l^u) \geq c_{tf}\end{matrix} \\ 0 & p_b^*>p_l^u/\alpha + \beta Q^{1/2} \end{cases}$$

$$(13)$$

When $Qp_l^{*2}/(\alpha p_l^u)<c_{tf}, EQ_d = 0$.

Discussion of the Equilibrium

The Nash equilibrium of this game is affected by the following factors:

1. Exactly what $f(p_l)$ is will determine the probability equation of a successful deal:

$$P = F(p_l^*) = \int_0^{p_l^*} f(p_l)\mathrm{d}p_l \qquad (14)$$

Different $f(p_l)$ values determine different P values, and there will be different p_l^* values as well. If $f(p_l)$ changes, so will the correct p_l^*. So, in actual cases, there will be different Nash equilibriums for different cases. We cannot directly apply the results of one case to another case. As time passes, even if we confirm that the deal is successful in one instance, we cannot know for sure that it will be successful at any time in the future.

2. According to the assumptions, BPP will not know whether the deal is successful or not until meeting the farmer. BPP must incur a fixed cost, c_{tf}, to complete a deal with the farmer. In this model, c_{tf} will be a constant. But in actual cases, the decision variables will include both p_l^* and c_{tf}, which influences each other's values. From a broader perspective, we can consider c_{tf} as a fixed cost on a wider range. If purchasing biomass from a particular area, BPP may need to set up a transit center, which represents an additional fixed cost for BPP. BPP must make an optimal choice of the location and scale of the transit center to maximize benefit. Whether the decision is right or not is determined by

the specific condition of the asymmetric information. A benefit-maximizing decision made right now might turn out to have the opposite effect in the future.

3. In this part, only BPP faces uncertainty. In reality, the farmer may not know when BPP will purchase biomass and how much they will buy. According to the basic assumptions, the farmer and BPP are both risk neutral. In actuality, the farmer is always risk averse, and how the farmer makes his decisions when facing uncertainty, which will generate an additional transaction cost, is also an important problem to consider. Every parameter of the information structure of BPP ($\{c_{tf}, p_e, \delta_2, L_e\}$) could become part of asymmetric information. So the game could become very complicated. We cannot know whether or not there exists a Nash equilibrium with which BPP and the farmer can strike a successful deal. The player facing the problem of uncertainty might not have enough information to grasp the condition of asymmetric information.

4. The reality is that these players are not always intelligent enough to deal with the complex calculations caused by many kinds of asymmetric information. The cost of solving the problem of uncertainty will increase. In an actual scenario, the farmer might not be able to calculate the value of p_b^* but knows the exact benefit of selling his labor to the market. BPP will neither determine the value of p_b^* obtained from this game model nor know how much biomass could be supplied from the farmers because the assumptions of the model will not have been satisfied.

In the following section, we will briefly investigate how much these costs will increase.

As mentioned above, the first game's Nash equilibrium could be considered to be a standard with which we assess the transaction cost. Now, we make a slight modification. We assume that the farmers in an area are no longer exactly the same. There exists the same probability distribution $f(p_l)$ without the asymmetric information. BPP can distinguish among different farmers according to their p_l.

Because of the asymmetric information, there are some losses for both parties. We can make the following inferences:

Some of the farmers cannot carry out the transaction to increase their income. This ratio is

$$\Delta P = F(p_l') - F(p_l^*) = \int_{p_l^*}^{p_l'} f(p_l)\mathrm{d}p_l$$
$$= 0.5\alpha\left(p_e\gamma - \varepsilon - Lc_{tr} - 2c_{tf}/Q - \beta Q^{1/2}\right)/p_l^u \qquad (15)$$

BPP's income will be reduced as follows:

$$\Delta E\pi_{21} = Qp_l'^2/\left[2\alpha(1 + \delta)p_l^u\right] - Qp_l^{*2}/\left(\alpha p_l^u\right) + c_{tf} \qquad (16)$$

When they do not reach a deal, no farmer can increase his income, and BPP's income reduced by $\Delta E\pi_{21} = Qp_l'^2/\left[2\alpha(1 + \delta)p_l^u\right]$.

These losses are known as the transaction cost. Any method that reduces the transaction cost also incur some additional costs for BPP, but any method that makes the additional cost less than the transaction cost could theoretically be adopted.

The first common method is for BPP to employ some farmers as brokers. They can earn the price difference between BPP's purchasing price and the price they offer. Some labor times and other costs are still involved. BPP can distinguish among these farmers' conditions at a relatively lower cost compared to knowing all the farmers' information. The exchange of information between them will be easier. However, $f(p_l)$ might change over time, and the farmer who chooses to be a broker is likely to change jobs at some point.

Another method involves the specialization of labor, that is, the labor allocation is separated from the biomass collection. The labor spent in biomass collection comes from the labor market.

Conclusion

The shortage of feedstock supplies despite rich straw biomass resources hinders the sustainable development of biomass power generation technology. The Chinese government has introduced many policies to promote biomass power generation and increase the environmental benefit. The most problematic part of the government's optimal policy is uncertainty because of the complexity of information. According to our study, the government should investigate the information situation in addition to technical condition to examine the policy's effect.

Based on the above discussions, we recommend the government emphasize on the following aspects: (1) Simplify the information structure for farmers. Information complexity is attributed to the large population of farmers and information uncertainty from widely distributed decisions. Therefore, the government shall assist in reducing peasant population and unify information for peasants who are engaged in agricultural activities, namely homogenization of peasants as a resource in agricultural activities. (2) Promote information communication. The government shall establish proper information platforms to reduce the cost of information exchanges for both parties. (3) Enhance the service of intermediary agencies and logistics.

AN EVOLUTIONARY GAME-THEORETIC ANALYSIS OF THE GOVERNMENT'S ROLE ON THE RURAL ENERGY EFFICIENCY CONSTRUCTION

Basic Assumptions
1. The two players are the government and the farmers.
2. Two strategies of the government are strict supervision of energy-saving products' quality (shorthanded for strict behavior) and the opposite behavior (shorthanded for relax behavior).
3. The opportunities to gain information for the two game players are equal and symmetrical.
4. This game is a static and non-cooperative game. They make decisions at the same time.
5. They are of both bounded rationality.
6. The government does not mandate any consumer economic behavior of the farmers.

Game Theory Model
Let us consider the 2×2 noncooperative repeated game. Stage game payoff matrix is shown in Table 3.

Evolutionary Game Theory Analysis
Maynard Smith and Price introduced the concept of evolutionary stable strategy (ESS) and established the evolutionary game theory which was based on the assumption of bounded rationality. The results obtained through the method of evolutionary game theory analysis are more realistic and persuasive. ESS can be achieved through the game players' adjustment process of learning and imitating. t times repeated game between the two players is simulated by dynamic simulation equations.

The farmers' dynamic simulation equation is as follows:

Table 3: Stage Payoff Matrix of the Asymmetric Game between the Government and the Famers.

Farmers	Government	
	Strict (y)	Relax (1 − y)
Purchasing energy-saving products (x)	$a_1 - a_2 + a_3 + a_4, b_1 - b_2 + b_3 - b_4$	$c(a_1 - a_2 + a_3 + a_4) + (a_5 - a_2)(1 - c), b_1 - b_4 - b_6(1 - c) + b_3 c$
Purchasing traditional products (1 − x)	$a_5 - a_6, b_1 - b_2 + b_3 - b_5$	$a_5 - a_6 + a_7(1 - c), b_1 + b_5 - b_6(1 - c)$

$x, 1 - x$ = the proportions of purchasing energy-saving products and purchasing traditional products for the farmers. $y, 1 - y$ = the proportions of strict behavior and relax behavior for the government. a_1 = the use value of energy-saving products. a_2 = the monetary value of energy-saving products that the farmers paid. a_3 = the income of the farmers using energy-saving products. a_4 = the value of the psychological benefits because of energy-saving products bringing actual energy savings to the farmers. a_5 = the use value of traditional products. a_6 = the monetary value of energy-saving products that the farmers paid. a_7 = the value of the psychological benefits of farmers because they are not deceived. c = the genuine proportion in energy-saving products bought by the farmers when there are loopholes in the government's work. Assume that c is only decided by the degree of government's work loopholes. b_1 = government's tax revenue from the sale of relevant products. b_2 = administrative costs increased because the government takes the strict behavior instead of the relax behavior. b_3 = the social benefits like energy conservation and emission reduction because of energy-saving products using. b_4 = the expense paid in order to stimulate the consumptions of energy-saving products. b_5 = the revenue obtained by punishing dishonest behavior when implementing strict policies. b_6 = the value of the loss of the government's reputation when there are loopholes in the government's work.

$$F(x) = \frac{dx}{dt} = x(1 - x)[(a_6 - a_2 - a_7) + c(a_1 + a_3 + a_4 - a_5 + a_7)$$
$$+ y(1 - c)(a_1 + a_3 + a_4 - a_5 + a_7)]$$

(17)

We get the EES as follows: $y* = 1 - \frac{a_1 - a_2 + a_3 + a_4 - a_5 + a_6}{(1-c)(a_1 + a_3 + a_4 - a_5 + a_7)}$.

When $y > y^*$, only $x_2 = 1$ is the ESS, which means when government implements a strict policy to a greater extent than a certain value, farmers will take the strategy of purchasing energy-saving products. When $y < y^*$ only $x_1 = 0$ is the ESS, which means when the government's work loopholes reach a certain level, the farmers will lose confidence in the government supervision work and take the strategy of purchasing energy-saving products.

The Government's dynamic simulation equation is as follows:

$$F(y) = \frac{dy}{dt} = y(1 - y)[b_6(1 - c) - b_2 + xb_3(1 - c)] \quad (18)$$

We get the EES as follows: $x^* = \frac{b_2 - b_6(1-c)}{b_3(1-c)}$.

When $x > x^*$ only $y_2 = 1$ is the ESS, which means when farmers adopt the strategy of purchasing energy-saving products to a greater extent than a certain value, the government will be confident in the prospects for promoting energy-saving products and take strict policies strategy. When $x < x^*$ only $y_1 = 0$ is the ESS, namely when farmers adopt the strategy of purchasing traditional products to a greater extent than a certain value, the government will slack off and take relaxed policies strategy due to energy conservation promotion work with little success.

Policies Recommendations

From the above analysis, if the game is desired to reach the Pareto optimal equilibrium, it needs to make x^*, y^* as small as possible. It needs to meet the conditions $0 < \frac{b_2 - b_6(1-c)}{b_3(1-c)} < 1$ and $0 < \frac{a_1 - a_2 + a_3 + a_4 - a_5 + a_6}{(1-c)(a_1 + a_3 + a_4 - a_5 + a_7)} < 1$.

Because of $x^* = \frac{b_2 - b_6(1-c)}{b_3(1-c)}$ it is necessary to increase b_6, b_3 and reduce b_2 to make x^* sufficiently small. First, the government should adjust the relevant regulatory authorities' work to reduce cost of work. Second, the government should increase the investment in energy-saving technologies and raise the farmers' awareness of energy saving and emission reduction.

Because of $y^* = 1 - \frac{a_1 - a_2 + a_3 + a_4 - a_5 + a_6}{(1 - c)(a_1 + a_3 + a_4 - a_5 + a_7)}$, it is necessary to increase a_1, a_3, c, a_6, and reduce a_5, a_7, a_2 to make y^* enough small. First, promote the energy-saving product development efforts to increase the use value of energy-saving products. Second, promote the farmers' awareness of energy saving. Reward active farmers for purchasing energy-saving products. Third, provide incentives for the farmers to purchase energy-saving products. Fourth, lift the farmers' income to raise their demand for energy-saving products. Fifth, improve the efficiency of the government's work.

References

Cai, Y. Q., Qiu, H. G., & Zhi gang, X. U. (2011). Evaluation on potentials of energy utilization of crop residual resources in different regions of china. *Journal of Natural Resources, 26*(10), 1637–1646.

Hu, Z., Yang, L., Wang, Z., Gan, D., Sun, W., & Wang, K. (2008). A game-theoretic model for electricity markets with tight capacity constraints. *International Journal of Electrical Power & Energy Systems, 30*(3), 207–215.

Wang, J., Zhou, Z., & Botterud, A. (2011). An evolutionary game approach to analyzing bidding strategies in electricity markets with elastic demand. *Energy, 36*(5), 3459–3467.

World Bioenergy Association. (2010). Certification criteria for sustainable biomass for energy. *WBA Position Paper.* Retrieved from http://www.worldbio energy.org/content/news-and-comments-wba

Zhang, Q. (2005). *Biogas technology and application.* Beijing: Chemical Industry Press.

Zhao, J. H., & Tan, Y. F. (2009). Design of joint heating of biogas digester by solar energy and biogas fueled boiler in cold area. *China Biogas, 27*(3), 34–35.

16 Novel Energy Systems for Smart Houses

Yong Li and Ruzhu Wang

ABSTRACT

Purpose – This chapter will introduce three novel technologies demonstrated in Sino-Italian Green Energy Lab of Shanghai Jiao Tong University for the hot summer and cold winter climate zone.

Methodology/approach – Experimental and modeling works have been conducted on the application of these systems. A comprehensive review on the features of these novel technologies, their adaptability to local climate condition have been carried out, and some initial study results have been reported.

Findings – Solar PV direct-driven air conditioner with grid connection, home used small temperature difference heat pump, smart house energy information and control system are appropriate energy technologies with reduced CO_2 emission, which can be applied efficiently in the hot summer and cold winter climate zone. More useful data will be obtained in the future demonstration tests in Sino-Italian Green Energy Lab.

Originality/value – This work shows combining renewable energy technologies and information technologies is crucial to improve the energy efficiency and the comfortableness for indoor environment.

Keywords: Renewable energy technology; information technology; PV air conditioner; small temperature difference; smart house; general review

Introduction

China has seen a steady increase in energy use for more than 30 years and energy conservation is of vital importance both economically and environmentally (International Energy Agency, 2015). According to the statistics of Energy Information Administration, although its carbon emissions per capita are low, China's emission of carbon dioxide surpassed the United States for the first time in 2006 and ranked first in the world (Figure 1).

Carbon emission from the use of energy in buildings was one of the major components in the overall emissions (Price et al., 2006). In China, it was estimated that in 2002 buildings accounted for 33% of the overall greenhouse gas emissions (Martinot, 2001) and was projected to increase to about 35% in 2020 (Yao, Li, & Steemers, 2005). Hence, it is urgent to develop

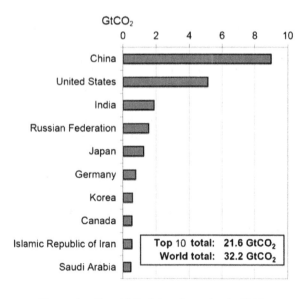

Figure 1:   Top 10 Emitting Countries in 2013.

energy efficient technologies and use more renewable energy in buildings.

On November 3, 2007, Shanghai Jiao Tong University and the Italian Ministry for Environment, Land and Sea signed an agreement to cooperate on the construction of a center of research, testing and dissemination of efficient and "low carbon" technologies in the building and housing sectors, at the Minghang Campus of Shanghai Jiao Tong University, China. This center is later named as Sino-Italian Green Energy Laboratory (GEL), which is a new generation green platform featured with integrated sustainable energy supply and low carbon emission (Figure 2).

GEL is expected to study novel building energy-consumption mode, building-based energy systems, energy saving devices with the merits of high efficiency, environmental friendly, and sustainable development, to realize low carbon emission during energy consumption, and to develop a study and test platform for international green energy technology.

GEL integrates more than 20 advanced technologies in terms of renewable energy, air conditioning, building automatic control, and green buildings. Different types of solar collectors with corresponding solar air conditioning systems (solar adsorption chiller, solar absorption system, solar desiccant cooling system, and solar ice-making system) operate inside GEL. Cooling and heating

Figure 2: Outside View of the Sino-Italian Green Energy Laboratory (GEL). *Source*: Authors.

power of GEL is provided by different heat pump technologies in terms of ground/river/air sources heat pump and CO_2 heat pump water heater. Also, GEL is equipped with many other advanced facilities, including high efficient independent temperature and humidity control system, floor heating terminal, cold radiant ceiling terminal, fan-coil terminal with small temperature difference, total heat exchanger, combined cooling heating and power system, heat storage system (phase change material, thermo-chemical heat storage), biogas power, hybrid PV/wind system, smart grid system, building energy management system, zero energy apartment and smart house, etc. GEL obtains gold medal of LEED Green Building Certification and has been regarded as one of the most advanced green building research platform around the world.

As a demonstration building itself, the technologies used in GEL are evolving and based on the research projects. Some new research projects for building energy and renewable energy application have been initiated in GEL in 2015. In this chapter, three new demonstration projects will be described and initial results of these projects will be discussed. The first one is the PV-driven air conditioner. The second is the GREE smart home. The third is the small temperature difference fan-coil units.

PV-Driven Air Conditioner

One important objective of the GEL is to find the appropriate building energy technologies in different climate zones in China. The most commonly adopted climate zones classifications is the one for thermal design of buildings, which is concerned mainly with conduction heat gain/loss and the corresponding thermal insulation issues. It has five major climate types, namely severe cold, cold, hot summer and cold winter, mild, and hot summer and warm winter (Ministry of Construction of P.R.C., 1993). The zoning criteria are mainly based on the average temperatures in the coldest and hottest months of the year. The number of days that daily average temperature is below 5 °C or above 25°C is counted as the complementary indices for determining the zones. Figure 3 shows location of the five major climates in China (Wan, Li, Yang, & Lam, 2010).

In recent years, the cost of solar PV system has been decreased steadily with the development of manufacturing technology and mature of the market (Barbose et al., 2015; REN21's Renewables, 2015). This makes the PV powered heat pump or

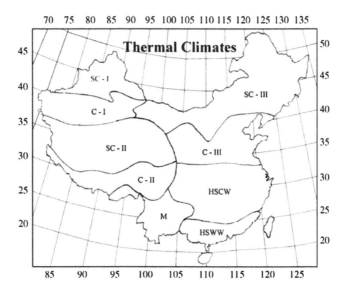

Figure 3:   The Thermal Climate Zone in China.

air conditioning system be competitive compared with other technologies.

SJTU started the investigation of PV air conditioner from 2010. A crystalline silicon (c-Si) solar photovoltaic array with 16 panels was installed on the roof of the room. In this system, four photovoltaic panels were connected in series as a group, then four groups of photovoltaic panels were connected in parallel. The system consists of PV panels, a controller, an inverter, a lead-acid battery bank, and a commercial variable frequency split type air conditioner (Li, Zhang, Lv, Zhang, & Wang, 2015). Figure 4 shows the main components of the experimental setup.

This experimental setup was used to investigate the performance of the PV air conditioner in the hot summer and cold winter zone in China. It was found that the PV-AC system can operate steadily to meet the cooling/heating load in different peak times in the hot summer and cold winter zone in China. The Solar Fraction (SF) of the present system was over 80% in normal summer daytime as well as winter daytime. The grid connected PV-AC might be a good solution to reduce the grid fluctuation as well as peak load generation capacity in this climate zone (Yao et al., 2005).

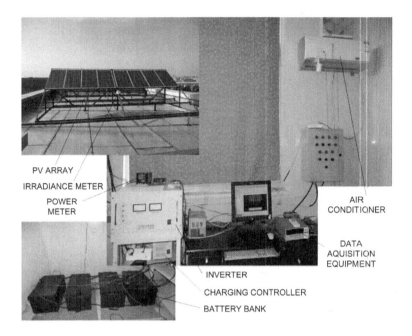

PV ARRAY
IRRADIANCE METER
POWER
METER

AIR
CONDITIONER

DATA
AQUISITION
EQUIPMENT

INVERTER

CHARGING CONTROLLER

BATTERY BANK

Figure 4: Experimental Setup of PV Powered Split Type Air Conditioner. *Source*: Authors.

In 2015, a new Variable Refrigerant Flow (VRF) air conditioner system driven by new installed solar PV array has been installed in GEL (Figure 5). The PV array is installed on the façade of the building. There are 38 panels and each panel has a capacity of 265 W_p. The total PV area is 62 m² and the total power of the array is 10.07 kW_p.

It can realize real-time switch over among different working modes in less than 10 ms according to the condition of photovoltaic power generation and cooling load demands. The fast switch over ensures the full utilization of PV power and the stable operation of air conditioning system. The specification parameters of the VRF system are shown in Table 1.

As shown in the schematic diagram in Figure 6, the system is grid connected. The system can work in five different modes based on the working load and the availability of solar electricity: (i) pure grid power mode. The air conditioner is driven by electricity from power grid when the PV electricity is not available. In this working mode, the machine works as a conventional inverter air conditioner; (ii) grid charge mode. When the air

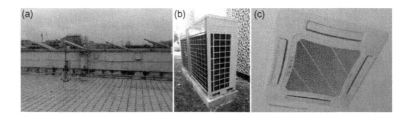

Figure 5:   PV-Driven VRF Air Conditioner System in GEL: (a) PV Panel, (b) Outdoor Unit, (c) Indoor Unit. *Source*: Authors.

Table 1:   Typical Parameters for PV-Driven Variable Refrigerant Flow System.

Parameter	Value
AC power supply	380 V to 3−50 Hz
DC power supply	370−800 V DC
Operation temperature	−25−60°C
Integrated part load value	7.6
COP	4.17
Cooling capacity	33.5 kW
Cooling input power	8.41 kW
Heating capacity	37.5 kW
Heating input power	9 kW
Switch time between operation mode	less than 10 ms

conditioning is not needed and PV electricity is still available, the PV system charges all its generating electricity into the public grid. This air conditioner functions as an inverter which converts the direct current into the alternative current electricity, and the overall system works as a PV power plant; (iii) photovoltaic air conditioning mode. When the load and the PV generated power is matched. Electrical power generated by the PV system provides all the power consumed by the VRF system; (iv) photovoltaic air conditioning and power generation mode. When photovoltaic generated power is more than air conditioning consumption demand, the photovoltaic power will give priority to the air conditioning operation, and then the excess power will be sent to the grid line; (v) photovoltaic air conditioning and power consumption mode. When photovoltaic generated power is less than

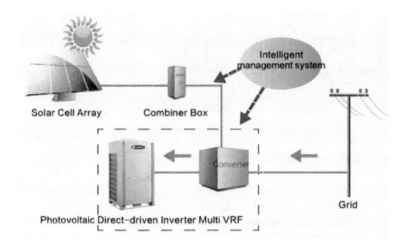

Figure 6: Schematic Diagram of the Photovoltaic VRF Air Conditioning. *Source:* Authors.

the air conditioning load demand, air conditioner is driven by the electricity from grid as well as from the PV.

A new research project has been established to study on the operation features of the PV-powered air conditioning system. Important performance parameters such as the power generation from the PV array, the cooling/heating power, the weather data, the electricity charged into and from the grid will be measured and analyzed. The economic and environmental issues related to the PV air conditioner will be studied comprehensively. Based on the experimental results, an accurate model will be developed to evaluate the performance of PV air conditioner in other climate areas in China. The design guidance will be proposed on the optimal ratio of PV capacity to the cooling/heating capacity, the tilted angle of the PV panel based on the location of the site and climate features.

GREE Smart Room

As home energy use is increasing and renewable energy systems are deployed, home energy management (HEM) system that considers both energy consumption and generation simultaneously to minimize the energy cost becomes a hot research topic (Page, Robinson, Morel, & Scartezzini, 2008; WBCSD, 2009). The HEM system offers the passive residential customer to be active in the energy market. The technical aspects include peak shaving, valley filling, load shifting, flexible load curve, strategic conservation, and strategic load growth. Further, previous researchers found that occupant behavior in buildings had large impacts on space heating, cooling, and ventilation demand, energy consumption of lighting and space appliances, and building controls (Nguyen & Aiello, 2013). Careless behavior can add one-third to a building's designed energy performance, while conservation behavior can save a third of the total energy use (Arens, Federspiel, Wang, & Huizenga, 2005).

In GEL, a new GREE smart room has started in 2015. Various system components including hardware elements, software algorithms, network connections, and sensors will cooperate with each other to provide monitoring and various services in smart home. The electrical appliances used in this room were all contributed by one GREE electric appliances, including which is one of the biggest public companies in the world. A HEM system App which is installed in a smart phone has been used. A user can monitor the energy consumption and control the home appliances such as air conditioner, refrigerator, air cleaner remotely through the smart phone (Figure 7).

Another aspect of smart home is healthy indoor environment. The indoor temperature, humidity ratio, air cleanness, and water quality will all be checked regularly. A new conceptual

Figure 7:   Layout of the GREE Smart Room. *Source*: Authors.

refrigerator will be added, the idea of the refrigerator is to make it "smarter," which can self-adjust during peak energy times, turning up the coolness when rates are down and cutting back when they're high. It is also expected to notify owners via mobile phones and tablets when, say, a door is left open. The smart phone will inform you the grocery lists, search recipes, upload photos, check the weather, control/monitor the machine's temperature, read news about food, discuss friends about the cooking method. It's like a cooker adviser in your kitchen. The objective of this room is to demonstrate and integrate the renewable energy technology with the information technology in home application. The energy use features will also be studied.

Small Temperature Difference Fan-Coil Unit

China is now one of the biggest energy consumers in the world. Its energy structure mainly depends on coal, which has led to serous air pollution problem. Heavy air pollution mainly happens in autumn and winter, particularly in winter, when coal burning significantly increases heating in north China. Many cities in China frequently suffer from thick smog, cutting visibility, and posing health hazards. Local government measures to try to limit the problem have included restricting traffic and halting industrial production. Heat pump is looked as an option to reduce the consumption of fossil fuel in urban area. However existing indoor units are not efficient in heating modes in winter. An important issue is that the air distribution is not optimal because the air conditioners in room are usually installed in an upper space, making heating temperature relatively high and energy efficiency reduced. In addition, defrosting frequently has influenced the heating comfort of the traditional air source heat pump. To solve these problems, a heat pump system with small temperature difference air conditioning terminal has been proposed.

The system includes a heat pump, which can be air source or ground source heat pump. Other source such as waste water or lake water can also be applied. Different from conventional system, the system use water as the secondary heat transfer fluid. The indoor unit is actually an improved fan coil, which is usually installed in the low level of the room. With increased heat transfer area and enhanced heat exchanger design inside, the hot water with temperature range of 35–40°C can provide comfortable heating for the indoor environment.

An experiment has been conducted for a residential house with 100m^2 indoor area in GEL. The variation of indoor temperature in January in Shanghai is shown in Figure 8. When the outdoor temperature is around 4°C, the indoor temperature can be kept over 20°C.

Figure 9 shows the variation of COP with time. It can be found that the COP is higher than 2.5, even when the capacity of the pump is oversized and the compressor is not in high efficiency.

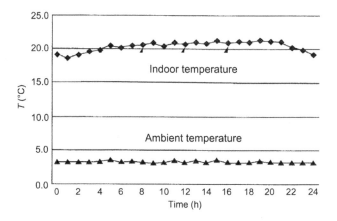

Figure 8: The Variation of Indoor Temperature in a Typical Winter Day.

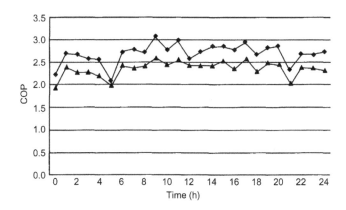

Figure 9: The Variation of System COP in a Typical Winter Day.

Conclusions

Three new building energy projects have started in GEL in 2015 which include PV-driven air conditioner, the GREE smart room, and the small temperature difference fan-coil units. Some initial results have been obtained. It is expected that the new research projects will make the building more comfortable, smart, and energy efficient.

Acknowledgments

This work was supported by POREEN—Partnering Opportunities between Europe and China in the Renewable Energies and Environmental industries, People Marie Curie Actions International Research Staff Exchange Scheme (FP7-PEOPLE-2012-IRSES).

References

Arens, E., Federspiel, C., Wang, D., & Huizenga, C. (2005). How ambient intelligence will improve habitability and energy efficiency in buildings. In W. Weber, J. M. Rabaey, & E. Aarts (Eds.), *Ambient intelligence* (pp. 63−80). New York, NY: Springer Berlin Heidelberg.

Barbose, G., Darghouth, N. R., Weaver, S., Feldman, D., Margolis, R., & Wiser, R. (2015). Tracking US photovoltaic system prices 1998−2012: A rapidly changing market. *Progress in Photovoltaics: Research and Applications*, 23(6), 692−704.

International Energy Agency. (2015). CO_2 *emissions from fuel combustion − 2015 edition*. Retrieved from http://www.iea.org/publications/freepublications/publication/co2-emissions-from-fuel-combustion—2015-edition—excerpt.html. Accessed on December 1, 2015.

Li, Y., Zhang, G., Lv, G. Z., Zhang, A. N., & Wang, R. Z. (2015). Performance study of a solar photovoltaic air conditioner in the hot summer and cold winter zone. *Solar Energy*, 117, 167−179.

Martinot, E. (2001). World bank energy project in China: Influences on environmental protection. *Energy Policy*, 29, 581−594.

Ministry of Construction of P.R.C. (1993). *Thermal design code for civil building (GB 50176-93)*. Beijing: China Planning Press (in Chinese).

Nguyen, T. A., & Aiello, M. (2013). Energy intelligent buildings based on user activity: A survey. *Energy and Buildings*, 56, 244−257.

Page, J., Robinson, D., Morel, N., & Scartezzini, J.-L. (2008). A generalised stochastic model for the simulation of occupant presence. *Energy and Buildings*, 40(2), 83−98.

Price, L., de la Rue du Can, S., Sinton, J., Worrell, E., Nan, Z., Sathaye, J., & Levine, M. (2006). *Sectoral trends in global energy use and greenhouse gas emissions*. LBNL-56144. Environmental Energy Technologies Division, Ernest Orlando Lawrence Berkeley National Laboratory.

REN21's Renewables. (2015). *Global status report*. Retrieved from www.ren21. net/gsr

Wan, K. W., Li, H. W., Yang, L., & Lam, J. C. (2010). Climate classifications and building energy use implications in China. *Energy and Buildings, 42,* 1463–1471.

WBCSD. (2009). *Transforming the market: Energy efficiency in buildings, survey report*. The World Business Council for Sustainable Development.

Yao, R., Li, B., & Steemers, K. (2005). Energy policy and standard for built environment in China. *Renewable Energy, 30,* 1973–1988.

Index